DYNAMIC STRATEGIC MANAGEMENT FOR THE 1990s

DYNAMIC STRATEGIC MANAGEMENT FOR THE 1990s

balancing opportunism and business planning

RALPH D STACEY

KOGAN PAGE

First published in 1990 by
Kogan Page Ltd,
120 Pentonville Rd, London N1 9JN

Typeset by DP Photosetting, Aylesbury, Bucks
Printed and bound in Great Britain by
Richard Clay Ltd (The Chaucer Press) Bungay

British Library Cataloguing in Publication Data
Stacey, Ralph D.
   Dynamic strategic management for the 1990s.
   1. Management
   I. Title
   658

   ISBN 0–7494–0134–6

Contents

Illustrations

Preface

This book is addressed to senior levels of management in business enterprises; those required to take the lead in dealing with the impact of change on their organizations. It is now widely accepted that such change will become even more turbulent in the 1990s than it has been over the past decade. And this will increase the pressures on those whose prime concerns relate to the long-term future of their businesses and therefore to the practical difficulties of managing in a strategic fashion.

But this is not a textbook intended to summarize or review the concepts of what is conventionally thought of as strategic management. Instead it puts forward, in what I hope is an integrated and practical manner, a framework and recommendations for managing which differ starkly from those to be found in conventional textbooks on strategic management, from what is recommended by most strategy consultants and from what now constitutes the 'received wisdom' on strategy of large numbers of senior managers themselves. My intention is to encourage such managers to question that received wisdom and the usefulness of the many expensive planning and reviewing rituals to which it has given rise.

The arguments the book develops and the recommendations it puts forward are derived from my own personal experience as a manager, corporate planner and management consultant. I have worked closely with senior and middle management in some two dozen companies during the 1980s, covering a variety of manufacturing and service sectors, operating both nationally and internationally. Part of the role of the consultant is the dispassionate observation of what managers do and how they do it. It is these observations over a number of companies and a number of years which provide the material for this book.

As a manager, or a consultant, essentially one is applying to specific situations a set of views and beliefs relating to the effective functioning of the business; views and beliefs which are derived from previous education and experience. But there is usually little time to set out coherently what those views and beliefs, or implicit structures, are. My opportunity now, in writing this book, is to take specific situations from my own experience, as well as many ideas from the literature, and to try to draw from them key generalizations to guide managers in meeting the challenge of the 1990s.

I have approached the writing of this book by reviewing what actually happened

in the consultancy assignments I was involved in and the management positions I occupied. I have used as case material a number of the consultancy assignments in which I have been involved. To maintain the required confidentiality I have not used the real names of these companies. Where my involvement was other than as a consultant, or the material has been published, I have used real company names.

Ralph D Stacey
Hatfield Polytechnic
Business School
November 1989

Foreword

This is a rare management book indeed. Starting where conventional thinking on mission, long-term objectives and strategic planning usually stops, Ralph Stacey confronts the challenge of open-ended uncertainty with compelling and practical advice. His canvass is wide: the political character of organisation; strategic control styles; and the encouragement of flexibility, experiment, trial and error, and leadership. To this Chief Executive Officer facing the accelerating waves of change sweeping over the British electricity industry and then wholly uncharted seas – circumstances we may all find increasingly familiar in the 1990s – *Dynamic Strategic Management for the 1990s* gives courage that a business voyage into the unknown can not only be survived but enjoyed on the way.

John Baker
Chief Executive (Designate)
National Power plc

Acknowledgements

I am particularly grateful to Richard Turton of the Hatfield Polytechnic, Martha Birtles of Doctus Management Consultancy, and John Sykes for the very helpful comments which they made on earlier drafts of this book. I also express my thanks to the colleagues I have worked with on assignments for Doctus Management Consultancy Limited; from them I have learned a great deal. Discussions with, and questions from, the first two cohorts of Hatfield Polytechnic MBA students provoked a number of thoughts. And last, but certainly not least, thanks to John Mant for his input and encouragement.

1
Introduction

This chapter sets out the central propositions which are developed in the ensuing chapters and provides a brief outline of the book.

Conventional strategic management

Conventionally, strategic management is seen as a separate and distinctive type of management concerned with the longer-term 'big issues'. It is a type of management to be distinguished from the ordinary day-to-day running of the existing business on the one hand and opportunistic entrepreneurial behaviour on the other. Proponents assure companies that they will improve performance by formulating a strategic plan, which anticipates change and provides a framework within which single strategic issues can be handled as they occur.

Formulating a strategic plan means determining fixed missions which set out what the company wants to be in the future; establishing clear, fixed, long-term goals and objectives for what the company wants to achieve at some point in the future; drawing up broad courses of action which the company is to take over some period into the future in order to achieve its objectives and fulfil its mission. The focus is on future change out in the market place with the emphasis on understanding market structures and competitive pressures. The aim is to identify sources of competitive advantage and match competitive capability to those sources.

The processes employed in this form of management are analysis, quantification and forecasting. Formal regular procedures are required to prepare and review long-term plans. Techniques such as portfolio analysis and SWOT (strengths, weaknesses, opportunities and threats) are available to assist in this. A corporation is seen in terms of a number of strategic business units, each of which prepares a plan matching its own ability to compete with critical success factors in the market. The corporate level then specializes in balancing portfolios of strategic business units, allocating resources and skills to them, transferring skills between them, building interconnections and synergies.

The result is an orderly 'grand design' for the future; a hierarchy of plans which are comprehensive, forward looking, internally consistent, which fit the resources

of the company to its environment and serve as a template against which to control the business over the long term. The analogy used is that of the general who deploys his forces tactically within a grand war strategy. It is a deterministic view of the world in keeping with the standard scientific traditions within which we have all been educated. It is a view which encourages us to focus on what we can understand in deterministic terms and to ignore small changes because in clearly specified, deterministic systems, small changes are conventionally accepted as having small consequences.

There have always been entrepreneurs who totally reject this whole approach to strategy. Apart from them, however, this overall philosophy of control in the long term has spread rapidly over the past 15 years and now has a powerful hold on the business community; many managers feel almost guilty if they cannot produce a strategy in these terms. Classes of MBA students and boards of directors alike now speak the language of fixed, long-term objectives and routes to them.

Even though there has been a significant move towards greater flexibility in the use of long-range planning by many companies in recent years, the basic conceptual approach remains intact in the minds of great numbers of managers. They react hostilely to any suggestion that the basic approach itself may be a fundamental nonsense in today's conditions, an approach which cannot be cured by any amount of flexibility. They recognize the limitations but still believe that long-range planning has real benefits in terms of communication, providing a focused, rational search for new opportunities and competitive edges and developing the strategic abilities of the management team. And the philosophy has spread deep into the public sector. Public health authorities and educational institutions in the UK now submit long-term strategic plans to their funding bodies and no self-respecting institution is without its mission statement.

Why conventional strategic management is inappropriate

This book uncompromisingly rejects the conventional strategic management framework, with its trite future-mission statements and flimsy strategic plans, as unrealistic, impractical and essentially static. It proposes more appropriate ways of developing and deploying the strategic abilities of the management team. The real cutting edge of strategic management lies in handling the unknowable, and the cast of mind generated by the conventional approach is a positive hindrance to such an endeavour. The time spent in preparing long-term plans which have to be changed within a few months is wasteful and diverts attention from the real issues. Conventional strategic management does offer some important insights and useful questions to ask when faced with problems, if used in an eclectic and flexible way. But as a form of control, a method of managing change, in the dynamic business

world of the 1990s it is totally inappropriate.

This is because conventional theory is based fundamentally on an assumption that change can be understood in terms of past experience, that probability is applicable, that small changes can be ignored, that clear frameworks can be established. It consequently conditions the thinking of managers in a manner which is highly dangerous in situations of true uncertainty. Managers so conditioned focus on matching existing resources to the environment; on competing with existing rivals who are assumed to think in the same way and play by the same rules. The result is planning for marginal adjustment rather than making imaginative moves.

Because managers with conventional strategic casts of mind are looking for clear, precise, long-term objectives, because they are concerned with working out in advance how to achieve those objectives, they frequently reject what appears to be the way out and the new. They are then no match for competitors who are not inhibited by a restrictive, conventional view of business strategy.

But, the reader will say, many successful companies have formal planning systems and conventional approaches to strategy. My reply is that such successful companies do not in fact use, and probably never have used, long-term planning as a method of control in dynamic situations. When it comes to actually managing change in conditions of true uncertainty, successful companies do something far more dynamic, whether they have long-term planning systems or not. They focus on single strategic issues and challenges, usually one by one; they develop implicit, dynamic strategic issue agendas; they focus organizational attention on the issues and challenges at many levels; they make experimental responses to such issues; and they back successful experiments with organizational energy and resource. In this way they develop and change their businesses organically and dynamically.

In short they do not control by grand design, they control by trial and error. The real analogy is not with grand war strategies but with playing games. Strategic management is a game in which a series of organizational and market moves are made, each with uncertain consequences in terms of customer response and competitor reaction. It is a dynamic, interactive game and companies play it because that is the realistic, practical thing to do in truly uncertain situations. It is the innovative, entrepreneurial behaviour which conventional strategic management treats as an alternative to planning, something separate, almost inexplicable and largely unsuited to large organizations. Innovative, entrepreneurial game playing is not an alternative to the planning mode of strategy, it is the only mode in conditions of true uncertainty. And it is so because we are dealing with open-ended change: that which is difficult to understand and where small changes escalate through the system with vast, unpredictable consequences.

But innovative, entrepreneurial game playing does not mean cowboy-like behaviour on the part of a single individual. In a corporation of any size it is a team

game, the effectiveness of which depends on the functioning of the business political system. Developing the strategic skills of the management team then has little to do with the arid formality and regularity of long-term planning. It has to do with creating and improving the political system of the company, the framework which provides opportunities for managers to exercise their intuitive and team skills in situations of true uncertainty.

If successful companies with long-term planning systems do not use them for 'real' strategy, then what do they use them for? They use them in fact to raise comfort levels by creating feelings of greater clarity; to communicate formally between levels in the management hierarchy on the 'big issues'; to gather and analyse data on the recent past; to back up complex procedures for approving capital expenditure. But they pay a price for these benefits — a way of thinking which inhibits really dynamic strategic management. The planning system wastes valuable time and diverts attention from the truly strategic.

As a consequence such companies are less flexible players of business games than they otherwise would be; they make fewer innovative moves; they react to more nimble competitors' moves instead of initiating them. In fact conventional strategic management tends to have the opposite effect to that intended — its practitioners are forced into reacting, when planning is supposed to enable them to anticipate.

Unconventional perspectives and prescriptions

This unconventional view leads to perspectives and prescriptions which are totally different from those of the conventional:

- Strategic management is not a separate kind of management at all, it is simply management. You cannot separate day-to-day and 'long-term' control; they are too interconnected. Effective day-to-day management requires tight, short-interval control, state of the art Management Information and Control Systems. Without them there will be little management time for the 'strategic' and there will be no tool to implement it. Such systems provide some short-term order in what is fundamentally a disorderly situation.

- Strategy is not some hierarchy of grand designs with fixed future missions and objectives, which precedes and provides a framework within which to deal with single strategic issues. Strategy is a consequence of the way in which challenges are created for the organization; the manner in which single strategic issues are dealt with; the experiments which are conducted; the games which are played. Strategies are built by the organizational backing of successful experiments. Strategy is not comprehensive, anticipative long-term planning at all; it is the consequence of innovative experimentation and entrepreneurial behaviour. And

in this kind of behaviour we do not find rigidly fixed missions and objectives. It is too opportunistic for that.

- The processes required to play games successfully in uncertain situations, and to conduct innovative experiments, are primarily intuitive and political rather than analytical and formal. The key to real strategic management is an effective political system in the business. This means visionary leadership, determination and effective teamwork.

- Successful strategic management does not mean preparing long-term plans — the future is far too uncertain for that. Instead it means improving the total control system of the organization so that it is fit and flexible enough to play dynamic business games in highly uncertain environments.

- To be fit and flexible in total control terms, businesses need to develop highly effective analytical, quantified, short-interval control subsystems for the day-to-day. They also have to develop highly effective political subsystems which encourage and enable intuitive behaviour and innovative experimentation. These two overlapping subsystems of the total control system have diametrically opposed requirements in terms of the processes applied, as well as in many other ways. But both have to be used at the same time because the business is bombarded simultaneously by day-to-day and other kinds of change. Using two different, overlapping subsystems at the same time creates control tension. And an essential part of strategic management is resolving that tension, walking a tightrope between diametrically opposed requirements placed on organization and behaviour.

- The corporate and business unit levels are intertwined in one political process which actually determines strategy. Differentiating between their roles in terms of their contributions to formal planning and review processes, or in terms of types of plan, is therefore not practical or helpful.

- What the conventional mentality does is foster ritualistic behaviour. Enormous effort goes into an elaborate annual budget tied to annually prepared five-year functional, business and corporate plans. Much less effort goes into more frequent budget updates to keep them credible. Annual staff appraisals concentrate on filling in forms rather than regularly reviewing specific performance against objectives. Most of the effort has little real impact on the control of the business. This book recommends scrapping expensive and distracting rituals.

The problems of strategic management are approached in this book within a conceptual framework in which control (ie accommodating change) is seen as the

central problem. The organizational and management problem is one of control in the sense of maintaining a continuing match between customer requirements and the competitive capability of the firm in the face of continuous change. Strategic management is the total control of the business, the management of change of all kinds, the handling of disturbances to business flows caused by change. Virtually everything about an organization is seen in terms of how it contributes to and is a part of control in this wide sense. And control is, in the end, a complex balancing act between short-term planning and opportunistic moves for the longer term.

I do not claim that anything in what I have written above is new. The reader will be able to find each idea or conclusion in one or another article or book. In terms of what successful companies are actually doing today, and have done for years, there is also little in the above which is new. What is different about this book is its attempt to put ideas spread across many branches of the management literature, together with observations on what actually happens, into an action-orientated conceptual framework. The aim is to redirect attention to what is practical, realistic and dynamic and away from an approach which I am convinced is diverting effort and wasting valuable management time, even in successful companies, with potentially disastrous results.

Most senior managers I deal with these days have absorbed conventional strategic management views into their thinking. Strategy consultants are still pressing companies to install formal long-term planning systems. Textbooks are still being churned out in the conventional mould and being used in Business Schools to condition the approach of both today's and tomorrow's managers. This book is offered as an antidote.

Outline of subsequent chapters

Chapter 2 explains why it is useful to think about strategic management in terms of playing games in uncertain situations. It introduces the idea that businesses simultaneously face different change situations. At one extreme there are closed change situations where the causes and consequences of a change are easily understandable and can be predicted. At the other extreme there is the open-ended change situation where causes and consequences are very difficult to comprehend and forecasting is totally impossible. These two change situations require different forms of control — tight, short-interval control in the one case and innovative experimentation, or control by trial and error, in the other. But these two forms of control make diametrically opposed demands on the total control system of the organization and create control tension. Strategic management is not simply about market moves: it is also about organizational moves aimed at continually resolving control tension.

Short-interval control in closed change situations — scientific management — is explored in Chapter 3. The two following chapters outline conventional strategic management and explain why it cannot work in the 1990s. Chapter 6 presents my perception of how successful companies do actually control in open-ended change situations — control by trial and error. Chapter 7 looks at typical control styles, where style is seen as the pattern of choices which companies make to resolve the tensions generated by the need to apply short-interval control and innovative experimentation simultaneously. The following two chapters address the question of how to improve control, the total strategic management of the business, and make 18 recommendations to assist in this. The final chapter summarizes the argument and the recommendations.

2
Conflicting Approaches to Management and the Nature of Change

Senior managers looking for advice on how to control their businesses most effectively are confronted with two fundamentally conflicting approaches. On the one hand they are exhorted to manage in a creative, intuitive, entrepreneurial manner. And on the other hand they are strongly advised to take the rational approach and plan for the future. Successful practice finds ways of combining both approaches, ways which change in sympathy with the needs of effective control in different circumstances. Successful managers walk a tightrope between opportunism and planning. And this complex balancing act is set to become even more difficult in the 1990s than it is now.

This book is about striking a balance between opportunism and planning; a balance which recognizes the nature of the change situations in which control has to be exercised.

Entrepreneurial games versus rational planning

Conflicting advice
There are increasing numbers of articles and books which talk about management in terms of planning for the main chance, opportunism, intuition and innovation.[1] The metaphors used relate to games, gambling, trade-offs, placing bets, calling odds, holding cards, battles, skirmishes and wars. Managers are exhorted to stop over-analysing problems, tear up rule books, throw away manuals, abandon rigid organizational structures and inflexible procedures. They are pressed to concentrate instead on listening to their customers, improving quality, involving everyone in everything, taking action in an experimental manner, either aggressively determined to win or cooperatively seeking alliances.[2] Mission statements are dismissed as useless, bland documents; and top-down strategies, with their five-year plans, are rejected in favour of letting the tactics dictate the strategy.[3]

At the same time the outpouring of textbooks and articles which focus on strategic management proper continues, on the whole, to present strategy in terms

of rational, analytical, long-term planning. Look at the contents of the vast majority of these books and they all run along the following lines:

> The corporate planning process and the need for planning. Beginning the planning process. Objectives, goals and standards of performance. The corporate appraisal. Analysing the competitive arena. Risk and uncertainty. Strategic planning. A closer look at strategy. A portfolio approach to strategy. Financial planning. Planning for human resources. Operating plans. Market planning. Project plans — capital investment appraisal. Making plans action. Completing the cycle.[4]

Different practice

The dichotomy between management as an entrepreneurial game and strategy as a logical, almost scientific procedure is present in the attitudes, pronouncements, discussions and actions of managers themselves. Consider some extracts from a speech made by Anita Roddick.

> In just 11 years the Body Shop has become by far England's most international store. We produce over 300 products sold in over 300 Body Shops from the Arctic circle to Adelaide ... We've done this with humour, intelligence, a sense of joy, magic and fun, which have always been our essential ingredients ... Marketing departments — like planning departments, management development departments and advertising departments are usually camouflages to cover up for the lazy or worn out executive ... So how do we do it? First know your differences and exploit them, then know your customers and educate them, then talk about the image of your company as well as of your products and finally be daring, be first and be different ... find out what your original features are and shout them from the roof tops ... never attempting to read a book on marketing or employing marketing skills ... we have found that when you take care of your customers extremely well, and make them the focal point, never once forgetting that your first line of contact is your own staff, profitability flows from that.[5]

Well she, in company with most conspicuously successful entrepreneurs and self-made millionaires, clearly belongs to the 'games' school of management. In fact catch most managers off their guard and you will hear them use the language of games and battles.

But the other approach to strategy, the rational and scientific approach of setting objectives and putting together five-year plans, now occupies a powerful place in the minds of very large numbers of competent and well educated managers. They may use that gaming and battle language over lunch and in unguarded moments at board meetings, but mention strategy and they switch mode to objectives and plans. Any suggestion that five-year plans are useless and should be avoided arouses a strong reaction: 'How else are we going to make long-term investment decisions?

You have to think about the future and plan for it. We have to establish where we are going. The company needs a strong sense of direction and that means a plan.'

In 1988 British Aerospace hired McKinsey and Co to recommend a framework for achieving its aims of turning its existing divisions into profit-driven businesses, accommodating acquisitions and sustaining long-term objectives. McKinsey recommended the adoption of a Strategic Architect style, in which the centre was to concentrate on establishing overall strategic direction and managing the business portfolio, while divisions responsible for making their own profits were established to run the businesses. A new planning and control process was set up with four stages:

- Each business will prepare a spring business plan for approval by the main board, which will focus on long-term strategic objectives.
- A new committee, the Business Investment Committee chaired by the corporate finance director, will review major projects required to achieve the strategy ...
- Operational programmes for achieving the strategic plan will be presented in the autumn budget and profit plan. This will give the milestones and financial targets for the coming year that will mark the progress of each business towards the long-term objectives laid down in its spring forecast.
- Quarterly reviews against budget will be provided by each business on the basis of exception reporting.[6]

A major British company, advised by one of the world's leading strategy consultants has therefore apparently just implemented a 'textbook' approach to strategic management. Others, no less successful, reject such goings on with outright contempt.

The purpose of this book is to try to put the fundamentally conflicting approaches to strategic management — the opportunistic view and the conventional textbook procedure actually implemented by many — into some kind of perspective. And that perspective is provided by considering the nature of changes facing the business. One change situation will leave you with little choice but to play entrepreneurial games and another change situation will have you thinking in coldly rational planning terms. So let us start with the games analogy and see how far it takes us.

Management as a game of business poker?

Winning depends on the cards your opponents play

Winning at poker depends on the cards you play relative to the cards your opponents put on the table. And the hands that both you and your opponents hold

change at each step in the game. This means that the set of important variables you have to deal with changes as you play. There is a strong parallel with the game of business, at least in some situations. The cards you hold, the set of variables you can operate with, are output prices and input costs, quality and service levels, product features, output levels, image, investment and so on. But the profit impact of any change you make in these variables depends very much on other variables: market size, demographics, commodity price changes, exchange rates and so on. Even more important, it depends on competitor offerings and moves. And the composition of the competitor group can change at any step in the game.

The set of really important variables you have to deal with changes as you play, just as it does with poker:

Alcatel of France has taken over ITT's European telecommunications activities to form the largest telephone equipment supplier in the region. Thomson in France, one of the two largest European defence electronic suppliers along with GEC's Marconi, has been reorganising this side of its business and has also taken over the RCA television business in the US. Ericsson, the Swedish telecommunications company, has moved into France's public exchange business with the purchase of CGCT. GEC tried to join the action three years ago with its abortive bid for Plessey, which was eventually scuppered by the Monopolies Commission ... Siemens made a similar move in 1986, when it was rebuffed in an attempt to acquire CGCT ... General Electric Company of Great Britain and Siemens of West Germany are in many ways very similar companies. Yesterday they gave their answer to the 1992 question mark in the most emphatic way possible — their joint £1.7bn bid for Plessey.[7]

But the game is by no means over:

Matra, the French privatised defence and electronics group, is negotiating a major new European partnership for its defence and space activities with Britain's General Electric Company (GEC) and Daimler-Benz of West Germany. The negotiations involve share exchanges between the three companies which would give GEC and Daimler-Benz a stake of 20 per cent each in Matra's defence and space operations ... In return, Matra would be keen to take a 20 per cent stake in GEC's Marconi subsidiary and in Deutsche Aerospace, the planned new Daimler-Benz subsidiary, grouping the West German car group's aerospace interests, including Dornier, the MTU aero-engine company, the aerospace sector of AEG and its proposed acquisition of Messerschmidt-Bolkow-Blohm. The Matra discussions bring a fresh twist to ... GEC's ... joint bid with Siemens of West Germany for its main UK rival, Plessey.[8]

With all this going on — and as we can see from newspapers every day, it is very widespread — is there really any point in preparing a five-year business plan? Surely what you have to do is improve your ability to play market poker. You are dealing

with a highly volatile set of variables; it is not just that the value of any one variable changes, it is the set of really important variables which is changing as well — some competitors disappear, others merge or establish special relationships and you do the same thing. As with poker it makes it very difficult to call the odds, or forecast, at any step in the game. Competitive capability is changing in unforeseeable ways over which you have only partial control.

But calling the odds is even harder because the rules change — open-ended change situations

At least with poker you know the rules. A particular combination of cards always gives you a certain number of points. But in the business game the rules, or parameters, can change. You cannot count on the customer continuing to pay the same price for the same product. Customer requirements change with changes in life styles and demands for higher quality, better service levels, lower prices and faster delivery. Other rules change too: rules on polluting the environment; rules on health and safety; legislation on employment and equal rights for minorities. Technology changes, altering the relationships between inputs and costs and affecting production efficiency. Relationships with customers and suppliers change.

Once again, newspapers every day contain ample evidence of these changes:

The screw tightens on machine makers

Can big corporations put the squeeze on their equipment suppliers? Yes, they can: and this is just what is happening to the manufacturers of special production machines in the US auto industry. Tighter tolerances, heavy warranties, the running of training courses for the car maker's employees, far tougher testing before installation; all these are being thrown at machine makers as requirements they must meet. This means that machine builders are being sucked into closer relationships with car makers, taking in both machine design and future component manufacture. The process is known as simultaneous engineering. 'People who do not change or meet these requirements are finished', says Dario Gianetti, sales and marketing vice president for Cross, one of the big three US special machine suppliers.[9]

You will easily find similar articles in a US newspaper about a UK component supplier, or in a French newspaper about a German equipment manufacturer. And in all these countries there are increasingly familiar articles along the same lines on just about any sector you care to think of. The story is always the same — more demanding customers. The very parameters within which businesses have to operate are therefore being subjected to widespread, rapid change.

Consider further extracts from the same article, on US machine builders:

Pressure on US manufacturers is being increased by foreign competition ... Three

European suppliers are dipping a toe into the US market ... US equipment makers are also wary of the Japanese.[10]

So it is not just the parameters set by customers, governments and technology which are changing; the set of variables we discussed earlier is changing at the same time. We therefore have a change situation which is clearly open-ended in the sense that everything is changing. It is poker with a difference; the hand of cards changes with each step in the game and so do the rules. The outcome of any move a company makes in this change situation is therefore highly unpredictable; highly unpredictable by definition. You have no hope of forecasting if the set of variables and the parameters are changing all the time. You are dealing with true uncertainty, the unknowable.

The immediate consequence of this open-ended change situation is that it becomes difficult to decide what the really important questions are because the variable set is changing. In the example of Cross, the US machine builder, the following questions are immediately raised by the changes it faces. What basis will the foreigners compete on? How big a resource are they intending to put in? Will they acquire a local competitor? What will the other local competitors do even before the foreign competition becomes intense? How will the customers respond? Should Cross take action now or wait? What action should it take? What will the market share consequences be? What needs to be done to meet the more stringent demands of the customers? Are these the important questions or are there others we have missed? On which of these questions should the most attention be focused?

The other consequence of the open-ended change situation is that we cannot feel very confident of the results of a change in a particular variable. We cannot reliably say what causes what. Forecasting is then an impossibility. We are in the same situation as a poker player.

Fortunately it is not always a game — closed change situations

Consider the nature of change involved in price pressures applied by customers to suppliers, by no means an uncommon occurrence in business today:

Jaguar's pre-tax profits plunged 51 per cent ... in 1988 ... Earnings are expected to fall further this year under the impact of continuing heavy currency losses ... the company would be profitable in 1989 ... The company is pinning its hopes on the success of a cost cutting programme, begun last year, which is aiming to reduce costs by 5 per cent ... It is squeezing component suppliers and expects around half of its savings in 1990 to come from a cut in its £600m materials purchase.[11]

Now there is little that can be described as open-ended in this particular change

situation, as far as either Jaguar or its component suppliers are concerned. The set of variables determining Jaguar's 1990 profits and cash flow is constant. The dollar exchange rate imposes a limit on car prices in the company's major market, the USA. Wage inflation in the UK will push up costs and the need to invest will consume cash. The set of important variables is clear cut. One variable in the set which the company can most easily influence is the price it pays for components. The causal connections between exchange rates, wage rates and component prices are clear, the parameters are constant. Both Jaguar and its component suppliers face a closed change situation in this particular instance.

Cross, the US machine builder discussed in an earlier example, faced an open-ended situation. But once the customer requirement for higher quality and better service levels was established, it faced a closed change situation. The variables which determine quality and service levels constitute a relatively fixed set and the manner in which they cause quality and service level improvements can quite easily be specified. Higher quality will be secured by installing detailed testing procedures, better materials purchasing and control, changes in work practices and worker motivation. Cross then simultaneously faces both open-ended and closed change situations.

In closed change situations we can call the odds, we can forecast with considerable accuracy because the set of variables and the parameters are constant. Sometimes business is not a game and bears no resemblance to poker.

And sometimes it is a game but the odds can be called — contained change situations

This particular change situation can be illustrated with another example taken from the *Financial Times*:

> In the last three years Japanese vehicle producers have implemented an extraordinary cost-saving programme designed to combat the impact of ... an appreciation of the Yen ... The share of bigger and better-equipped high value added vehicles has been increased. At the same time, Japanese producers have managed to bring forward programmes for further rationalising production processes, while also driving down procurement prices for components ... The Japanese automotive industry is steadily increasing the value of the parts and materials purchased outside Japan ... The re-sourcing of components is moving towards lower cost countries such as South Korea, Taiwan and Thailand ... The Japanese transplant operations in North America started out as relatively unprofitable ventures to head off protectionist measures in the US but they have become an economic imperative as a result of the soaring value of the Yen.[12]

This is really the same problem as that faced by Jaguar in the example on closed change situations. There we were talking about Jaguar squeezing UK component

suppliers — the set of variables was not changing and the causal connection between a change in any variable and profit was rather clear.

Here, in the Japanese case, we have a somewhat more volatile set of variables, involving product composition (the move from lower to higher value products), production processes, re-sourcing of components (to South Korea, Taiwan and Thailand) and geographic shifts of production (to the USA). And the causal connections are not as clear cut. For example the impact on profit of a shift in production from Japan to the USA is much more complex than the connection between price pressure applied to component suppliers and Jaguar's profits. The parameters in the Japanese case are rather more volatile. But neither the variable set nor the parameters are as volatile as they were in the example given on the European electronics industry.

We therefore have a situation which is neither closed nor open-ended, one which we may call contained. In such situations it is possible to call the odds. The situation is not unique; there is some comparable experience from the recent past upon which we may call. We are not dealing with truly uncertain situations but with risk; and in risky situations it is possible to apply probability, to talk about most likely outcomes. Forecasting can be performed with some degree of reliability, or at the least we are able to develop a small number of likely scenarios. Identifying what the issues are in the first place is not all that difficult and there is a fairly good understanding of what causes what, what the consequences of specific changes are likely to be.

Change situations

We can now draw together the discussion and look at what we might call a map of change situations. The three change situations have all been identified in terms of the volatility of the variable set, broadly speaking the factors constituting competitive capability, and the volatility of the parameters — that is, the causal connections between the variables and what the business is seeking to achieve, namely profit. The parameters we are talking about broadly correspond with customer requirements, or the sources of competitive advantage, the technological and cost structures of the business and the government regulatory framework within which it has to operate.

Parameter and variable set (including variable) volatility are shown on the two axes in Figure 1. Where both are highly volatile we get open-ended change situations, where both are relatively constant we get closed change situations and in between there are the contained change situations.

The business problem, the management problem, is one of control, where control means anticipating or accommodating the impact of change on some

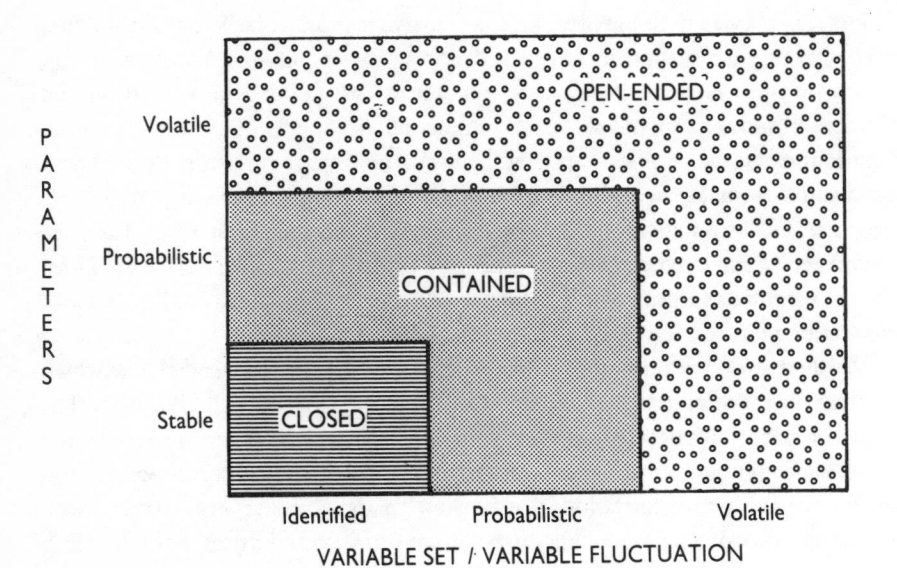

Figure I Change situations

desired state, for example profit or market share. Control means heading off the changes which rivals might provoke, and the best way of doing this is to create change which keeps rivals off balance, forces them to react and leaves them little time to provoke change of their own. Control is about benefiting from the impact of change on a desired state; it is about coping with disturbances to the desired state in an interactive way when others are also making moves. The starting point for understanding control is change.

Change in a desired state occurs when the value of some variable affecting that desired state alters or fluctuates, when new variables become important or old ones cease to be, or when the parameters connecting them to the desired state alter. Distinctive change situations are created by differences in the volatility of variables, the volatility of the set of variables, the volatility of the parameters and by the clarity with which they can be identified and understood.[13]

Closed change

So in a closed change situation, the set of variables is clearly identified and constant and the parameters are stable. Change occurs only because one or more of the variables in the set fluctuates within reasonably narrow bounds. In this change situation we can say with a very high level of confidence that a particular change

will affect the desired state and we can also say how it will affect the desired state. Control can then take a rather precise form and we can set clear quantitative objectives, prepare detailed plans, regularly monitor outcomes against plans and take corrective action swiftly.

Contained change

In a contained change situation there is an additional set of variables which is not constant — during some periods the set contains certain variables but later some drop out and others are added. But they do so in a probabilistic manner — we can identify which are likely to be important and which are not, using past experience; we can identify them in advance using probability. Individual variables in the set fluctuate more widely than in closed change situations, but we can still use probability based on past experience to form a judgement on the bounds within which they will fluctuate.

Furthermore, in this change situation the parameters connecting the variables to the desired state are not precisely known, but they can be estimated, using past experience, with a reasonably high level of confidence. Change to the desired state now occurs because variables fluctuate, the set of variables changes over time and so do the parameters, but all in a manner upon which past experience sheds considerable light. In this change situation we cannot say that a particular change in a variable will affect the desired state. All that we can say is that it probably will and we can estimate, with some confidence, how it will affect the desired state. We are dealing with a risk situation where the odds can be estimated. We can develop a limited number of scenarios which will in all probability capture the change.

Clearly, in this change situation we cannot apply exactly the same form of control as we could in closed change situations. Objectives will have to be less precise and more qualitative, plans somewhat more tentative, monitoring rather vaguer and action less swift.

Open-ended change

Finally, in open-ended change situations there is yet another set of variables. This set is highly volatile and difficult to identify; individual variables within the set fluctuate wildly. The parameters are also volatile. Here we cannot rely on past experience in any probabilistic way and scenarios become too many to handle — the situation is unique and truly uncertain; the outcome is unknowable. In this situation we cannot be all that certain which variables are important and which are not. We simply do not know how any variable change which may occur will affect the desired state. The only way to deal with this situation is to try things out and learn from our mistakes. The only form of control we can possibly practise is that of experimenting or playing games.

Unfortunately the definition of the change situations which face us are even more complex than that outlined above. Business is a dynamic system in the sense that the value of the desired state achieved in this period, say profit, becomes one of the variables determining the outcome in the next period, and so on through time. It is also a complex system in the sense that many of the relationships between variables are nonlinear, for example an increase in output can cause an accelerating decline in costs, the consequence of economies of scale. Such complex, dynamic systems can, at certain parameter values, give rise to fluctuations in the desired state which are for practical purposes 'chaotic', even when the parameters and the variable set are constant.[14]

Such systems are very sensitive to what is called initial conditions and this means that a small change now, one that is virtually unnoticeable, will escalate through the system over time and have a major impact on the desired state later on. Some new competitor arrives almost unnoticeably on the scene and ten years later you have lost your market. Open-ended change will then occur even in circumstances in which we believe it ought not to.

Combined change situations

It is possible to face change situations which combine closed, contained and open-ended aspects. There may be a set of variables which we know always affects the desired state in a way which is clear; another set may affect the desired state in a manner which we can estimate; and yet another set may be lurking around, difficult to detect and even harder to specify how it will affect the desired state. Given that small changes can have major impacts in dynamic systems we are ill advised to approach this hybrid change situation as if it were closed or contained and to treat the rest as unavoidable 'noise' or error; that little error could destroy the business. Where open-ended change is present we cannot rely, over the long run, on control forms which are appropriate for closed or contained situations.

Change situations and time frames

A closed change situation does not imply any definite time period. The description applies to any period extending into the future where one can be confident that change will be confined to a constant set of variables and confident of the manner in which change in any one of these variables leads to change in the others.

In past centuries, for example in feudal agricultural systems where the magnitude and pace of change were both modest, closed change applied to periods stretching decades ahead. In the 1950s and 1960s many companies could confidently think of change in closed terms for some years into the future. For most businesses today, facing major changes within short time periods, closed change can only refer to some months ahead. We are therefore talking about the short term, in practical

terms often less than a year. We are talking about the forms of control which are appropriate to accommodate change occurring now which has consequences within this time period. We are talking about the day-to-day management of the business.

The set of variables dealt with in day-to-day management is fixed and clear cut — customer demands, prices, material and manpower costs, equipment reliability, productivity, quality and so on. Each of these variables will of course fluctuate from day to day and it is the purpose of control to accommodate the disturbance which this kind of change causes in the short term to the basic flows through the business of orders, manpower and materials requisitions, inputs, outputs and money. Day-to-day management relates to producing at a profit to meet those orders already placed or about to be placed for existing products and services, using existing technologies and competing with existing rivals.

The presentation of substantially different customer requirements, the introduction of new technologies and the re-grouping of competitors may all be occurring at the same time, but they are creating a different change situation. This is so because their consequences stretch much further out into the future and the disturbances they create must be accommodated, controlled, in a different way.

Note that the problems and opportunities presented by these two different change situations all constitute today's problems and opportunities, to be dealt with and controlled today. The difference lies in the time period over which their consequences will be felt. The difference lies in the nature of the change situation, the volatility of variable sets and parameters, to which control is to be applied. The difference lies in the most effective form of control to be applied. This point needs to be stressed so heavily to head off the mistaken perception that day-to-day management is what you have to deal with today, while change outside this situation, the strategic, can be put off until tomorrow. Both are today's problems, they simply have to be dealt with differently.

What determines the combination of change situations
Every business continuously faces some combination of the three change situations. And the particular combination will depend upon three factors:

- The time frame we are considering. The shorter the time frame, the more predominant will closed change be and the longer the time frame the more dominant open-ended change will be.

- The magnitude and the pace of change occurring in the industries or market segments in which the business operates. The bigger and more rapid the changes, the shorter will be the time period to which the labels 'closed' or 'contained' can be applied. Substantial, fast-moving change means that in anything but the very

short term the business will have to deal with a high level of open-ended change.

- The extent to which the business is diversified in interconnected ways across a number of market segments. A number of different operational activities may serve the same customer base. Or activities serving different market segments may be interconnected in operational terms. One consequence is a far more complex causal connection between any variable, say investment in any one activity, and the total profit of the business. Parameter volatility is therefore likely to be greater. The set of variables is also expanded to encompass those that affect synergy between the interconnected activities. Variable set volatility is therefore likely to be greater. Once again, greater volatility means shorter time periods within which closed and contained change situations are likely to apply.

Change situations facing two companies — Plessey and Laing

Plessey, with its interconnected electronics activities in world markets characterized by large-scale restructuring of the competition, must occupy a very different position on the change situation map from, say, John Laing plc. The latter operates predominantly in the UK housing, building and civil engineering markets. Its major activities are not strongly interconnected and the scale and pace of change in its markets is relatively more modest than in the electronics and defence markets. The change situations which these two companies face in given time periods, say the next three to twelve months and the period three to five years hence, are very different. Figure 2 illustrates this.

What we are looking at is the consequences over the next three to twelve months and over the next three to five years of changes which are occurring now. In the first of these periods, Laing faces a predominantly closed change situation, while Plessey will have to deal with a much more diverse one.

The contrast between the situations faced by the two companies becomes even more stark if we take the longer-term view. If we are thinking about the consequences, in three to five years' time, of changes occurring now, then Laing faces a combination of closed, contained and open-ended change, predominantly the latter two. It has a number of long-term contracts, and it can predict many of the consequences for its housing and other activities of changes occurring in the demographic composition of the population.

But the possible consequences of changes in the European Community in 1992 and what this means for competition for European contracts is open-ended. And there may be changes in say the housing market which are as difficult to foresee now as the sudden rise and demise of timber-frame methods of construction were to foresee in the late 1970s and early 1980s. Plessey facing takeover bids from GEC and Siemens, in markets well known for their volatility, is confronted by a change situation which is much more open-ended.

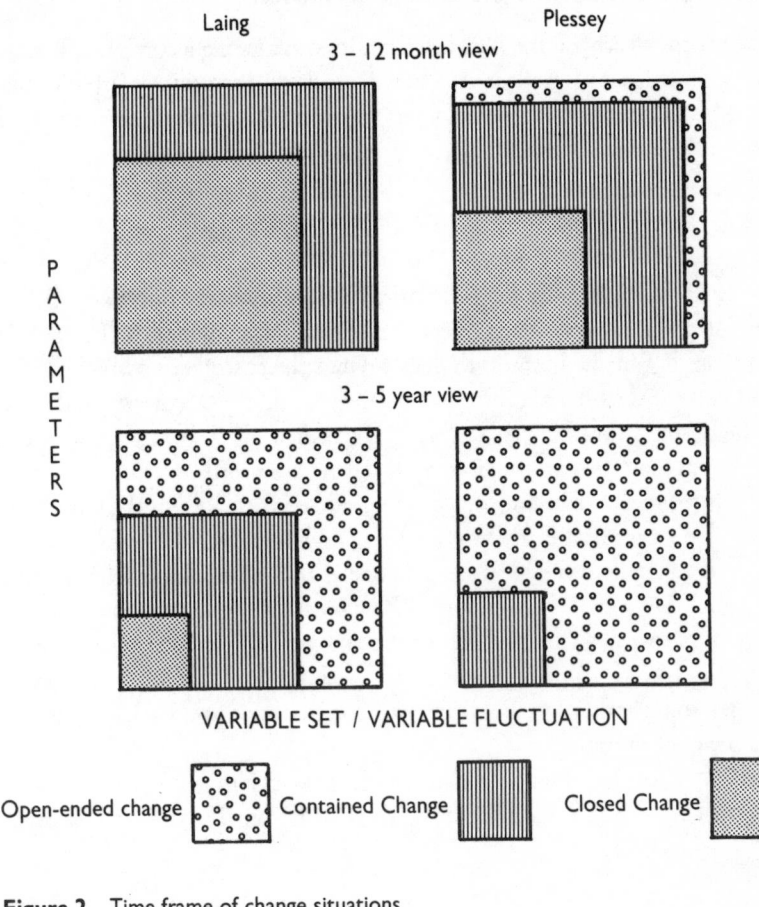

Laing　　　　　　　Plessey

3 – 12 month view

3 – 5 year view

P
A
R
A
M
E
T
E
R
S

VARIABLE SET / VARIABLE FLUCTUATION

Open-ended change　Contained Change　Closed Change

Figure 2　Time frame of change situations

Despite the different composition of change situations, both companies face open-ended change over the medium term. It really does not matter much that one faces relatively more of it than the other. Both have to deal with it, because ignoring this kind of change can have disastrous consequences. And there is only one way of dealing with this kind of change and that is by trying things out, by experimentation, by trial and error. Focus on the contained aspects of change and conclude that demographics point to a declining housing market. Conclude from this that you will not invest in a new plastics plant to manufacture drainpipes and you may find that a competitor does, secures lower costs, drives you out of that market and then uses the cash flow generated to mount competition against you in a completely different market segment. Thinking in contained change terms could destroy your business.

Effective control matches the change situation

It is vital to focus clearly on the likely change situation facing a company, because the form of control which will be effective depends on the nature of that change situation. The very meaning of control alters from one change situation to another.

The meaning of control

Change disturbs, or has the potential for disturbing, the basic task patterns and flows of inputs, outputs and money through a business. Some disturbances are problems which, if left unattended, will impair the ability of the business to deliver what the customer now wants. Others are opportunities which, if taken, will improve the ability of the business to deliver what the customer now wants. The purpose of control is to handle these disturbances so that task patterns and flows through the business continuously enable the fulfilment of customer requirements more effectively than the competition, and so generate profit.

Control, then, means 'directing and guiding' the performance of the business so that change can be profitably accommodated. Directing and guiding have no real meaning unless there is some idea of what one is trying to achieve, that is some purpose or goal. But a goal is not enough. There must also be some idea of the path to be adopted in reaching that goal. Directing and guiding can also have no useful outcome unless there is some opportunity to check on progress along the selected path and then some ability to take corrective action either to get back on course or to change the goal or path.

Control[15] therefore has three clear elements, all of which must be present in some form if control is to mean anything in any change situation. These control elements are:

- goal (or purpose) and path selection;
- progress checks;
- corrective action.

But the meaning of each of these three elements of control changes significantly as we move from closed, through contained to open-ended change situations. This is because the meaning of each element of control is different and because the focus of attention shifts from the planning to the monitoring element.

The meaning of control in closed situations

In closed change situations constant variable sets and constant parameters mean that all the elements of control have precise meanings. Goals become precise objectives which are comprehensive and clear cut. The paths to be taken to achieve

those objectives can take the form of detailed action plans with reliably predicted outcomes. Precise objectives and reliable forecasts become a plan. Checking on progress is a precise, quantitative comparison of actual events against outcomes, yielding variances. It becomes monitoring. Corrective action is simply a response to the variance, a response to get back on to the predicted outcome path.

The form of control can accurately be described as control by variance or exception and the prime requirement of this form is attention to detailed and precise planning.

The meaning of control in contained situations

The nature of the contained change situation, with its higher degree of variable and parameter volatility, means that the elements of control cannot be so precisely defined. Goals may still be firm, fixed and quantitative, but these are likely to be far less detailed and supplemented by more qualitative missions. The paths which are to be taken to achieve the goals and missions become more uncertain, because forecasting is less reliable and it is somewhat harder to specify the causal connection between any action and its outcome. Less detailed goals, qualitative mission statements and generalized actions constitute a strategic plan, essentially a grand design which the business is to follow.

But the difficulty in specifying causal connections creates real problems for the control element of checking on progress. Does an unforeseen outcome mean that we are no longer on the path to the objective? We cannot be all that sure. The difficulty with 'monitoring', if we can call it that in this change situation, immediately leads to some confusion as to the appropriate action to take. In this situation the form of control still focuses on planning, particularly the setting of goals and missions in the form of some 'grand design' for the future of the business. But the rest of the control activity becomes vaguer than it was in closed situations. We can call the form of control appropriate to contained change situations after its most prominent feature — control by grand design.

The meaning of control in open-ended situations

When we come to open-ended situations, the problems of control are compounded. It is difficult to identify the issues — the set of variables is highly volatile. We cannot forecast with any degree of reliability — the parameters are highly volatile. Consequently there is no point at all in setting fixed objectives, or overall goals and future missions. Purpose, or objective, becomes tentative — it may have to be changed as we go along. The path to the goal cannot be reliably specified in advance; it has to be clarified by experimentation, by trial and error.

Monitoring in the sense of detecting, understanding and paying attention to change becomes the most difficult part of the whole control process. The

monitoring element of control, in the sense of detecting change, in the sense of identifying important single issues, comes to dominate. Monitoring in the sense of checking on progress has a very limited meaning, because it is impossible to produce a reliable template against which to check progress. All it can mean is checking progress on a single issue, not the whole set of interrelated issues.

Planning in the sense of predicting change, setting fixed, detailed objectives and paths to them over time, is quite impossible. So the meaning of planning in open-ended situations also changes — it means trying out responses in as small and safe a way as possible to detected single issues; it is about planning as trial and error, as experiment, not as grand design; it is about developing agreed areas of operation, sets of values and senses of direction within which to experiment, to take opportunistic action.

Consequently, action is not deterministic, it is opportunistic. The form of control has more to do with experimenting, trial and error, games and gambling. A business in the open-ended change situation is very much in the same position as a research scientist working at the frontiers of knowledge. The scientist proceeds from tentative hypothesis to experiment. Experimental trial and error leads him or her to change the experiment, to alter or refine the hypothesis, until success is achieved. And sometimes success will mean a discovery far different from that which was sought in the first place. A business facing open-ended change situations has no option but to follow a similar procedure. The form of control is that of control by trial and error.

Trial and error may not sound all that controlled, but it is. There is purpose, albeit tentative. There is an approach to achieving the purpose, albeit experimental. There is a check on progress, although it may be only a judgement on the outcome of the experiment so far. And there is corrective action even though it may only be a decision to continue with the experiment, try another one, or abandon the whole thing.

A point of major significance is that the form of control which is appropriate to open-ended change is the diametric opposite of that which is appropriate to closed change. The former is about intuitive opportunism, while the latter is about analytical planning or determinism. But a business has to deal with both closed and open-ended change at the same time. Control becomes a balancing act between planning and opportunism, a continuing attempt to resolve the tension created by the need to apply two diametrically opposed forms of control simultaneously.

Management perceptions of change situations

The form of control which is appropriate to a given change situation alters as a logical consequence of the nature of that change situation. But the form of control which any organization actually adopts will depend on the change situation which

the managers in that organization in fact perceive and their understanding of, or belief in, what constitutes control and how it relates to the change situation.

Change situations in the 1990s

We cannot forecast what will happen in the 1990s. But we can list what is obviously happening now, the consequences of which will clearly extend well into the next decade.

In the next decade final consumer markets will continue to be characterized by accelerating change: the age structure of the consumer population will change markedly over short periods of time, bringing with it important changes in the composition of demand; the same is true of tastes and fashions; consumers now have far more money to spend and they demand higher quality. The requirements of industrial customers are becoming more and more stringent as they strive to improve profitability while meeting final consumer demands for new product offerings, better quality and higher service levels. Relationships between supplier and purchasing companies are changing, requiring more cooperation and different attitudes.

Competition is increasing, with traditional competitors becoming more efficient, falling to acquisitors, or disappearing. Competitors merge and, increasingly, joint ventures, cross-shareholding relationships and special understandings obscure the nature of competition. New companies enter markets, often from unlikely directions. And these markets increasingly exhibit what often look like contradictory trends towards fragmentation or changing segmentation on the one hand and globalization on the other. Companies, therefore, now more frequently face difficult market segmentation decisions and also choices between exporting and substituting for imports, or extinction.

The rate at which new technology is being applied in the search for competitive advantage is accelerating. The internal problems which companies face in keeping up with new technology and other competitive pressures are mounting.

Government policy changes are adding to the pressure with deregulation, privatization, tighter environmental controls and more stringent health and safety requirements. Supranational bodies, such as the European Community, with the proposed dismantling of frontiers and the establishment of common standards, are adding to the pressures for change and the need for adaptation.

Exchange rates and interest rates fluctuate wildly. And then there is the growing deregulation and internationalization of the capital markets, as well as the concentration of investor power in the hands of more sophisticated institutional investors with tight short term performance targets to meet.

What all this means is change of greater magnitude and faster pace affecting even

more industries and market segments than it has already done in the 1980s. New forms of cooperation, cross-shareholdings and joint ventures, all indicate more widespread interconnection between businesses. It is safe to bet then that most businesses will increasingly face open-ended change situations within shorter periods of time as we go through the 1990s.

But recurring features in all the likely developments outlined above are cost pressure, higher quality, better service levels, faster delivery. And once established, these are all about closed change situations. The framework within which they can be achieved is fixed, the parameters are constant. The set of variables you need to operate on to secure them is clear cut and well understood, at least until further changes in customer requirements lead to a new closed change situation.

Polarizing of closed and open-ended change

So in the 1990s businesses are likely to face, simultaneously, the increasing importance of both closed and open-ended change situations. This will call for the simultaneous practice of two fundamentally different forms of control — control by variance alongside control by trial and error. Trying to do two fundamentally different things at the same time creates tension. The 1990s can only sharpen the control tensions to which organizations and management have already been subjected for some time.

The rest of this book explores the tensions which are created by this need to adopt control forms that are polar opposites. It explores the fundamental difficulties of strategic management: difficulties created by the nature of open-ended change situations and the strain placed on business organizations and their managers by the need to practise simultaneously two diametrically opposed forms of control. And it puts forward practical recommendations for improving control.

We turn first to a consideration of some of the key points relating to control in closed change situations, short interval control or control by variance. Here control must be based on detailed planning — opportunism has disastrous consequences.

Notes
[1] Some examples are: R Evans and P Rusell, *The Creative Manager*, Allen & Unwin (1989); H Mintzberg, 'Planning on the Left Side and Managing on the Right', in J Quinn, H Mintzberg and R James, *The Strategy Process*, Prentice-Hall (1988); A Bhide, 'Hustle as Strategy', *Harvard Business Review*, September–October 1986; 'Planning for the Main Chance', *Australian Accountant*, December 1988; P Harper, 'Intuition; What Separates Executives from Managers', *Business Horizons*, September–October 1988.
[2] T Peters and R Waterman, *In Search of Excellence*, Harper & Row (1982); T Peters, *Thriving on Chaos*, Macmillan (1988).
[3] A Ries and J Trout, *Bottom-Up Marketing*, McGraw Hill (1989).
[4] T Hussey, *Introducing Corporate Planning*, Pergamon Press (1988).
[5] Reported in *Marketing*, 3 December 1987.

6 'British Aerospace', *Business Review*, January 1989.
7 *Financial Times*, 17 November 1988.
8 Ibid, 17 March 1989.
9 Ibid, 30 September 1988.
10 Ibid, 17 March 1989.
11 Ibid, 17 March 1989.
12 Ibid, 23 January 1989.
13 There is another complication which is mentioned later on. Where causal relationships between variables are nonlinear it is possible to get unpredictable change even when variable sets and parameter values are constant.
14 J Gleick, *Chaos*, Cardinal (1987).
15 Control is frequently used in the sense of checking on progress, or monitoring, and then taking some corrective action. In this sense it is seen as an activity to be distinguished from planning — it is the implementation of planning. Throughout this book the word control is used in its full meaning to encompass the planning element.

3
Control by Variance

Management information and control systems in closed change situations

The purpose of this chapter is twofold. First it is to develop the view that the short-term, day-to-day control of a business, using modern Management Information and Control Systems, is the initial step in, a precondition for, and in fact an integral part of, strategic management. Main stream textbooks on, and specialist consultants in, business strategy present strategic management as a separate kind of management which deals with the long term out in the market place.

These textbooks and consultants normally make little reference to that other kind of management which is seen as having much more to do with the short term inside the company. And this separation is now part of the received wisdom of large numbers of modern managers. In my experience, such separation, accompanied as it usually is by the logical proposition that the strategy comes first and the system is designed to fit, often leads to a failure of effective control.

The second purpose of this chapter is to establish the specific demands which Management Information and Control Systems, at their most effective, place on organizations and the behaviour of the people within them. It sets out those organizational and behavioural features which produce optimal control in closed change situations, in isolation from the need to practise control in any other change situation. In this way a framework is constructed within which to explore the fundamental problem of control — the tension placed on organization and behaviour by the directly conflicting demands of effective control in different change situations. The tensions themselves are explored in subsequent chapters.

Closed change and scientific management — systems

The form of control which is most effective in the closed change,[1] day-to-day situation is well understood and there is little argument about it. It is, basically, scientific management. The control problem is one of specifying causal connections between profit, quality, productivity, materials requirements and so on. The causal

connections are specified by analytical processes and detailed measurement. The values of key variables within an easily identifiable set are forecast and their consequences are projected in the form of a quantified plan. Actual outcomes are then compared to plan at short intervals and variances from plan trigger action; action which is predetermined, as far as possible, by assigning clear responsibilities to specific individuals. The thousands of day-to-day disturbances which change causes for the flows through the business are transformed into a much smaller volume of 'automatically' detected variances. Responses are required only when there is a variance. Responsibility for action on most variances is localized as far down the management hierarchy as possible, freeing the top levels to deal with other, more difficult, change situations; dealing with them today, not tomorrow.

This approach to control in closed situations focuses on disturbances which: have short-term consequences; can be localized and compartmentalized; are easily identifiable and accompanied by information adequate for rapid, effective action. The problem of control in closed change situations is very much internal to the company. Attention is directed to developing and supporting quantitative systems for handling change. The systems used to handle these disturbances, Management Information and Control Systems, constitute a given, fixed framework within which the disturbances can be handled. Once set up, they do not have to be adjusted as the disturbances arising in closed change situations are handled.

Components of Management Information and Control Systems

Management Information and Control Systems consist of the following typical components, all with the aim of accommodating disturbance to the basic flows through the business caused by changes in a constant set of variables:

- marketing and sales control — control of the whole process of obtaining orders from customers and linking these to requisitions;
- operations control, covering control of product and service outputs, quality and reliability, flexibility and responsiveness, timely delivery to the customer, facility capacity utilization, manpower efficiencies, materials usage efficiencies;
- control of materials procurement and availability;
- manpower control;
- facility control and maintenance;
- cost and revenue control — the budget;
- control of debtors and creditors;
- control of capital expenditure and financing.

These systems may be fragmented or integrated with each other. They may be manual or computerized. They may be effectively or ineffectively applied. But the

underlying principles are the same; it is only the degree of sophistication, the application of technology and the extent of effectiveness which varies.

In closed change situations, then, you can apply scientific management. But the need is far stronger than that — in closed situations you have to apply scientific management if you are to survive. The next three sections explain why.

Systems first to make time for strategy

The first powerful reason for establishing effective day-to-day control as a precondition for strategic management is that it releases the time and energy of senior management. It enables them to attend to strategic matters, matters which also have to be dealt with today, at the same time as the day-to-day. Effective Management Information and Control Systems transform the nature of day-to-day disturbances into a much lower volume of variances. Control can then be pushed down the hierarchy, leaving the top levels to deal only with certain selected, important variances. Time is created, the top levels are freed, to handle disturbances arising from the other change situations; and it is handling these which ultimately leads to a strategy.

So without detailed and comprehensive Management Information and Control Systems you will not have time to build strategies. The simple, conventional view is that you first develop a strategy for the business and then you decide on the appropriate systems. The more sophisticated and logically correct view is that strategy and systems are interdependent and circular. But the practical demands of management dictate the systems first, strategy next approach.

The mere existence of such systems does not in itself guarantee that senior managers will have the time to attend to the strategic. It all depends on how these managers use such systems. And there are three very common problems in this regard, all relating to senior management's fear of letting go on the day-to-day and their failure to perceive the true nature of this form of control — it is control by variance or exception. If senior managers do not concentrate on its exceptional nature then the benefit of time to focus on strategy building will be lost.

Problem — the quantity of information

The first problem is the sheer quantity of information which is fed up the management hierarchy. The frequent result of the generation and analysis of the vast quantities of information made possible by modern information technology, is thick reports with masses of detail landing on senior managers' desks every day. They either get bogged down in trying to absorb it or, more sensibly, they ignore it.

A parcels delivery company I worked with generated vast quantities of

information on all its customer accounts. But the information could not be extracted and summarized in a form which could be used to answer basic questions about the business. In fact there was so much of it, that it was normally stored in files and rarely used by managers at all.

Another client, a producer of building materials, segmented its markets in every conceivable way and collected data on market shares, volumes, prices and many other matters for each segment. The result was a number of substantial volumes published each year and updated during the year. But again there was so much of it, that it was simply ignored by the hard-pressed managers.

Other managers are not so sensible and plough through the detail, using up the valuable time which should be devoted to more fundamental issues. This problem is solved by focusing on the nature of control by variance. Information fed up the hierarchy should be based on exceptions, not on detail. Each level up the hierarchy should receive only information on the variances upon which it is required to take corrective action. Detail should decline dramatically as information flows up the hierarchy: a well-known requirement, but one frequently ignored.

Problem — wasting time
The second problem relates to the time which is spent at senior management meetings on discussing and reviewing the information fed to them by the systems. Even where the quantity of information is not excessive, it is common to find senior managers devoting well over half the time they spend together in reporting on and discussing day-to-day matters upon which they are not, as a group, required to take decisions.

For example — board meetings
As part of a consultancy assignment, I was required to attend, for some time, the monthly meetings and quarterly board meetings of a holding company with a number of subsidiaries in the road maintenance and building products industries. It had adequate information and control systems with regular procedures for reviewing results. Each of its subsidiaries held regular management meetings and quarterly board meetings to review performance against budget and discuss major issues facing that subsidiary company.

But in fact, the quarterly board meetings were rehearsed set pieces, where most of the time was spent on reviews against budget and administrative matters. These board meetings functioned almost purely as a vehicle for informing the holding company chief executive and securing his formal approval to changes which the subsidiary board wished to make.

At the holding company level there were also regular management and board meetings which involved the managing directors of the subsidiaries and key head

office executives. These too were largely occasions for information exchange on past performance and discussion, mainly of administrative matters affecting all the subsidiaries. From time to time major issues would be raised, for example the effects of a local authority expenditure moratorium, or the problems of moving into the small contracts end of the civil engineering market. But these major issues were simply referred to and never followed up.

The Management Information and Control System was therefore performing a vital function of bringing major issues to the surface, but the focus of its use did not lead to any follow up. Far from using its systems to free top management to attend to strategic issues, these managers devoted most of their time together to short-term control, leaving little time to address strategy.

Inappropriate use of Management Information and Control Systems therefore results in a narrow focus on negative variances from profit, rather than in a focus on fundamental issues. Furthermore, it is usually only the negative variances which receive much attention. But positive variances could also have a story to tell — the unexpected success could well lead to significant new opportunities if properly interpreted.[2]

Problem — failure to delegate

A third problem is where senior managers fail to use the delegation possibilities opened up by effective control systems. Middle management is granted little discretion, and absurdly small expenditures, already in approved budgets, still have to be referred up for approval. Budgets are scrutinized in immense detail by those right at the top of the management structure. The consequence once again is too little time to attend to changes occurring in other change situations.

Systems first to generate information for strategy

The second powerful reason why systems are a precondition for strategic management is that they generate crucial information on where the business is now: how it is performing and is likely to perform in the short-term future. If you do not know where you are now and why, you will be in no position to develop strategies. Strategy starts from where you are.

Once again the existence of a system does not guarantee that it will generate information which will be useful for the management of the business. There are a number of common deficiencies in the information generated.

Problem — accounting bias

The first problem is an excessive accounting bias in the selection of those variables in the business which are to be targeted, monitored and reacted to. Management

Information and Control Systems will only achieve their maximum effectiveness if the most relevant and action-orientated variables are the ones which are targeted, monitored and acted upon. At the sharp end of the business, operations and sales, we tend to find that immediately relevant and forward-looking variables are monitored and form the basis of corrective action. The focus is on order flows, prices, quality measures, measures of service levels.

But typically, as information is fed up the management hierarchy, these variables of central relevance to the business, and those which are forward-looking, tend to be dropped and what the higher levels of managers see is generally sales values and profits. Individual one-to-one contact between one level of manager and another, and group meetings of managers, then tend to discuss and focus on variances from profit targets which are at least one month old and frequently older. The whole focus inevitably becomes backward-looking and the lags between identifying a problem and taking corrective action tend to lengthen. Information on what is happening now is inadequate.

The solution lies in centring attention on forward-looking indicators and those directly relevant to the conduct of the business; those which lead to or cause profit — order flows, key prices, margins, market indicators, quality measures, customer complaints and so on.

Problem — poor linkage

A second problem is poor linkage between the different components of the Management Information and Control Systems in a company. This most often takes the form of very weak links between the accounting and budgetary components of control and those components which relate to operations control. The profit consequences of under-utilization of, for example, a transport fleet, may then be impossible to determine.

For example — operational components and profit

A company I worked with in the parcels delivery industry provides a good example. An aspect of this business which is of crucial importance in operational terms is the weight and size of the parcel delivered. The management saw its market and operational strength as lying in the delivery of the larger, heavier parcels and claimed that this constituted the major part of its business.

But the control system was incapable of yielding information on the numbers of heavier parcels handled or on the costs of handling these as opposed to the lighter parcels. A specially mounted exercise revealed that 60 per cent of the business was accounted for by lighter parcels. Some estimates showed that these were being delivered at a loss, but there was considerable argument among the managers as to the reliability of these estimates. There was also little clarity as to why so much light

45

parcel delivery business was being generated. It seemed to have something to do with the pricing structure, but information was not readily available to confirm or reject that supposition.

Problem — poor relationship to market segments

A third problem lies in the poor relationship of the Management Information and Control Systems to the market segments in which the company is operating. The whole purpose of Management Information and Control Systems is to drive the business towards its short-term goals by enabling its managers to know where they are now in business terms, what is realistically achievable in the foreseeable future and when they are falling short of achievement.

The information flows therefore have to be closely related to the nature of the business and to its markets if it is to achieve its purpose. There must be a clear relationship to the market segments in which the business operates and ready identification of where the business is making or losing money.

For example — agricultural merchanting

This company produces fertilizer which it sells through agricultural merchants, but also through its own retail team. This retail team also sells other products, in particular agricultural chemicals. The whole structure of the company and its Management Information and Control Systems did not reflect the fact that it was operating in two market segments — the fertilizer segment and the agricultural merchant segment. As a result there was no clear and regular answer to the question — where is the company making a profit and where is it making a loss? In these circumstances it is unlikely that managers will in effect be controlling costs. In fact, this company showed the major part of its sales costs as an unallocated overhead for which there was no clear responsibility.

Problem — purpose of the budget

A fourth problem which obscures what is likely to happen in the short-term future relates to the purpose which the budget, a key Management Information and Control Systems component, is meant to serve. One purpose the budget serves is that of a target which people believe in and strive for. Another purpose is to provide some standard against which performance can be judged. Yet another purpose is to provide a realistic judgement of what will be achieved by the existing business in likely market conditions.

Emphasis on the performance standard aspect leads to the view that the budget is fixed and cannot be revised as the year progresses — by hook or by crook, managers must achieve budget. The realistic judgement view, however, suggests that budgets should be revised in the light of reality. The whole process of

formulating performance standards in a large corporation creates pressures for budgets to be prepared early in the year to meet top management and accountants' desires for orderly procedures. But the need for credibility, motivation and realism point to preparing the budget as close to the start of the next year as possible. If budgets are to provide reliable information on likely short-term performance, then their preparation should not be governed by elaborate reporting arrangements and they should be regularly updated.

Fixed annual versus quarterley rolling budgets
It is a widespread practice nowadays to prepare an annual budget. Much effort is put into its preparation and into elaborate reviews at board meetings. It must be questioned whether elaborate annual procedures are appropriate in conditions of rapid change. The calendar year is quite artificial in terms of real change; change does not fall into calendar years, it occurs all the time.

In today's conditions, annual budgets soon become out of date. Objectives and specific action plans tend to be lost sight of; there are too many of them and they are stretched over too long a period. The whole expensive ritual diverts management attention for months every year. What is needed is rolling quarterly budgets, with small numbers of shorter-term objectives which are more frequently reviewed, and for which managers are held accountable. These objectives should not be purely financial. Continual preparation of quarterly updates instead of the comprehensive annual thrash around will have to take up less time and therefore be less accurate; but the accuracy of the annual budget is spurious; it so soon becomes out of date.

Problem — reluctance to see the defects
Why is the frequent poor use and inadequate information not corrected? The short-term, financial control of a business, or part thereof, is quite rightly closely tied up with the manager's own self-assessment. It is also tied up with the view his or her colleagues have of the manager. Many (male) managers seek the 'macho' image which goes with tight control. They will therefore be most reluctant to admit that there are problems with short-term, financial control. It is acceptable to own up to strategic problems; after all they are difficult to deal with. But criticize the short-term control systems of such a manager and you take the chance of diminishing his manhood.

A frequent problem encountered therefore is the received wisdom that Management Information and Control Systems are working. Allied to this is the view that the measurement of every single aspect of the basic business flows is not necessary. Managers claim that they know what is going on.

So, at the parcels delivery company referred to above, managers took some

persuading that better measurement of vehicle capacity was necessary. At first they did not regard it as a matter of pressing importance to measure depot capacities. As they developed their plans for related diversification into other segments of the parcels and letter delivery market, they came to see depot capacity utilization as a major determinant of the flexibility they would need. They then installed ways of measuring and monitoring capacity utilization as one of the tools they would need to implement their strategies. And this brings us to the next connection between Management Information and Control Systems and strategy.

Systems are part of strategic management — the implementation tool

An effectively functioning Management Information and Control System provides some degree of automation of control tasks, or at least a higher degree of clarity on when and what sort of action needs to be taken. It also provides an ability to cope with a high level of detail and complexity as well as the large volumes of information which are relevant to business success. These major benefits are of tremendous significance in five areas which are vital to the achievement of competitive advantage: productivity improvement/cost reduction; consistent provision of required service levels; consistent provision of required quality; consistent delivery on time; flexibility of operations and responsiveness to short-term changes in customer requirements.

For example — delivering consistent quality

A manufacturer of bitumen-coated roofing felt cannot deliver consistently to a predetermined quality standard unless that manufacturer sets standards at each step in the manufacturing process, establishes testing procedures at important points and has the ability to trace every piece of material back through the production process when any fault is detected. In other words quality delivery is impossible without a carefully specified Management Information and Control System. And this is exactly what BS 5750 is all about. The British Standards Institute grants a BS 5750 certificate to an establishment only when that establishment demonstrates that it has installed a detailed, functioning Management Information and Control System which enables control at each step in the production process.

The McDonald fast-food business is a classic example of securing competitive advantage through the provision of consistent quality and service levels. The Roman Catholic Church is perhaps the only other institution in the world which delivers exactly the same service anywhere in the world — only the language changes in both cases. The secret of the hamburger with the same taste, delivered with the same speed and friendliness the world over, lies in the complex, hard to

copy, Management Information and Control Systems with their tremendous attention to every detail of product quality and service delivery. This system is backed by detailed and comprehensive training (the McDonald Hamburger University!) and reward schemes. The result is a thriving, worldwide business.

A similar example is provided by the theme park business of Disney. Visitors to Disneyland are always struck by the smooth way in which very large crowds are handled by armies of uniformed and smiling young people, who have been trained to be 'entertainers' at the Disney University. These same visitors are also struck by the almost neurotic speed with which every piece of discarded paper or abandoned cigarette end is picked up by white-coated sweepers roaming the park with dust pans and brooms. The result is a clean, orderly and, for some, exciting environment, as well as a high level of quality service which attracts millions of visitors each year.

So the Management Information and Control System is all about delivering competitive advantage. It is a key part of competitive capability. It is the tool for the implementation of strategy. There is not much point in developing strategies if there is no tool for implementing them or consistently sustaining them. And you cannot implement strategies, or at least sustain them and give them continuity if there is no tight, short-interval control system. Not only is short-interval control a precondition for strategy, it is an integral part of it, because implementation is an integral part.

But systems make specific demands on organization and behaviour

Management Information and Control Systems then are a precondition for effective strategic management because they release senior management time, they generate vital information and they provide the tool for the continuing delivery of a strategy. They do all these things if senior managers use them properly, but all too often they do not. There is, however, a far more fundamental problem. Such systems impose specific requirements on organization and behaviour which are the polar opposites of those required by control in other change situations. The rest of this chapter examines the demands made by control by variance. Later chapters explore the control conflict which they create. For the moment then we ignore the requirements of control in other change situations and look for answers to this question. What specific organizational and behavioural features do Management Information and Control Systems at their most effective call for?

Detailed short-term, definite, tightly constrained objectives
The effective use of Management Information and Control Systems demands that goals should be precise, quantitative objectives which are fixed for specific points in the short-term time frame. These objectives take such forms as a level of orders

from customers which is to be achieved by the end of a time period; a level of production by the end of each time period; standards of output per person per time period; cost levels or standards; profit to be earned in a set time period; safety levels to be achieved; pollution standards to be satisfied; and so on.

Ideally there can be no extraneous excuse for failure to achieve the objectives if the Management Information and Control System is to operate at the maximum level of effectiveness. The most effective short-interval control does not excuse non-achievement of an objective in subsidiary A on the grounds that achievement would have harmed subsidiary B. If such an objective is set then the consequent harm to B must be assumed to be acceptable. If it is unacceptable then the objective should never have been set in the first place. The same point applies to health, safety and environmental impact. If impact on the environment, on health and safety and on other parts of the corporation is to be taken into account then objectives need to be set for this. The impact of achieving them will have to be incorporated into other performance and financial objectives.

Unless objectives are tightly constrained, in the sense that they mean exactly what they say, then major benefits of Management Information and Control Systems will be lost. As soon as judgement is allowed as to when objectives are to be achieved and when they can be allowed to slip, the variances thrown up by the system will no longer reflect specific categories of disturbance to be handled by particular levels of management in a prearranged way. Higher levels of management will not be able to rely on a largely automated system, and more and more disturbances resulting from change will have to be fed up the hierarchy for attention.

I am not advocating that, once set, objectives should always be achieved no matter what harm this does to the total corporation or to the rest of society. All I am doing is establishing that the Management Information and Control System operating at its maximum effectiveness has this implication. It is what really tight, short-term control means — you have carefully thought about all the important matters and realistically reflected them in the objectives which you have set for people to achieve. Once you have done this then only the remaining unforeseeable matters will be reflected in variances which have to be referred up the hierarchy. And there should not be all that many because you are dealing with a closed change situation where it is possible to determine interconnections and make forecasts.

Analytical, quantitative, formal and instructing processes applied to the planning element of control

The dependence on detailed short-term objectives which are interpreted by people in the organization in a tightly constrained, definite way underlines the importance of careful, comprehensive and accurate planning. Of the three elements of control,

planning, monitoring and action, the prime emphasis in control by variance has to be on planning: not only in the setting of precise objectives, but in the comprehensive specification of how they are interrelated and what paths are to be followed in achieving them. Such careful planning reduces monitoring and action to relatively easy tasks.

Achieving this result calls for the application of specific groups of processes. Detailed analysis of the flows of orders, requisitions for materials and manpower, inputs, outputs and money is required. Detailed quantification is necessary at each step. Comprehensive formal rules and procedures need to be laid down in manuals. Formal, precisely defined communication becomes necessary, as do regular, formal review meetings to establish plans, monitor variances and pass on instructions about corrective actions.

The result is an interconnected set of objectives and action plans cascading down in increasing detail from the top level in the management hierarchy. Flowing the other way is formal, regular information of decreasing detail; information which focuses on variances or exceptions. Instruction on corrective action then flows down the hierarchy.

Particular role attributes and constraints

It is of course people who apply processes to the elements of control. And in any group context people operate through roles. The role of any individual in a group is the part they play in the group; how and where they fit, what is expected of them in broad terms and how they are expected to behave in broad terms. The role is not the same thing as the tasks those individuals are to perform or the processes they are to apply, just as in a play, the words the actor speaks can be distinguished from the role he plays.

Management Information and Control Systems, the application of formal rules and processes to sharply defined elements of control at clearly specified levels in the hierarchy, obviously require well defined roles for those who are to operate them. The definition of roles must establish who is required to determine the goals and time paths (planning); who is required to monitor the variances; who is required to collect and put information on actual events into the system; who is required to take corrective action on the variances. The variances which are to trigger action by each level of the hierarchy will have to be clearly established. This in turn will call for specific information flows which are appropriate for each level in the management hierarchy.

Management Information and Control Systems impose particular attributes and constraints on roles. They require an emphasis on specific bodies of knowledge and experience. They require skills or competences in leadership, particularly those aspects of leadership relating to the exercise of authority and the delegation of

responsibility. They also require the ability to accept and exercise responsibility for the performance, or control, of the area of the business allocated to that role. And Management Information and Control Systems impose significant constraints on roles through the formal definition of position in the organization and through the resources which are allocated for the performance of that role.

Particular role perceptions

But no matter how clear and precise role definitions are, they will only partially determine the role. Individual perceptions of that role will also determine the attributes which are in reality applied and the constraints which actually count. At its most effective, control by variance requires that people have parochial perceptions of their roles. The main focus of the perception is one of the role in the specific part of the organization to which the person belongs. Such parochial perceptions actually reinforce the specific, definite and tightly constrained objectives which are set. The whole point of clearly defining roles and allocating very specific responsibilities is to get a particular manager or worker to focus very clearly on one part of the organization and take responsibility for the performance of that part. At their most effective, Management Information and Control Systems actively discourage perception of the role in terms of the organization as a whole.

Particular role relationships

There is another demand which the control by variance approach makes on roles, this time to do with the relationship between one role and another. The separation of the control problem into clearly defined parts, each with very specific objectives and roles, means that relationships will be of the directing kind. Where there is no pre-programmed rule for dealing with a variance thrown up by the system, the matter is referred to the next level in the hierarchy and corrective action is taken as the result of an instruction. Relationships are instructional and characterized by vertical referral up and vertical instruction down. The point of the detailed system is to cut down on the need for much collaboration at the same level in the hierarchy.

Particular approach to matching people to roles

Any specific approach to control creates certain requirements of the role, and people need to match these if the approach is to be effective. People need to fill roles. Putting people into roles cannot, of course, be left to chance. Instruments which match people to roles are an integral part of any effective control system. And these instruments are selection, training and development, and reward systems. Management Information and Control Systems impose certain conditions on each of these matching instruments.

Management Information and Control Systems set particular criteria for the selection and development of people because of the role attributes they call for and the constraints they impose. The principal criteria are specific bodies of knowledge and experience and a number of fairly easily defined competences and skills which have to do with motivating teams, exercising and accepting authority, delegation and so on.

And at their most effective Management Information and Control Systems call for personal rewards which are clearly tied to individual performance. Rewards which depend heavily on the achievement of well specified and quantitatively measured objectives will strongly reinforce the whole operation of control by variance.

Simple/flat, decentralized organizational structures supported by conservative cultures

The essence of control by variance is the separation of the control problem into clearly defined parts and the clarification of what everyone in each part is required to do. This demands an organizational structure which is simple and easy to understand; one in which responsibilities are clear cut and do not overlap. This condition is most effectively met when the structure of the organization is one of decentralization into clearly defined profit centres with independent operational systems corresponding to specific, independent market segments. The complication of information flows up and down the hierarchy are minimized by structures which are flat, that is having few levels of management. Such structures impose constraints on roles, by formally defining positions in ways which are clear and easy to understand.

But no matter how well everything is defined, measured and clarified, every system has to contend with people in groups. And people in groups never behave in the automaton mode which the ideal Management Information and Control Systems would call for. The systems must therefore be supported by the culture of the organization. Organizational culture is an instrument of control. Shared values, beliefs and ideology are indeed the most powerful instruments of control.

A strong organizational culture cuts down on the need for communication; common understanding replaces the need for much information exchange. A strong organizational culture can either powerfully reinforce or seriously impede the operation of any form of control. The short-interval control approach will be strongly supported by conservative cultures; cultures where objectives are accepted rather than questioned; cultures where people focus on narrowly defined tasks rather than on wider experimentation; cultures where people know their place. Such cultures promote ideology, strong beliefs in central values such as quality or

low cost. Conservative cultures match the nature of closed change situations, create stability and reinforce control by variance.

Missions, and their written form, the mission statement, are usually presented as part of longer-term or strategic management. But they are much more clearly a part of day-to-day management.[3] Systems for quality control are now widely accepted to be insufficient on their own. The wider concept of quality assurance incorporates systematic control within an ideological framework, where all involved believe in and value quality. The same point applies to matters such as customer service, low cost and high productivity. Control by variance must be supported by central, shared values, by beliefs and missions. And it is strong, conservative cultures where missionary zeal thrives.

Control by variance and its requirements summarized

The operation of Management Information and Control Systems, at their most effective (ignoring the need for simultaneous control in any other change situation), places specific demands on the organization and the behaviour of the people in it. These demands relate to the nature of objectives, the relative focus on the elements of control, the categories of process to be applied to control, the attributes demanded of and constraints placed on roles, the kinds of role perceptions and relationships, and the nature of organizational structures and cultures. These specific demands are summarized in Figure 3.

What I have been describing is scientific management accompanied by a number of well understood rules of organizational behaviour. It is a standard approach adopted by successful management consultants who design and install Management Information and Control Systems or improvements to them. This activity of installation and improvement is a substantial industry on which companies spend sums running into many millions every year. There is ample evidence that it works and that it produces significant results in remarkably short periods of time. And it works because it matches realistically the nature of the change situation it is intended to deal with. It focuses on detailed analysis and forecasting, precision and comprehensiveness, where such things are possible. They are possible because they are applied where change is occurring within given parameters in relation to a constant set of variables.

But business has, simultaneously, to face other change situations as well. And control by variance, the Management Information and Control Systems approach, is not at all appropriate to these. Conventional strategic planning recommends an approach to control in these situations which we may call control by grand design. This approach is discussed in the next chapter.

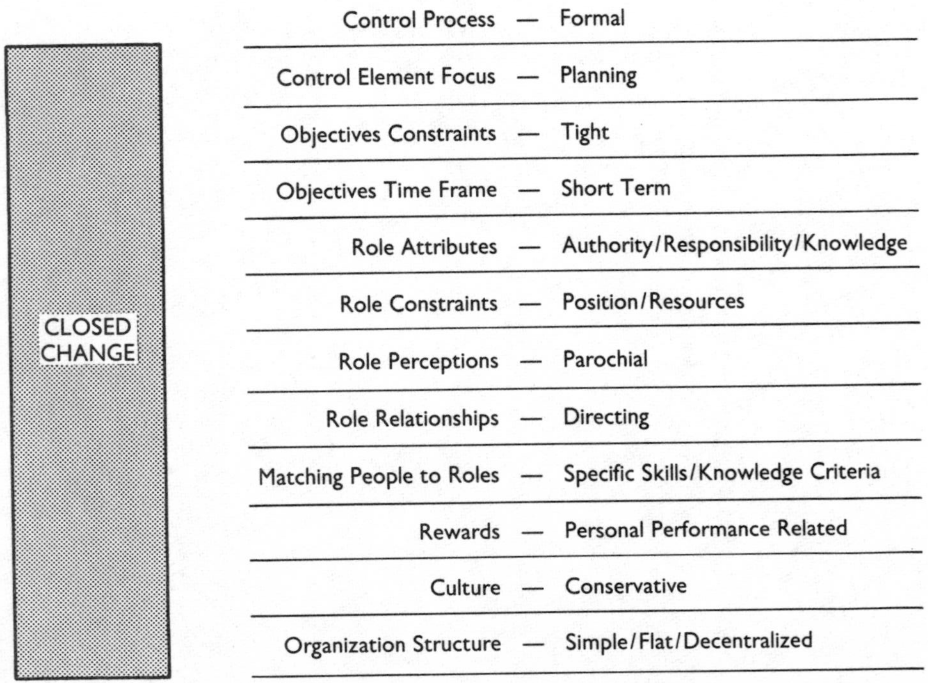

Control Process	— Formal
Control Element Focus	— Planning
Objectives Constraints	— Tight
Objectives Time Frame	— Short Term
Role Attributes	— Authority/Responsibility/Knowledge
Role Constraints	— Position/Resources
Role Perceptions	— Parochial
Role Relationships	— Directing
Matching People to Roles	— Specific Skills/Knowledge Criteria
Rewards	— Personal Performance Related
Culture	— Conservative
Organization Structure	— Simple/Flat/Decentralized

CLOSED CHANGE

Figure 3 Requirements for control by variance

Notes

1 See Chapter 2 for a definition of closed change.
2 P Drucker, *Entrepreneurship and Innovation*, Heinemann (1985).
3 See Chapter 2.

4
Control by Grand Design

Conventional strategic management

Control in closed change situations is relatively simple. The real problems surface when you have to confront change outside those situations. It is this kind of change which conventional strategic management addresses. The purpose of this chapter is to identify the distinctive features of conventional strategic management as a form of control. This leads to three questions:

- What is conventional strategic management as it is understood by managers and those recommending its practice?
- What does the form of control it proposes add to the control of the business?
- What is the outcome in practice of applying the principles of conventional strategic management?

By conventional strategic management I mean the body of views and prescriptions which is to be found in most textbooks on the subject; that which is practised by most strategy consultants; that which is visibly adopted by companies with formal long-term planning systems of some sort, perhaps accompanied by corporate planning functions. The next two sections describe this conventional strategic management approach. These sections do not try to provide a comprehensive or critical summary of the literature, a description of the problems encountered in practice, or an analysis of the effectiveness of conventional strategic management. What they do is try to get at the advice which the main body of conventional strategic management gives to managers on what should actually be done to practise control outside closed change situations, what consultants who recommend it and managers who use it demonstrate they understand it to be. The focus is on an overall view of the manner in which control outside closed change situations should be exercised, what tensions this creates when it is added to control by variance and what results it achieves.

We deal first, then, with the question: What is the advice conventional strategic management gives? At its most basic, its recommendation to the manager is to

prepare a blueprint for the future and then use it to control the business over the longer term.

Prepare a blueprint for the future — the grand design

The blueprint, or grand design for the future, consists of clearly understood, perhaps written down, missions, long-term objectives, strategies and quantified financial plans. It results from a careful analysis of methodically collected information on the business and its markets, and projections of the consequences of likely changes and the intended responses to those changes. Such analytical processes are not applied haphazardly, they are part of regular, formal procedures.

The blueprint is then used as the framework within which the business is to be controlled over the next few years, that is, the framework for the budget, for specific action plans at all levels in the business, and for the specific tactics which are to be adopted. Organization structures, cultures, short-interval control systems, just about every other aspect of the business you can think of, are developed to fit the grand design.

The grand design starts with a mission

It is now rather widely received wisdom that effective long-term control requires a business to have a mission which is believed in by, and which drives the behaviour of, all who work within it; that the leaders of the business should have a vision of that business which they share with those whom they lead. These terms, mission and vision, are used in two rather different senses. The first has to do with the here and now, while the second has to do with the future.

Here and now missions

In the here and now sense, the mission of the business is an expression of what it stands for, the central values and beliefs which drive the behaviour of its people. And the vision of its leader means much the same thing, being what he or she sees as important in the real world now, in much the same way as the vision of the artist refers to what he or she has selected from complex reality to present in picture form. The mission and the vision are then expressions of the company's ideology, its chief cultural values. Missions and visions are expressed in the way people talk, the way they behave and sometimes in what is written down in a 'mission statement'.

The retail chain, Marks & Spencer, is well known for its mission, the vision of its founders, to provide only the highest quality. On one occasion I know of, Marks & Spencer inspectors insisted that workers in a factory supplying them with tin cans for wrapped toffees should wear hairnets and hats, that cigarette ends should not be dropped at the canteen door and that graffiti should be removed from the toilet

walls. These requirements had little to do with quality in any practical sense. But they do demonstrate how pervasive, how believed in, the quality value is in that company. Real missions, then, are reflected in almost obsessive behaviour, not just in carefully worded statements. Missions, in the here and now sense, generally relate to quality, customer service, integrity, treatment of employees, attitude to profit, attitude to the environment, to health and safety and any other vital values or beliefs relating to the conduct of the business. In this sense mission, vision and organizational culture mean much the same. And in this ideological sense they are vital to the day-to-day control of the business, to Management Information and Control Systems, to control by variance in closed change situations.

Future missions

It is in the other, future-orientated sense, that missions are relevant to control outside closed situations. Here mission and vision refer to what the business and its leaders want to be, where they want to be, at some point in the future. And this point is usually five or ten years hence. Mission here is all about direction into the future. Managers find it much harder to set out this kind of mission.

The kinds of answer you get to a question on future mission are: to continue to stress existing values; to maintain the existing customer base; to improve quality; to become a highly flexible producer with much faster delivery times; to reduce dependence on one major customer; to increase the proportion of, say, package deliveries in the next-day segment from 40 per cent now to 60 per cent in five years' time; to become the market leader; to have 40 per cent of the business in the USA; to penetrate the German market; to operate in defined market segments and geographic areas; and so on. Missions in this sense begin to fuse with long-term targets and objectives, the latter tending to be more quantitative. Typical long term objectives relate to market shares, profit growth rates and rates of return on capital.

Whether they be written down, or simply clearly and widely understood, the firm recommendation of conventional strategic management is that missions, visions and objectives, in their future-orientated sense, should be established; that they should be firm, definite, relatively fixed and therefore inevitably restrictive. This view of missions and objectives is central to the conventional strategic management approach to control and it is one to which we shall be returning later.[1]

The grand design develops long-term plans

Long term plans, or strategies, set out how the business is to achieve its missions and objectives. They are broad courses of action which are to be followed over, say, the next five years. So a mission or objective of shifting 20 per cent of the package delivery business to the next-day delivery segment of the market will be accompanied by strategies such as: refocusing the attention of the sales force from

heavy engineering companies to those in the financial sector; identifying ten sites for smaller collection and delivery depots; investing in a larger fleet of small delivery vans; improving systems of tracking packages between consignor and consignee, and so on. These broad courses may or may not be written down, but conventional strategic management would recommend that they are.

The grand design concludes with the financial plan

Finally, in the conventional approach, the financial implications of likely market changes and intended courses of action are reflected in a quantified form. Projections are made of the financial implications in terms of sales revenues, profit levels, capital expenditure required and cash flows for each of the next five years at least.

And this is the blueprint, or grand design, for the future. It sets out clearly what the business intends to achieve, how it intends to go about achieving it and what the financial consequences are likely to be. It presents a snapshot of the business now and a snapshot of what the business will be in five years' time. It also maps out a pathway from the current snapshot to the future snapshot. It is a clear direction to a point in the future.

The grand design flows from analysis of the business and its markets

Conventional strategic management provides direction on how to develop the grand design for the future. The literature on the subject and the consultant practitioners make all sorts of qualifications about the order in which preparation might proceed, the techniques which might or might not be used and whether it is ever possible to practise strategic management in a strictly logical order or not. But whatever the sequence, whatever the techniques, whatever the misgivings, there are specific components and specific processes which are recommended. The components are summarized briefly in Figure 4 and described in the following sections.

Analysing the current situation

A thorough analysis, using comprehensively collected information, of the current situation in which the business finds itself is an obvious and practical starting point. This normally involves clarifying the nature of the business and setting out a definition of it; analysing the markets it operates in, the technologies it uses, the customer requirements it satisfies, where it is making money and where it is losing it. Considerable stress is laid on the need to segment markets according to customer groupings, common sets of customer requirements, common groupings of competitors, common technologies and common products. The point is to establish clearly the distinct, independent market places in which the company operates. As

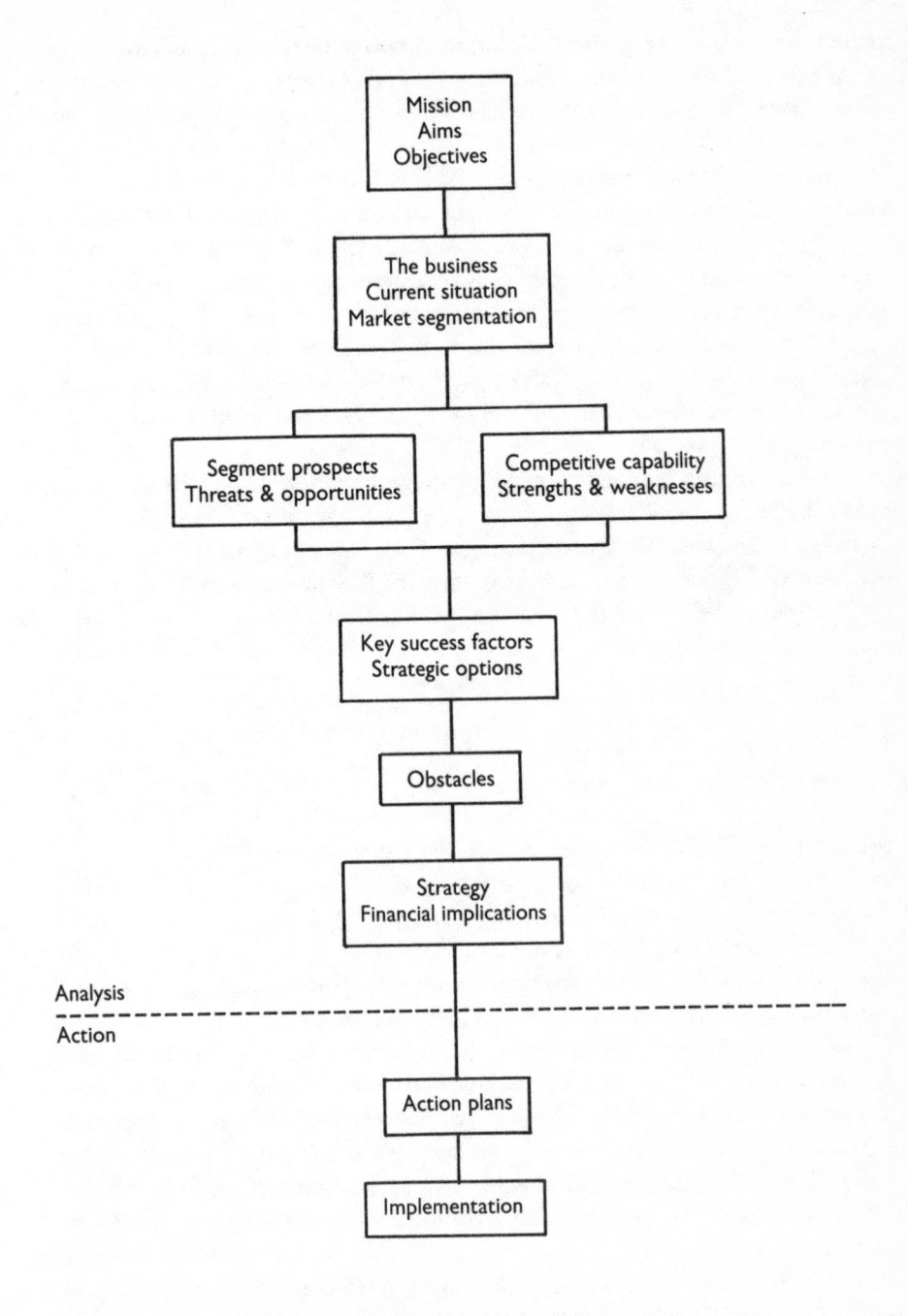

Figure 4 The conventional strategic management process

part of this analysis of the current situation, missions for the future and long-term objectives may be established, but they may also emerge later, on a further repetition of the whole analytical process.

Analysing market segments

Having established clear, independent market segments, each of these must be carefully analysed. And there are well developed approaches and check lists for examining customer requirements, growth determinants, industry and market structures, competitor capabilities and strategies. What we are seeking to do is to identify growth trends or the lack of them, the sources of competitive advantage, likely competitor moves — in short the opportunities and threats facing the business. We are identifying those market factors which will determine the possibility of making money.

The outcome is an improved understanding of the forces likely to shape the market in the future and a set of predictions or forecasts of what is likely to happen in the markets in which the business operates. These predictions may be in a detailed quantitative form, in a more qualitative form, or they may be a small number of likely scenarios. Whatever the form, the requirement of conventional strategic management is that some view be taken as to what is likely to happen, out in the market place, over say the next five to ten years.

Analysing competitive capability

Another clear requirement of the conventional approach to strategic management is that the competitive capability of the firm in each of its market segments should be carefully analysed. This means comparison of every key contributor to meeting customer requirements with those of the most successful rivals. It involves critical comparisons with competitors in relation to organizational structures, control systems, marketing capability, operational capability, research and development, design, distribution and so on. The whole point is to identify clearly the company's competitive edge, its specific competences, its strengths and weaknesses.

The market analyses and competitive capability analyses must then be brought together to identify critical opportunity or improvement points. And there are a number of approaches suggested for doing this: Strengths, Weaknesses, Opportunities and Threats analysis (SWOT); business portfolio techniques such as the Boston Grid or the Shell Directional Policy Matrix, basically devices for comparing the relative market attractiveness and competitive capability of a number of different market segments or businesses; or Profit Impact of Market Strategy (PIMS), which uses a large sample of companies to estimate relationships between profit and possible determinants of profit such as market share, quality and investment levels.

Strategic options

The point of bringing the analysis together in this way is to identify key success factors and generate the strategic options open to the business. What we are essentially looking for is how we can take the competitive advantage, how we can build competitive capability, how we can use interrelationships, how we can exploit the synergies between one business and another, how we can optimize and manage our portfolio of businesses, how we should allocate our resources to best long-term advantage.

The strategy

From the options generated by the whole analytical procedure it is necessary to extract those that will form the strategy. It is therefore necessary to consider how each option might fit the organization and its environment, what the obstacles to realizing it might be, and whether the consequences are acceptable or not. The options with the best fit, the most surmountable obstacles, the most acceptable consequences, the greatest feasibility, are then chosen to form the strategy. Its financial implications in likely market conditions are projected, usually for five years ahead. What we have at the end is a hierarchy of plans. There are business plans which set out the broad courses of action of the business units and functional plans which spell out what the business plan means for each function. Then there is the corporate plan, which pulls together the plans for all the business units and sets out corporate direction, portfolio balance and resource allocation.[2]

A key point about the whole process described above, one to which we shall be returning, is that it is all about the application of analytical, quantifying and forecasting processes to the control element of planning. It is about analytically establishing a grand design, firm objectives and broad paths by which they are to be reached over the next five years.

The grand design and regular, formal procedures

The aim is to draw up a robust blueprint which will remain realistic over a number of years. But conventional strategic management recognizes that a change situation, in which consequences extend over a five-year period, must at the very least be what we have called the contained variety. The set of variables relevant to the performance of the business and the parameters through which they have an effect on the business are likely to show some volatility. There is a need therefore to reappraise the grand design and update it.

In any but the smallest businesses there is also the need to involve those close to the markets in the analytical processes, in order to widen the perspectives taken into account, to extract up-to-date information which they are likely to possess, and to secure their commitment, since they will have to implement the strategy.

Conventional strategic management is therefore usually accompanied by regular, formalized procedures by which managers of business units are required to prepare and update five-year plans. Top corporate management is thereby assured that business unit managers do take time off from the day-to-day to think about the future of their businesses. The formal procedures also provide a regular vehicle for informing top management of the thinking of those lower down and for securing approval and resource backing from those top managers.

Conventional strategic management therefore recommends formal annual, or biannual, procedures for preparing grand designs which look something like the following:

- **A timetable.** Each year there is a similar sequence of events with which business units and functions must comply. Typically this starts with a 'planning letter' from the chief executive, perhaps setting out some common assumptions about the future, to be used by each unit in drawing up its plan for the next five years. Draft plans must be submitted by a certain date.

- **A given format.** Some more or less fixed format will be prescribed with headings directing attention to markets, competition and resource requirements. There will almost always be a requirement for financial projections over a five-year period — a form to be filled in.

- **Prescribed or suggested techniques.** Attention may be directed to analysis of strengths and weaknesses, opportunities and threats. The use of product portfolio or policy matrix techniques of one sort or another may be required. Market segmentation or strategic business unit approaches may be called for. There may be pressure to consider market and industry structures and generic strategies.

- **Prescribed or suggested issues.** Business units may be directed or requested to consider the impact which particular issues may have on their business. For example they may need to consider how they are going to take the benefits of modern information technology, or what they are going to do about the single European market scheduled for 1992.

- **Forecasts.** Forecasts of the major financial variables for fixed time periods are almost always required and the pressure to forecast may be extended to market changes. The inherent difficulties of forecasting may be recognized by insisting on the use of scenarios or a range of possible outcomes, derived from different sets of assumptions about the future.

- **Planning roles.** Formal planning systems are based upon, and fall within, formal organizational structures and hierarchies. These may be the same formal

structures as those applied to the day-to-day, or in some cases entirely separate formal structures of great complexity are set up to accomplish strategic planning tasks.[3] The planning role in some systems is very much a staff one, with large corporate planning staffs performing most of the planning tasks. Or, far more popular nowadays, the focus is on line managers as the planners with corporate staff providing information and analytical back-up services.

● **Formal review and approval meetings.** Draft plans are considered at review meetings for each business unit. The focus of attention at all these meetings (and there are usually a large number) is the 'plan', rather than a few specific issues. A central concern is usually the availability and allocation of resources, particularly financial. One level of management probes and questions the next level down, or top management considers the plans put together by staff planners. The plans are then approved or rejected by the top corporate board but, having been through various review meetings, they are rarely rejected.

The grand design and organizational structure

Since the formal planning procedures are usually conducted within the formal organizational structure, the shape of that structure comes to have an important bearing on the outcome of formal planning. The decentralized structures called for by effective day-to-day control are unlikely to promote the identification of synergies, the building of competitive advantage across business unit boundaries, or the rationalization of business portfolios which is so much a part of conventional strategic management. More complex organizational structures with centralist features may therefore be installed to improve the development of strategies. For example, centralized international product organizations may be superimposed on local geographic subsidiaries.

So a normal aspect of conventional strategic management is the application of formal rules, procedures and methods of communication to the planning element of control. The whole approach can have significant impacts on role relationships and on organizational structures, and it views strategy as the determinant of such role relationships, structures, systems and cultures. You decide what it is you want to do and then you design structures and systems, you change role relationships and cultures, to support the strategy. These too are key aspects of conventional strategic management to which we shall be returning.

Using the blueprint — implementing the grand design

The grand design is used in three important ways. The first is communication down the hierarchy — there is written or verbal communication of detailed objectives and

broad courses of action down the line. Each level in the hierarchy then develops detailed action plans to implement the broad courses of action.

The second way in which the grand design is used is as a framework within which the budget is formulated. The budget is seen as the first year of the five-year plan, the first of a set of milestones along the five-year road, the most immediate set of detailed action plans. The formal long-term planning timetable therefore usually incorporates the budget preparation and approval timetable.

The third way in which the grand design is meant to be used is as a point of reference when it comes to dealing with single strategic issues as they arise. For example an unforeseen opportunity for profit may arise. An important consideration in deciding whether to take this opportunity or let it pass should be whether it fits in with the grand design or not.

But to qualify as control, there should also be periodic reviews of performance against the grand design and action to correct any deviation. Is the organization travelling along the path towards its long-term objectives? Are those objectives still likely to be achieved? At this point conventional strategic management runs into a practical difficulty. We can only monitor what is occurring now. Monitoring the five year plan therefore becomes exactly the same as monitoring the budget and other short-term plans. But variable set and parameter volatility means that we cannot be all that sure that short-term plan achievement will actually lead to long-term objective achievement.

Conventional strategic management does not have anything additional to offer in terms of monitoring; it has to fall back on the same monitoring devices as those used in the Management Information and Control Systems applied to closed change situations in the short term.

Having outlined what conventional strategic management is actually recommending, we now come to what it adds to the control of the business — its key features as a form of control.

Grand design and control tension

The description over the past few pages of what conventional strategic management is actually recommending you to do, if you are to manage strategically, has highlighted five key features:

- Missions and objectives for the future should be clearly established. They should not be tentative and vague, but relatively fixed and constrained.

- The focus of attention should be on the planning element of control, on planning to deal with change out in the market place in the future. As such

changes arise they are handled within the plan framework in which they have largely been foreseen.

- The processes applied to planning should be analytical, quantitative and predictive, together with formal rules, procedures and modes of communication.

- The culture should be strongly ideological, with behaviour being driven by well understood, uniform beliefs and values. These are the hallmarks of conservative cultures.

- The short-term control systems, organizational structures, culture and role relationships should all be designed to reinforce the strategy.

These five key features represent fundamentally the same demands on the organization and the behaviour of those within it as are imposed by control by variance in closed change situations.

But there are two important differences. First, the objectives are those which are to be achieved in the long term rather than the short term as they are in Management Information and Control Systems. Second, planning attention is directed to the future out in the market place, rather than the now within the business which is the chief concern of Management Information and Control Systems.

These two differences amount to a recognition that we are no longer dealing with closed change situations. We are dealing with change arising from situations where there is greater volatility in the set of factors changing (the variables) and in the manner in which they affect each other (the parameters). But the continued use of formal and analytical processes, particularly forecasting, amounts to an assumption that this volatility is not extreme — where volatility is extreme, forecasting is by definition impossible and the information available for stringent analysis is inadequate.

Conventional strategic management therefore clearly presents a form of control which is applicable to contained change situations. The approach is designed to deal with higher levels of volatility than Management Information and Control Systems; it is designed to consider and respond to a wider set of change factors and more complex interconnections; it is designed to look for and take the benefits of synergy and integration. Management Information and Control Systems are designed to deal with a narrower range of change and to take the benefits of separation and localization.

So as we move from control in closed change situations to control in contained change situations some of the demands on organization and behaviour remain the same: processes applied to control continue to be formal and analytical, the centre

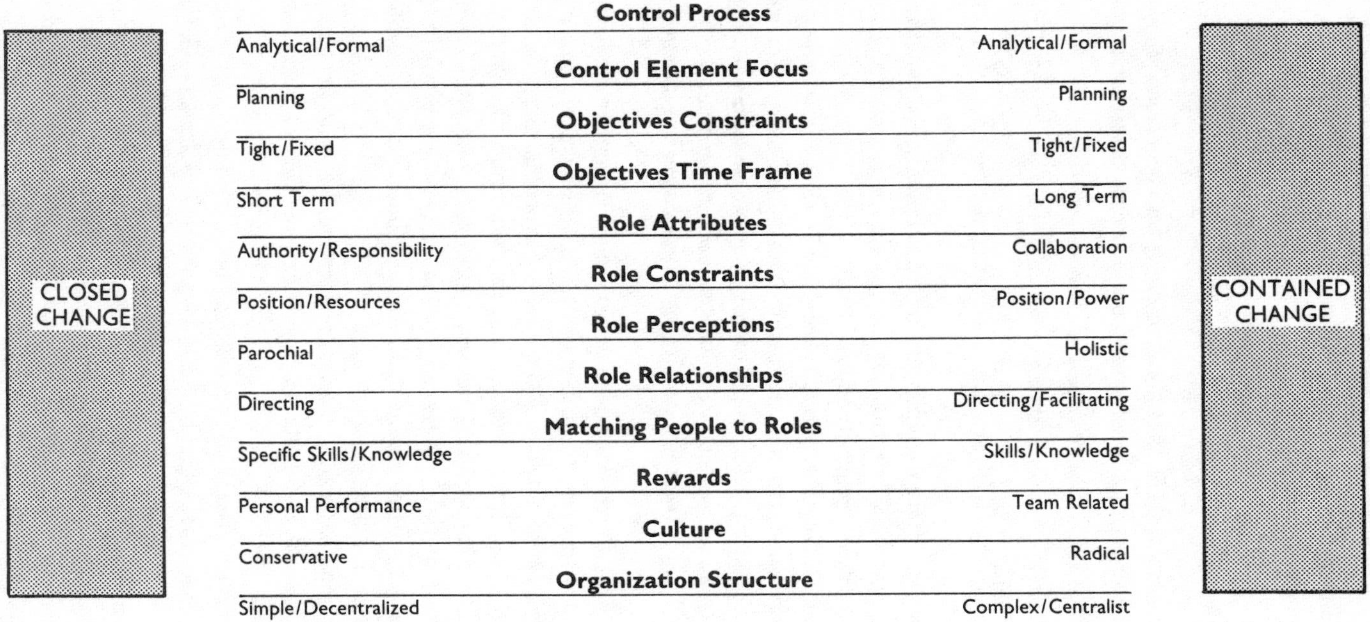

Figure 5 Closed and contained control tensions

CLOSED CHANGE	Control Process	CONTAINED CHANGE
Analytical/Formal	**Control Element Focus**	Analytical/Formal
Planning	**Objectives Constraints**	Planning
Tight/Fixed	**Objectives Time Frame**	Tight/Fixed
Short Term	**Role Attributes**	Long Term
Authority/Responsibility	**Role Constraints**	Collaboration
Position/Resources	**Role Perceptions**	Position/Power
Parochial	**Role Relationships**	Holistic
Directing	**Matching People to Roles**	Directing/Facilitating
Specific Skills/Knowledge	**Rewards**	Skills/Knowledge
Personal Performance	**Culture**	Team Related
Conservative	**Organization Structure**	Radical
Simple/Decentralized		Complex/Centralist

of attention remains on the planning element of control; objectives are still fixed and constrained, strongly ideological, conservative cultures are still required.

But there are also some very important differences in the demands which control in contained situations places on organization and behaviour. And these relate to objectives time span, management roles, instruments to match people and roles, organizational structure. The similarities and the differences are summarized in Figure 5. The requirements which control in closed situations, short-interval control, places on organization and behaviour are listed down the left-hand side of the Figure. The right-hand side shows the corresponding requirements for effective control in contained change situations, using conventional strategic management. The major differences between these two sets of requirements are discussed over the next few pages.

Both forms of control must be practised simultaneously, but in some important respects they place diametrically opposed demands on organization and behaviour. The result is control tension which management has to resolve in some way. Since you cannot simultaneously satisfy diametrically opposed demands, choices have to be made. Choosing to satisfy the demands of short-interval control means paying a price in terms of loss of effectiveness in longer-term control and vice versa. We turn now to a consideration of the nature of these tensions.

Long-term versus short-term objectives

The central objective in the control by variance form is immediate short-term profit, while that in the control by grand design form is profit over the long term. These two objectives can be diametrically opposed to each other. We all know that you can make profit over the next few months by chopping out people, cutting costs, putting a stop to investment, lowering quality, reducing service levels and abandoning training as well as research and development. The exact opposite is required if it is long-term profit you are after. Building market share, penetrating new markets and developing new products may all require short-term losses in return for longer-term profit. But do all those things necessary for long-term profit and you may well fall prey to acquisitors as you incur short-term losses.

For example — research and development expenditure

This time-span conflict of objectives comes up in practice with great regularity. A while ago, as part of a consultancy assignment, I attended the board meeting of a holding company at which one item on the agenda was the review of recent performance of subsidiaries. One recently acquired subsidiary, a small company developing new electronic products for the road and rail signals market, was making losses. The discussion centred on whether it was now time to make cost cuts in order to bring the company back to budget. But cost cuts would affect product

development. After nearly an hour's discussion, which covered the place of the new subsidiary in the group's long-term future, the decision was taken to run with the losses for a while longer in the interests of the long term.

Another example is provided by an assignment I did three years ago for a company in the packaging market, then recently acquired by a hungry and rapidly growing conglomerate. A strategy for the ailing packaging company to regain market share was developed. This strategy might or might not have worked, but it was never given the chance — within a year, the conglomerate refused to accept short-term losses and sold the business to a competitor. The pressures to secure short-term profit growth to satisfy investors were too great to allow time for longer-term strategies.

Simultaneous control in closed and contained change situations requires management to concentrate either on short-term profit or on long-term profit, or to strike some balance between the two. And any balance struck is likely to shift between the long- and short-term ends of the spectrum, depending on the circumstances as time passes. A shift in the balance alters the trade-off between short-term and long-term profit.

Parochial role perceptions versus holistic role perceptions

Effective control by variance in closed change situations demands that managers and workers perceive their roles in parochial terms — they must take responsibility for the part of the organization in which they are located, to the exclusion of any concern for other parts. Strong role identification with a part of the organization, rather than the whole, improves motivation and focuses attention. The results of this perception are functional barriers and walls between one business unit and others; barriers and walls which are actually conducive to the tight short-term control of each part.

Control by grand design in contained change situations demands the direct opposite — if the long-term profit of the whole organization is the principal concern, with its search for synergy and interconnections between the parts, then managers and workers must perceive their roles in holistic terms. What matters is the good of the whole even at the expense of the part and barriers and walls are severely detrimental to the good of the whole organization.

Simultaneous effectiveness of both forms of control would require managers to have two diametrically opposed perceptions at the same time. A tall order! In practice a choice will have to be made on the emphasis which is to be attached to these two perceptions at any one time. And a price will have to be paid in the form of a lower effectiveness in one or other of the forms of control. As organizations become more decentralized, as they are organized into smaller profit-responsible units in order to increase short-interval control effectiveness and the ability to

respond to rapid market changes, this tension of role perception increases. Such tension has the potential to turn the short-term benefits of decentralization into a longer-term disadvantage.

The tension between roles in relation to the parts and the whole is at its most evident at the senior level within both the business unit and the corporation. Senior managers of director level clearly have organization-wide responsibilities for performance, but most directors also have other functional or business unit responsibilities as well. Some companies, for example ICI and Hanson plc, recognize this tension very clearly and do not have divisional managing directors sitting on the main board. But this tends to be exceptional. Most senior managers therefore have personally to find some way of resolving the tension.

For example — the role of the group board

The question of roles and the perception thereof was the specific subject of one of my consultancy assignments with a roads and building products group of companies, organized into distinct, profit-responsible subsidiaries. The managing director of each of these subsidiaries sat on the group board together with top head office executives. A key concern of this group of senior managers related to what the role of the group board actually was and how it could effectively be carried out.

It took some discussion to agree eventually that the group board had an important part to play in managing the group and that this required members to contribute to and influence each others' businesses; it meant that members accepted joint responsibility for decisions and looked for team support. Agreement on the part of some of the members to this conclusion was somewhat reluctant; they took the view that their role was one of responsibility for their own business; they did not believe that board colleagues had the necessary knowledge to contribute to and influence their businesses; they were reluctant to assume joint responsibility for businesses of which they knew comparatively little; they saw this joint responsibility concept as weakening the responsibility and control of individual subsidiary managing directors. The conflicting role perceptions among this group of senior managers resulted in an inability to practise the grand design form of control. Strategy related to each business unit and there was little that could be referred to as group strategy; little attempt to take advantage of synergies.

Clearly the way in which managers perceive their roles affects their decisions and actions; it could lead to totally different outcomes to any strategic issue. For example an individual managing director of a subsidiary may take the view that a potential acquisition is not appropriate, because the acquisition would be much bigger than his or her own company. But if that director's role is seen as one of furthering the progress of the whole group, then he or she may take the view that a significant share increase in this particular market is just what the group needs.

Similar points apply to functional roles. So many accountants and even finance directors seem to see their roles purely in functional terms, producing accounts which are legally required and are correct in all respects. This leads them to lose sight of financial information as a management tool, where rapidity is more important than precise accuracy, and where market segments count for more than accounting conventions. The functional divides between production, engineering, development and design can all hinder product development.

The functional divide between production and purchasing can reduce the overall effectiveness of control. But the answer to these problems cannot be a simple recommendation to destroy the divides and get everyone to accept responsibility for the whole. This would destroy all the important benefits of the division of tasks and the establishment of clear responsibilities. There is no way out of having continuously to make the complex choices arising from the tension of role perception.

Directing versus facilitating relationships between roles

The tension between the need for parochial role perceptions in short-interval control and the need for holistic perceptions in longer-term forms of control has implications for the relationships between roles. One extreme is the tough, directing form of relationship, using the instruction process, which goes effectively with parochial role perceptions in short-interval control. The other extreme in the relationship spectrum is the more caring, participative, facilitating form, using the processes of persuasion and negotiation. Holistic perceptions may be better fostered by the facilitating form of relationship.

So once again, control by variance in the short term pulls in the opposite direction to control by grand design. But it is even more complex. Relationships of the facilitating kind help to foster holistic role perceptions in decentralized businesses. But you could adopt directing relationships and use more complex, centralist organization structures to foster holistic perceptions. So the form of role relationship adopted follows from a choice between short- and long-term control. But there is also another choice within long-term, or grand-design, control. And that choice is between directing relationships in complex structures and facilitating relationships in decentralized structures. The former is what is referred to as top-down strategic management and the latter as bottom-up.

Role attributes and constraints

Management Information and Control Systems, with their parochial role perceptions and directing relationships, call for particular management role dimensions. The attributes which are emphasized most are those of authority and responsibility, while the constraints are mainly in terms of formal position and the

availability of resources. But effective control by grand design, with its holistic role perceptions and rather more facilitating role relationships, requires a shift in attribute emphasis to collaboration. Managers have to work less in compartments and far more with each other across functional and business unit barriers if the benefits of long-term synergy, interconnections and integration are to be achieved. There is a consequent shift in the way roles are constrained; it is power and personality which provide the principal constraints, with formal position and resource availability becoming of lesser importance.

Change role perceptions and relationships and you change the dynamics of people working together. Change the dynamics and you require people to fill roles which are defined in a different way; you call for rather different skills and competences and you impose rather different constraints on how the role is to operate. And this leads to other important tensions in the total control system.

Criteria for selecting and developing people

As you move from one control form to another you change the dimensions of the roles required to make that form of control effective. Roles for effective control by variance relate to specific tasks in localized parts of the organization. The selection and development criteria for people to fill these roles therefore relate primarily to the specific bodies of knowledge, experience and expertise, as well as to the specific skills which clearly depend on the particular tasks called for.

When you are selecting a supervisor for a tin can production line, or developing a training programme to improve that person's performance, your selection procedures and development programmes focus on technical knowledge and supervisory skills. But the roles required for the effective operation of control by grand design are substantially different; they relate to broader issues for the whole organization. Key selection and development criteria will have to do with more generalized analytical and collaboration competences. The simultaneously practised forms of control call for different 'bundles' of competences, which may be difficult to find and develop in one person.

Individual performance-related rewards versus organizational performance-related rewards

The effectiveness of Management Information and Control Systems is clearly enhanced by closely tying monetary rewards to personal achievement of precisely specified objectives; there is ample evidence that well designed profit sharing schemes, bonuses and piece work payments boost short-term, localised performance. There is also the widespread view that they harm longer-term performance for the organization as a whole.

Control by grand design is about the long-term performance of the organization

as a whole and it requires individual rewards to be tied to that performance. Management is therefore confronted by another choice: this time between rewards closely tied to individual performance, those tied to total organizational performance, or some balance between them. The choice is complicated by the problems of designing reward systems which relate to results in the more distant future and which motivate individuals more distant from the end result.

Control tension relating to organizational structures

Control by variance calls for simple decentralized structures because we are trying to localize problems and opportunities and allocate clear personal responsibilities. But when it comes to control by grand design we are trying to take account of interconnections and take advantage of synergies. The ideal organizational structure to achieve this will be one which stresses centralization and reflects complex interconnections.

Once again this is a choice between either extreme or an attempt to find some balance. Attempts to find a balance lead to considerable variety in the centralization and decentralization of different functions and in dual or matrix type organizations. So an essentially decentralized group of companies may try to achieve balance by strong centralized finance, corporate planning and personnel functions. Or it may superimpose project structures on functional ones, or product structures on geographic or operational ones. Structures will have a powerful impact on role perceptions, and complex, centralist structures aim to promote the holistic perceptions so necessary for control by grand design.

The resolution of control tension — control style

The particular manner in which managers resolve the important conflicts relating to the time frame of objectives, the nature of roles and the structure of the organization, constitutes the style of total control which they adopt. Control style, then, is a description of the choices made to deal with control tensions. Within the framework of conventional strategic management thinking, three frequently observed patterns of choice, or style, have been described by Goold and Campbell.[4] There is no evidence that any one of these choices is always superior to the others. Style success depends on the circumstances: the type of company and the nature of the markets in which it operates.

Financial control style

One choice is to operate in market segments which are highly stable so that the change situation faced is predominantly of the closed type. Control tensions are

thereby avoided and the company is able to adopt a clear control style dictated by the requirements of control in closed change situations. It can adopt an uncompromisingly simple, flat, decentralized organizational structure where role perceptions are purposely parochial and role relationships largely of the directing kind. It can focus firmly on short-term objectives to the personal achievement of which rewards are clearly tied.

Such companies practise tight control using Management Information and Control Systems. This has been identified in research carried out by Goold and Campbell as a style successfully practised by a number of UK companies. They call it the Financial Control style. Such a style will be appropriate only in stable, mature industries where substantial changes in customer requirements and competitor groupings are judged to be highly unlikely. The risk it runs is that this condition will not be satisfied.

Within the framework of conventional strategic management thinking, the Financial Control style represents a choice to reject the grand design approach to handling the disturbances arising outside closed change situations. This does not mean that such change situations are completely ignored, that strategic issues are never addressed. It simply means that some way other than grand design is used to deal with them. Changes arising outside closed situations are dealt with by the 'entrepreneurial' initiative of the managers closest to the action and/or by an 'entrepreneurial' approach at the corporate level. The 'entrepreneurial' with its 'opportunistic' flavour does not sit easily with the grand-design concept of conventional strategic management.

Strategic planning style

The opposite style choice is to satisfy all the requirements placed on organization and behaviour by contained change situations in the grand-design concept. Here companies actively utilize the grand-design control form outlined earlier in this chapter and they adopt complex, centralist structures and encourage holistic role perceptions. They foster directing, top down relationships. They place great weight on the achievement of long-term objectives and are tolerant of non-achievment in the short term. They make these choices because they are pursuing interconnections and synergies; they are trying to develop competitive advantage and achieve balance in the portfolio of businesses under their control.

This style choice will be appropriate where the company has to face change arising in contained change situations, that is, where changes in customer requirements and competitor groupings which have to be accommodated are reasonably predictable. This choice is also appropriate where there are significant interconnections between business units in terms of shared customers or shared operational processes and technology. The Goold and Campbell research has

identified this as a frequent style choice by successful companies in the UK and they have called it the Strategic Planning style of control.[5]

Strategic control style
The third choice which it is open to companies to make is that of striking some balance between the demands which closed and contained change situations place on organization and behaviour. These companies also actively practise the grand-design form of control outlined earlier, but they strike a balance between short- and long-term objectives, sacrificing short-term profit where there is a reasonable prospect of this leading to greater long-term profit. They usually choose simple, flat, decentralized organizational structures to allow effective short-term control, but try to promote collaboration and holistic role perceptions to enable some interconnections and synergies to be taken advantage of. To lessen the parochial role perceptions fostered by structural decentralization, they adopt the more facilitating form of relationships between roles, relying far more on the processes of persuasion and negotiation than on instruction. Planning is then of the bottom-up type. This style choice is far less clear than the other two, but it does offer advantages of flexibility. It is likely to be appropriate where the company operates in markets characterized by change arising in contained situations, but with businesses which are not significantly interconnected in customer or operational and technology terms. It too has been identified as a frequently made choice which meets with success. Goold and Campbell have called this the Strategic Control style.

The nature of the style choice
Within the conventional strategic management framework, there is essentially a choice of style between Strategic Planning (top-down) or Strategic Control (bottom-up). The choice is determined by the strategy — the market segments targeted by the strategy, the kind of operation required to deliver the strategy and determine the systems, structures, roles and culture which the organization needs.

If you choose a strategy which focuses on synergy and which requires integrated operational responses and common approaches to customers, then a successful choice is the Strategic Planning style, with all that means in terms of structures, roles and cultures. If you choose to sacrifice some synergy and operate in rather more independent market segments, which do not have common customer bases and do not require integrated operational responses, then Strategic Control is the successful choice. And this leads to particular structural, cultural, role and systems requirements. Having made the choice and developed the grand design you handle single disturbances arising from change within that grand design; they become a matter of tactics.

The style of the corporate level in the organization

The above description of control style applies to the corporate level of the organization. The conventional approach to strategic management, with its grand designs and its central focus on planning, draws a sharp distinction between the roles of the corporate level and the business unit level in the strategic management of the whole business. Control, or management, styles are then seen in terms of the manner in which each of these levels carries out its particular control or management functions.

Within this conceptual framework, the corporate level and its corporate plans should be concerned with: the shape of the business portfolio, that is, the areas within which the business units are to operate and the resources which are to be allocated to them; restructuring the business units to improve performance; creating synergy by fostering cooperation and transferring skills between business units; and adding skills to the business units.[6] The role of the corporate level is to ensure that a high level of strategic thinking takes place in the business units by dictating direction or suggesting themes to them, prodding their strategic direction, establishing long-term objectives and processes for planning, and reviewing plans and results. The corporate level should also be concerned with setting short-term objectives, reviewing them, and holding managers responsible for achieving them.

The control style of the corporate level is then described in terms of: relative emphasis on short-term versus long-term control; the organizational structures and systems which are established to carry out that control; the procedures adopted for formulating and reviewing plans; the degree of intervention in supervising business units and allocating resources to them.[7] So the Strategic Planning style emphasizes long-term objectives, has complex, centralist structures, long-term planning procedures, intervenes strongly in the planning process and has elaborate formal procedures for reviewing plans. The Financial Control style, on the other hand, stresses short-term objectives, has simple, decentralized structures, no long-term planning procedures and leaves strategy to its business units. The Strategic Control style adopts a position between these extremes.[8]

The conventional approach then sees the business unit and its strategic planning as being primarily concerned with competitive advantage. It is at the business unit level that market analysis, competitor analysis and operational response become important. Business unit plans are all about competitive advantage while corporate plans are all about portfolios, restructuring and synergy.[9] Functional plans are then components in business unit plans, concerned with more detailed implementation.

The results of control by grand design

The key question now is whether conventional strategic management, control by

grand design, delivers the results it promises to. Is it a practical and successful form of control for dealing with change outside closed situations? Does it actually deliver a useful blueprint, or grand design, for control purposes? Does it provide a realistic framework within which single issues or disturbances can be handled as they arise?

Some successful companies practise conventional strategic management

The first point to make is that many of the world's major successful companies actually do appear to practise control by grand design. The Goold and Campbell study has identified a number of the UK's most prominently successful companies as practitioners of the Strategic Planning and Strategic Control styles; companies such as BOC, BP, Cadbury Schweppes, Courtaulds, ICI, Plessey, STC, and Vickers.

In the USA some of the major successful companies have pioneered and developed the whole approach. One such is General Electric. It is true that GE has changed many aspects of its strategic management system in recent years, but their approach is apparently still one which falls within conventional strategic management:

> Soon after he became chairman of US General Electric, Jack Welch took an axe to the company's renowned strategic planning system. Out of a total planning staff of more than 200, the headquarters team was slashed by two thirds. The group's constituent businesses gave their own planners similarly vicious treatment ... What GE has done is not to dump the discipline and rigour of strategic planning, but to streamline and de-bureaucratise the process, shifting the main planning responsibility away from the centre and out to line management ... 'the plan is never put to bed, as it was in the strategic planning era — but rather constantly tested and revised, based on changing events in the real world. And it is well communicated and shared by the organisation.' ... Since GE's dramatic change of planning direction in the early 1980's, many other companies in the US and Europe have broadly followed suit.[10]

So the approach has not been abandoned, it has been streamlined and brought closer to line management, while the plan is revised more frequently.

Other successful companies reject the conventional approach

On the other hand, many prominent and successful companies totally reject the conventional strategic management framework. In the Goold and Campbell study a number of companies are identified as Financial Controllers and they do not practise formal long-term planning; they include BTR, Ferranti, GEC, Hanson plc, and Tarmac. These companies are described as using an 'entrepreneurial' approach for dealing with strategic matters.

Then there are those conspicuously successful, individual entrepreneurs who openly reject strategic management. I have already quoted Anita Roddick on this

topic in Chapter 2 and the views of Alan Sugar and Richard Branson will be discussed in Chapter 7. All these people and many many more, who have built multi-million-pound businesses in short time periods, reject by word and deed the whole grand-design approach.

The research evidence in favour of long-term planning is suspect

A number of academic studies have attempted to test scientifically the relationship between success and formal planning. Some find a positive connection and others fail to do so.[11]

But there is a fundamental problem with much of that research evidence. It is based on asking managers to describe how they plan and control in complex strategic situations, rather than carefully observing what they do in practice. Observing what they do is difficult and would require working closely with a number of managers involved in the same strategic issues over fairly lengthy periods of time. The resulting observations would be subjective. Consider some of the drawbacks to asking managers what they are doing and then collating this as research evidence.

One problem relates to the question being asked. If you ask how they plan, they will describe their planning system. This does not mean that they actually use it for long-term control purposes.

During my period as a corporate planning manager, I was asked by questionnaire and interview to describe how my company planned strategically. I described the formal planning system. I did not describe how many of the strategic moves, some highly successful and some little short of disastrous, had in fact been made as a result of the 'gut feel' of one or other of the more powerful executives. I did not go into the political intrigues which promoted one project or killed another. After all, this was not planning, it was the kind of haphazard behaviour I thought I was being employed to combat. I did not point out that the five-year projections of cash flows always had the familiar 'hockey stick' shape — cash outflows to year two, followed by an increasing bonanza to year five. After all none of us ever believed the projections. The recipient of the questionnaire and the interviewer could only have concluded that my company was seriously using formal long-term planning as a control procedure, but in reality it was not.

Another problem has to do with the selective memory of those who are closely and personally involved in making major decisions over lengthy periods of time. I have frequently been surprised by the memory lapses which many senior managers experience some time after a strategic decision is taken. The story which they tell quite seriously and genuinely is one of carefully considered reasoning which led to a particular decision. On many of these occasions I knew that the information and reasoning had come after a decision taken on much more intuitive grounds. Many

managers seem to feel that it is somehow wrong to rely on intuition.

A further problem is the rapidity with which myths about success grow up. The penetration of the US motor cycle market by Honda is often described as a carefully planned operation. In fact it was a series of trials and errors.[12] I suggest therefore that the existence of formal planning systems and descriptions by senior managers of how they use them cannot reliably lead to the conclusion, in highly complex business situations, that such systems are actually being used and therefore add value. Where there have been careful observation of what managers actually do in strategic situations, a process is detected which is far more complex and much more intuitive than the planning mode would have us believe.[13]

Clearly, the evidence on the success of the grand-design approach to control is highly inconclusive. The correlation between its application and sustainable business success is low. Such correlation is no evidence that success is due to planning.

Companies visibly adopting conventional strategic management may well not be actually using it as a form of control. Is control outside closed change situations actually practised within the framework we have been describing? Or in reality is it other processes which are applied? Does the real control action take place in some other way, even in those companies visibly using the conventional strategic management framework?

Some clues that this might be the case are contained in several references, in the Goold and Campbell study, to informal contacts and decisions being made outside the formal processes. For example, with reference to BOC and Cadbury Schweppes, 'heavy reliance is placed on informal contacts to provide the centre with a view of progress in implementing agreed strategy and of any changes in the environment that might lead to a need for a revision of strategy.'[14] There are also some indications that the formal long-range planning systems may be fulfilling functions which are only peripheral to the real control of the organization outside closed change situations. 'The formal system provides legitimacy and a rationale for decisions that get taken.'[15]

My experience over the past 18 years as a corporate planner in a large corporation and as a management consultant to about two dozen companies in the last five years has convinced me that real control takes place outside any conventional strategic management framework that may be employed.

The visible output of most of the strategic planning exercises I have witnessed is poor stuff indeed. Most future mission statements are a bland collection of self-evident truths which could apply to just about any sensible company. They normally talk about continuing to make efforts to satisfy customers, provide quality, make profits and treat employees well. Or let us take the usual written corporate or business plan. The result, with a very high frequency rate, is a bland

collection of statements and bullet points, long lists of SWOTs (strengths, weaknesses, opportunities and threats), in which are lost the really important issues facing the company. In fact they do not really deal with the future at all and the written output is soon out of date; it rapidly finds a home in a filing cabinet and is occasionally referred to by those with a strong interest in history.

A major weakness with all these plans is that no one seems to know how to monitor performance against them in a way which leads to definite action. And most telling of all, important strategic matters, which always seem to arise as single issues, are handled with very little reference indeed to any plan which might be in the filing cabinet.

Companies do not use conventional strategic management for control purposes — but it does contribute insights and questions

I am not saying that the whole body of conventional strategic management has nothing at all to offer. I have been involved in many exercises which have played an important part in focusing senior managements' minds on the really important issues, but issues arising now, not in the future. Such focusing of minds has led to concerted action. This has occurred when the exercise has been exceptional in the sense that it is a special event, a one-off occasion, or the first in a series of annual exercises; and when it was highly participative, involving all the key decision makers who felt free to express their opinions.

But even then success was not in terms of plans or projections within which to handle single issues as they arose, but in terms of raising the important questions, structuring the issues as they stood at a particular point in time and building consensus and a sense of direction. The success lay in the quality of the team-building exercise itself. Any mission statement which emerged was still bland to the outside world but, as a result of the discussions leading to it, it had real meaning to the participants. Any written plan might still have appeared rather simple, but the process leading to it had clarified today's real issues. And the body of conventional strategic management had contributed some important questions and perspectives which had assisted the structuring of issues and the development of a sense of direction. But on those occasions the body of conventional strategic management had not been used as a coherent whole; parts of it were applied in a manner which seemed appropriate to a particular situation. Even then, the real activity of control, the decisions about and action taken on strategic problems and opportunities, occurred in other ways.

This raises three important questions:

- Why does conventional strategic management not produce a grand design which functions as a real control tool?

- If successful managers are not in fact controlling by grand design, then how are they dealing with change outside closed situations?

- If successful managers are in fact using some other form of control would it not be better to focus on improving this, rather than continuing to employ formal strategic planning systems?

The following chapters consider each of these questions.

Notes

1 See Chapter 5.
2 Sometimes the term 'business plan' is used to mean the financial part of the strategy, sometimes it refers to the first year of the strategic plan and is then synonymous with the budget.
3 See the Litton Industries and Texas Instruments case in J Quinn, H Mintzberg and R James, *The Strategy Process*, Prentice-Hall (1988).
4 M Goold and A Campbell, *Strategies and Styles*, Blackwell (1988).
5 This is the same as the Strategic Architect style installed by British Aerospace and described in Chapter 1 above.
6 M Porter, 'From Competitive Advantage to Corporate Strategy', *Harvard Business Review*, May–June 1987.
7 Goold and Campbell, op cit.
8 Ibid.
9 Porter, op cit.
10 'Why strategy has been put in the hands of line managers', *Financial Times*, 18 May 1988.
11 Pearce, Freeman and Robinson, 'The Tenuous Link between Formal Planning and Financial Performance', *Academy of Management Review*, 1987, Vol 12, No 4.
12 R Pascale, 'The Honda Effect', in J Quinn, H Mintzberg and R James, *The Strategy Process*, Prentice-Hall (1988).
13 J Quinn, 'Logical Incrementalism', in Quinn, Mintzberg and James, op cit.
14 Goold and Campbell, op cit., p 55.
15 Ibid., p 167.

5
Why Control by Grand Design Will Not Work in the 1990s

One of the principal features of the current business world, one which it was argued in Chapter 2 would become an even more important feature of the 1990s, is that more and more change arises in open-ended situations. My reason for taking the view that conventional strategic management is positively harmful to the control which must be applied in the 1990s, is that it is a fundamentally inappropriate form of control for accommodating changes arising in open-ended situations.

If you accept that the 1990s will be years of open-ended change for your business, then the harmful consequences of conventional strategic management follow for a number of clear reasons. These are summarized briefly in the next paragraph, before exploration in further detail in the rest of this chapter.

The first reason why conventional strategic management will not work in the 1990s is that grand designs are not robust enough — they fall apart in open-ended change situations. If you cannot have a comprehensive plan then the meaning of control alters. It is no longer monitoring against plan, that is, automatic detection of disturbance created by change, and taking corrective action determined by the plan. Instead control becomes coherent opportunism, that is, detecting the disturbance and tentatively trying out responses before backing successful ones. Opportunism has to rely on intuition far more than on analysis. It is not just that control by grand design is inappropriate, its application in open-ended situations is positively harmful because it restricts the innovative thinking required by opportunistic control.

But despite all this, conventional strategic management does contribute some important questions and insights when it is used in an eclectic and flexible way to assist in the identification of change and opportunistic response. And the analytical processes make substantial contributions to decision-making once the situation has been clarified and important single issues identified. In essence I am putting forward the proposition that the form of control recommended by conventional strategic management is completely inadequate for dealing with the most important changes which business is already encountering. But this does not mean totally rejecting the body of strategic management knowledge; that body contains important insights

and analytical approaches which can make significant contributions to that opportunistic form of control which is appropriate to open-ended change situations.

First let us consider why grand designs fall apart in open-ended change situations.

Grand designs fall apart in open-ended change situations

The open-ended change situation is one where the set of important factors causing change is highly volatile. It is not just any one of the factors in the set which is changing: new factors are appearing and existing ones are becoming less important or disappearing. So one year, very few managers are concerning themselves with a single European market in 1992 and the next year most are; one year most are focusing on the prospect of new controls on exhaust emissions from cars and the next it is no longer one of the most important factors.

In addition to highly volatile sets of variables, open-ended change situations are characterized by a high degree of volatility in the manner in which a change affects the business, the parameters within which it operates. So at one time a delivery period of six days is perfectly acceptable, but later this is reduced to two. At one time sample testing of 5 per cent of components is acceptable, but later, quality assurance of all components is required. At one time plate glass is produced by grinding and later the most effective technology is the float process.

What then are the characteristics of change in these highly volatile, open-ended situations, which make the application of the conventional strategic management framework of no value? First, the change is inherently unpredictable. Second, the change is difficult to detect and understand so that appropriate responses cannot easily be developed. Third, the change generates intense internal political activity — this always occurs when you cannot know what will happen and you even find it difficult to understand what is happening now or what to do about it. Grand designs developed analytically and based on forecasts do not stand a chance in these circumstances.

Open-ended change is inherently unpredictable

By definition, forecasting cannot be applied to a situation in which both the variables and the parameters are highly volatile. In fact it is no longer even clear which are the variables and which are the parameters. Such volatility means that there is insufficient relevant past experience, a lack of stable patterns, upon which to base any one forecast, or even a limited number of scenarios. The situation is not a repetitive one in which you get a number of opportunities to try out a particular response — each change is unique and you either respond successfully or you do not.[1] The simple fact is that, confronted with this kind of change, you just cannot

know what is likely to happen. And this is the kind of change businesses in even the most mature industries already face. Consider the situation facing one such business with which I have worked as a consultant and which I will call Company C.

For example — market restructuring

Company C is a subsidiary of a fairly large holding company. Its principal business is the manufacture of a building product and it operates in a mature, slow-growth market which is characterized by over-capacity, fierce competition and consequent downward pressure on prices and margins.

A meeting of the holding company board turns to the long-term future of Company C. The market can be segmented into a high performance segment, a standard, and a low cost/low performance segment. Company C operates mainly in the standard performance segment, where it has a 12 per cent share and where over-capacity is particularly great. It has not conducted any specific market research, but from some published information and a knowledge of its markets, the managing director of Company C puts together a table of market shares for his colleagues on the holding company board (see Table 1).

Table 1   Market shares of ten companies

Market Shares (%)				
Company	Total	High Perf.	Standard	Low Perf.
A	23	11	12	—
B	24	4	17	3
C	9	2	7	—
D	5	—	—	5
Others (6)	39	8	24	7

Options discussed are selling the company to a competitor; investing in new equipment to improve competitive capability in the somewhat more attractive high performance segment; rationalizing production; buying a competitor. It is thought that Company A cannot be acquired since it is part of a powerful group which seems to have no desire to leave the market. Company B cannot be acquired because the shareholder in Company C's holding company does not wish to be involved in a contested bid. There is little point in acquiring Company D since it is in the least attractive market segment. Perhaps some of the six smaller companies could be acquired, but each has a small market share and it will take a long time to buy two

or three of them. Anyway none of them is thought to be attractive.

Board members disagree on which option should be followed; one or two mutter about withdrawing from the market. The possibility of closing some of Company C's capacity is considered for a while and then dropped. In the end the decision is made to continue operating in the market and keep the situation 'under review.' The managing director of Company C 'believes' that the holding company should retain a position in this market and on the whole his colleagues agree with him.

The possibilities are so many and their outcomes so dramatically different, that any attempt by Company C to set detailed long-term objectives and project sales and profits over the next five to ten years would be quite meaningless. The members of this particular board are facing an inherently unpredictable situation; the consequences are unforeseeable. In this situation they fall back on expressions of belief and the exercise of intuition.

Consider what happened only a few months later. Company A acquired Company B and, to head off any objection from the Monopolies Commission, it offered to sell part of the acquisition to Company C. The consequence of such a deal, in terms of market shares, is shown in Table 2.

Table 2   Market shares — the effects of unforeseen circumstances

Company	Market Shares (%)			
	Total	High Perf.	Standard	Low Perf.
A	32	15	17	—
B	—	—	—	—
C	21	2	19	—
D	8	—	—	8
Others (6)	39	8	24	7

The holding company board of Company C rapidly agreed to the proposal; it was entirely consistent with the consensus belief that the company should stay in the market. As a result of this move, Company C now holds a share of nearly 30 per cent of the standard market segment. Companies A and C between them account for over half of this market segment. The option set in terms of factory rationalization is now completely different. This outcome could not have been foreseen as the most likely one; hours of analysis would not have added much to any decisions which were taken. What was important was the process of securing agreement on the kinds of move that would be acceptable to all. This had allowed

the company to respond rapidly when an opportunity presented itself.

Now these events occurred in a mature, low-technology industry and yet any grand design which might have been prepared within the conventional strategic management framework, other than one based on what actually happened, would have fallen apart. The point must apply with even more force in emerging, high-technology markets. But the problems facing conventional strategic management in open-ended change situations are not confined to inherent unpredictability.

Open-ended change is poorly structured

Take another example of managers dealing with change arising in open-ended situations. Managers across Europe are currently much preoccupied with, and are already anticipating, many of the changes which are scheduled to occur around 1992, when the European Community takes steps to create a single European market. The proposals relate to establishing common standards and regulations for all products and services throughout the Community; the removal of border controls; enforcing common rules on public sector purchasing; harmonization of taxation and company law; a common monetary system; and common social policies. At much the same time the Channel Tunnel will open and this will add a whole new dimension to competition.

Companies are already actively influencing the standards and regulations which are to be adopted for Europe as a whole. They are already repositioning through acquisitions and new alliances. They are looking for ways to benefit from the expected expansion of markets as country segments disappear. They are looking for opportunities outside their own domestic markets and means of repelling the attack from companies in other European countries. They are reconsidering organizational structures in the light of possible market changes. This is an example of the poorly structured problems and opportunities typical of open-ended change situations. The group of the most important factors causing the change is not clear cut; immediate past experience is not much of a guide; new variables are appearing and it is not all that easy to decide which are the really important ones or how they will impact on any individual business.

So, disturbances to the operation of a business which are created by open-ended change situations can be described as poorly structured in a number of senses: their true nature is not immediately apparent and their consequences are widespread and unclear.

The true nature of the disturbance is not immediately apparent

At first managers may think that customers are switching from tinplate paint cans to plastic containers because of rust problems. Further consideration reveals that the real reason is the poor service levels provided by tinplate manufacturers. The true

opportunity lies, then, not in research into rust-proofing techniques, but in installing the necessary control systems to be able to provide higher service levels. What starts off as apparently one problem, develops into another and may end up as an opportunity.

For example — small cars at General Motors

Through the 1970s General Motors in the USA was preoccupied with accommodating the impact of rising fuel prices and changes in regulations which reduced the permissible emission of noxious exhaust gases. Its response was to scale down the size of its whole range of cars — the focus was on vehicle size and smaller cars. With hindsight the really important disturbance occurring at that time was the (at first insignificant) attack on the luxury car segment by the Germans and on the low price segment by the Japanese.[2] The response required to head them off would have been one less concerned with vehicle size across the range and more to do with quality on the one hand and cost on the other, in specific market segments.

It is easy to see what the true nature of the disturbance was after the event; examples and case studies are always structured. But it is rather difficult to do so as the disturbance is just beginning to become apparent. And this is the real difficulty of poorly structured, or open-ended situations: to detect the really important disturbances among the great many barely noticeable, small changes which are occurring at any one time. Disturbances in open-ended situations are difficult to detect because they come from all directions at the same time and they start off in a small way. They are manifestations of true uncertainty; we cannot use past patterns to attach probabilities to outcomes as we can in contained situations, ones of risk rather than true uncertainty.

Consequences of change are widespread and unclear

The consequences of disturbances arising in open-ended change situations are widespread and unclear. The options for handling the disturbance are many and not immediately obvious. Effective responses require the participation of a number of parts of the organization. The launch of a new product will involve development, production and marketing functions and it may require the cooperation of business units in different geographic areas. Potential consequences then depend on the response which you and your rivals make to the disturbance. Your rivals may also bring out a new product and these new products, yours and your rivals', may damage one of your existing product lines. Other disturbances are thus set off by any response you or they make.

Open-ended change situations are dynamic ones in which it is hard to identify all the variables determining your profit and the causal chain from these variables to your profit. That is why you keep arguing in circles when you set out to discuss what to do in open-ended change situations.

Furthermore, the difficulty of identifying what the really important problems are, the lack of structure, is compounded by incomplete, difficult to obtain and biased information about the disturbance and its consequences.

Inadequate, biased information

Information on what your competitors are intending to do, or are actually doing now, is always partial and incomplete; much of it is rather unreliable gossip. And the interpretation managers place on that information could well be biased; they may not want to believe it; they may not want to inform those above them that competitors are gaining market share. I remember the managing director of a company producing building blocks who believed that the major marketing effort of his company should continue to be directed at architect specifiers. His competitor changed and was putting his effort into the merchant stockists. The managing director in question maintained for some time that information on the superior performance of his competitor was inaccurate. Later he accepted that competitor performance was superior but kept pointing to reasons other than what appeared to me to be the real one. There was never enough information to prove conclusively, analytically that he was wrong.

Since the information is inadequate to meet the requirements of any respectable analytical approach, managers have to fall back on perception and judgement; perceptions of the nature of the disturbance, indications of its consequences and approaches to dealing with it, all have to be based on incomplete and often unreliable 'bits' of information.

Information, moreover, is often politically conditioned; interpretations of it are biased by what individual managers are trying to achieve. Interpretation is therefore clouded by personal ambitions, values and beliefs. Managers only 'hear' the bits of information they want to hear and understanding between them may become defective. Calls for more information, often to delay having to deal with the disturbance, become commonplace. As one proceeds to deal with the matter, information about it and perceptions around it change.

Open-ended change generates a high level of political activity

The consequences of a poorly structured situation with inadequate information about it are paradoxes and contradictions, conflict and disagreement based on values and feelings. The situation is therefore one which is characterized by stress, by emotion and, initially at least, some considerable confusion.[3] This generates a high level of political activity.

For example — making an overseas acquisition

The managing director of the lightweight synthetic aggregates production

subsidiary of a major construction company with whom I worked, came back from a conference in the USA where he had met top managers of a similar company in Canada. He felt that he had identified an opportunity — the acquisition of this Canadian company. He persuaded his divisional director that there was some merit in the idea and pointed to the fact that the corporate plan contained a broad course of action to diversify the activities of the subsidiary into North America. In turn the chief executive of the group and other board members were also persuaded that it was worth exploring. Two people, the marketing director from the subsidiary and the group planning manager from head office were sent to Canada to assess the market for aggregates, the extent of the competition and market views of the company to be acquired.

At the same time the subsidiary company managing director returned to Canada to sound out the response of the management of the potential acquisition. All came back with a reasonably favourable report, although the group planning manager had some doubts about market growth prospects. There was a further round of discussion, lobbying and persuading before it was decided by the chief executive that the subsidiary company managing director could take the matter further.

A firm of lawyers was appointed to handle the legal side in Canada. The subsidiary company accountant then went out and came back with the latest accounts, which had not been available before — these showed a recent substantial increase in borrowing and some decline in profitability. After further discussions, a proposal was put together but the group finance director and the planning manager both opposed it because of the high debt levels of the proposed acquisition and the price that would have to be paid. The subsidiary managing director believed that he would be able to turn the company around; that good management would improve profitability to a point which more than justified the price. The finance director lobbied the chief executive. After considerable debate the proposal was dropped. The key issue in the end was not any analytical finding but differing judgements on management capability. The outcome was determined by power. The important process was political. In the end the grand design for this subsidiary to expand into North America fell apart.

This example clearly concerns a strategic issue, that is, one which threatens the existing order to a significant extent, which could relate to major changes in purpose or direction of the business unit or the corporation. Two consequences follow. First, it is outside the competence of any single manager, or even of any single level, to handle alone. Second, the process by which the disturbance is handled becomes more complex and somewhat disjointed. A sequential process of planning and action is not followed. Information emerges gradually and is not always adequate. The political persuasion element in the process takes on major significance. And the dynamics of this political process are not explicitly part of

conventional strategic management or any grand design.

Grand designs fall apart in open-ended change situations, and conventional strategic management is not a suitable control form in them. This is because you cannot forecast and you cannot apply analytical procedures when the problems and opportunities are ill-structured and accompanied by inadequate, even suspect, information and generate a high level of political activity. The conditions for a robust grand design simply do not exist in such situations. And this changes the whole meaning of control.

Open-ended change requires a different way of thinking

The whole conventional strategic management way of thinking about the business world is conditioned by an underlying, but unstated, assumption that most change of significance arises in contained situations and that the remainder can largely be ignored. It is the kind of view which says that if you can understand how 90 to 95 per cent of change is caused, you can safely concentrate on this and ignore the rest, regarding it as inevitable 'noise', estimating or experimental error.

Now this is fine when you are dealing with static or rather simple deterministic or probabilistic systems, that is those which apply to closed and contained change. But where you have to deal with the open-ended, complex dynamic systems, where the outcome today is one of the determinants of what happens tomorrow and the causal connection between them is complex or non-linear, then such assumptions are highly dangerous. For certain parameter values such systems can give rise to turbulence or 'chaos'; they generate patterns over time which are never exactly repeated.

Furthermore the way in which such patterns develop is sensitive to initial conditions, which means that a scarcely noticeable difference today can lead to a totally different pattern tomorrow. Turbulence in gases and liquids provides an example of one such system, the weather is another and the world of business may well be a third. A small change in air flows in Peking can escalate up through the weather system and produce a violent storm in New York. The moves of a small new competitor from an unsuspected direction can escalate through the market system and lead to the demise of a powerful company. In complex dynamic systems it is not safe to assume that the 5 per cent you do not understand too well can safely be ignored.

The hallmarks of conventional strategic management, fixed long-term objectives, future missions, long-term plans developed by using simple deterministic, analytical techniques such as market structure, value chains, experience curves, product life cycles and so on, all presuppose that the past provides reasonably safe guidelines to the future. If you cannot apply probabilities, if you cannot identify

likely outcomes, then using the past as your guide, in anything other than the most tentative way, has to be dangerous. Wherever a small amount of open-ended change is present it undermines the whole conventional strategic management approach.

Managers who think in conventional strategic management terms inevitably focus on contained change. They look to past patterns and experience as their guide, they focus on the likely and the probable, where they have some idea of how change is impacting on their business. They want clarity on where they are going and how they are going to get there. The emphasis on clear, precise objectives, so necessary in closed change situations and so useful in contained change situations, and the belief that it is necessary to set out in advance how the objective is to be achieved, means that market and organizational moves not satisfying these criteria will be rejected. They will be labelled: 'not properly thought out.' The requirement for quantification, for bottom-line numbers and discounted cash flows, will mean that many innovative ideas to which it is quite impossible to attach realistic numbers, will be rejected. The search for a logical coherence and a fit of the company's capabilities to its markets means that innovative potential new directions will not even be considered. The small changes will not only be ignored, the cast of mind is such that they will not even be looked for.

Managers with conventional outlooks tend to assume that counterparts in rival companies view the world in the same way. They expect competitors to make similar moves and take similar considerations into account. They focus on existing competitors and on competition in existing markets. They therefore miss the competition which now so often comes from unlikely directions. Because they are thinking in contained change terms, their strategies are statements about the existing business projected into the future with some tinkering at the margin. The result is a rejection of ambitious, unlikely moves.[4]

And it is no defence for a particular manager to say that most of the change facing his or her company is of the contained variety. If there is any significant component of open-ended change to which the company is exposed, then thinking in contained change terms runs the great risk of ignoring the really important changes which could be of the open-ended kind. Any contamination by the characteristics of open-ended change makes the whole system potentially unstable.

Successful managers recognize all this, either explicitly or implicitly. Even if they do have formal planning systems, they do not really use them for control purposes. The next chapter turns to what they actually do in open-ended change situations.

Notes

1 There is also the point that even with fixed variable sets you can get relationships with certain parameter values in dynamic systems which generate outcomes which are not periodic — the pattern varies over time in a way which is not regularly repeated. The outcome cannot then be predicted.

² See General Motors Downsizing case study in J Quinn, H Mintzberg and R James, *The Strategy Process*, Prentice-Hall (1988).

³ L R Pondy, R J Boland and H Thomas, *Managing Ambiguity and Change*, John Wiley & Sons (1988).

⁴ C Hamel and C Pralahad, 'Strategic Intent', *Harvard Business Review*, May-June 1989.

6
Control by Trial and Error

What companies actually do in open-ended change situations

Even those companies which do invest considerable resources in the annual planning procedures and review meetings necessary to produce grand designs, do not in reality use them to handle the problems and opportunities thrown up throughout the year by open-ended change. Those successful companies with corporate planning, information gathering and market research staff functions actually control their businesses in open-ended situations in much the same way as those who reject conventional strategic management and proclaim a more entrepreneurial approach. Successful companies do differ from each other in the manner in which they practise control; there are different control styles. But the existence of formal planning systems and the development of grand designs are not real distinguishing characteristics of style.

In 1981 I was the planning manager for John Laing, one of the UK's major construction companies. After about five days of discussion, over a number of weeks, the main board adopted a grand design for the following five years. According to this, the company was to achieve profit growth and a high rate of return on its capital by maintaining its position as a leading building and civil engineering contractor in the UK, selectively widening the geographic area of overseas contracting where profitable, retaining its presence in building products manufacture, expanding its medium-sized housing activity in a limited way and diversifying the business into related markets.

By 1988 overseas contracting was smaller and more specialized, building products activities had virtually disappeared, some limited diversification had occurred and the private housing activity had expanded tenfold in revenue terms to contribute nearly 60 per cent of profits. The grand design had fallen apart. But the company certainly had not. John Laing's turnover had grown in real terms, its profits had increased at least tenfold and its rate of return on capital exceeded 30 per cent. So, the company never adhered to its grand design; it recognized the open-ended nature of the change facing it and did something else, something far more entrepreneurial, which proved to be highly successful. And this, in my experience, is what happens in other successful companies as well.

Successful managers do not use long-term plans to control

My contention is that, whatever they may say to the contrary, successful managers do not actually exercise long-term control by means of corporate and business plans with their fixed future points. They do not actually use such plans because they face true uncertainty, the unknowable, which cannot be captured in plans. Formal long-term planning may achieve some things but it has nothing to do with real life strategic management. Reasons for this view were given in Chapter 5.

They use them to raise comfort levels

But if successful managers do not in fact use their plans to control over the long term, why do they continue to prepare them? The answer is that the preparation procedures themselves raise comfort levels. Unstructured situations, lacking in clarity, promote confusion and create stress, especially in large corporations where it is very difficult for top managers to stay in touch with the whole business. Formal planning gives at least the impression of structure, it gives some assurance that those lower down are attending to strategic matters and provides an opportunity for communication with the top. Comfort levels, particularly for those at the top, consequently rise. But if this is all that formal plans provide, how are successful managers in fact controlling the business in open-ended change situations?

Successful managers start from where they are, the existing business, and extend the boundaries of that business by a process of experimentation, trial and error, playing games and taking chances. This involves detecting change and identifying the disturbances such change is causing, or could cause, to the business. It involves developing or clarifying the issues raised by change and developing dynamic strategic-issue agendas, using intuitive and political processes. Successful managers conduct small-scale experiments wherever possible and back those where there is some evidence of success. Where small experiments are not possible, they take major gambles, some of which succeed dramatically and others of which fail disastrously. Strategy is not predetermined, it emerges opportunistically in the form of strongly backed single-issue responses or experiments. It is dynamic and organic. It is not comparatively static as the long-term plan is.

This chapter explores the dynamics of control in open-ended change situations. It looks first at what is being done — managers start with the existing business and extend its boundaries. We then look at how it is done — developing strategic-issue agendas, experimenting and building single-issue responses into strategies.

Starting from where you are and extending the boundaries by experiment

The reality of strategic management is not a journey along a predetermined path to

somewhere, as conventional strategic management would have it, because in today's world that somewhere cannot be known. What strategic management is trying to accomplish in reality is an opportunistic journey from somewhere and that somewhere is known; it is the existing business. In reality you start with what you already have. There is an existing area of operation: the present markets in which the company operates and the technology it employs. There is an existing set of values which condition the operation and the image of the company in the market place. There is at least some direction created by the momentum of the existing business — because it cannot be changed overnight the existing business carries the company forward into the future. And there is an existing total control system which is being utilized to accommodate the impact of change on the business. The area of operation, the values, the direction and the total control system constitute the existing boundaries of the business.

As that business travels through time, its managers test its boundaries by continually experimenting with new opportunities and solutions to problems — they conduct numerous trials, some of which inevitably turn out to be errors. Successful experiments are backed by organizational resource and energy, so reinforcing or changing existing areas of operation, sets of values, directions and the control system itself. Control in its long-term sense is exercised by trial and error.

Direction from somewhere, not to somewhere
The direction of a company is in reality a dynamic, organic development from where it is now, by a process of testing the boundaries, conducting experiments, trial and error, behaving entrepreneurially and opportunistically. You do not know where you are going because you are travelling on uncharted seas. You cannot know what the area of operation, the set of values, the direction or the control system will be in five years' time because you face true uncertainty, the unknowable. What they will be all depends on the experiments you conduct and those you back during the coming five years.

But you can still have direction. It is simply from somewhere rather than to somewhere and you do not know where it will end up. This does not mean that you are failing to deal with the future. It means that you are doing it in a way which is realistic. You are doing the sensible thing in a truly uncertain situation; you are feeling your way forward through experimentation, a process of adaptive learning.[1] It does not mean that your behaviour is haphazard or uncontrolled. The type, size and progress of each experiment can be controlled. Or to put it another way, the control you exert is that of the game player.

Playing games successfully requires control
Control in games is exercised, first, by choosing the game to be played, the game

where one's skill can most successfully be exploited and where the rewards are greatest. In business this means choosing the markets in which to play; that is, an area of operation. It also means developing appropriate control systems and operational responses, the skills you have to play the game. And it means backing those responses to the market for which there is a demonstrable track record; that is, pursuing a distinct, continuing direction. If you have little skill in the game, or its potential rewards are small, you avoid it. If your performance in the game is good you continue to play.

Control is exercised, second, by agreeing the rules by which the game is to be played. In business this means establishing the values and beliefs which are to govern moves in the market. If you cannot accept the rules you do not play.

Control in games is exercised, third, by placing bets, game by game, according to judgement, and limiting each bet to that which is affordable. In business this means testing the area of operation, the direction and the values by experimenting with trial marketing of products, new technology prototypes, and small-scale initial investments wherever possible. If the risks posed by the game are too high you avoid them, wherever possible.

The game plan of the professional, as opposed to that of the obsessive, addicted gambler, is not a grand design of fixed moves; it is not a scheme to break the bank. It is a set of flexible, intuitive responses in a dynamic situation where control means limiting risks, judging what to try and what to avoid, when to press ahead and when to stop. The game plan of the professional business strategist, as opposed to the bureaucratic administrator, is much the same — the key to control in open-ended situations is limiting the risks of the unknowable, by keeping your options open, by trial and error; a dynamic process of testing the relatively safe boundaries set by existing consensus values and beliefs, areas of operation and continuing direction derived from past success. And this means that strategy starts with the existing business.

So control in open-ended situations, the strategic management required in today's business conditions, is all about area of operation, sets of values, systems of control and direction, much as it is in conventional strategic management. But it is the present rather than the future state of these which is the starting point, and progress from that starting point is by testing the boundaries through a process of experimenting and so changing the boundaries as you travel in time. And it is a dynamically interactive process in which the control system changes as you practise control. Although successful companies, with a formal planning approach, set out a vision of what they want to be, they actually back successful experiments and end up somewhere different. The 'to somewhere' view is unrealistic, lifeless and static; the 'from somewhere', organically feeling your way by experiment and playing the game view, is dynamic and realistic.

Since area of operation, set of values, control systems and direction are what are being tested and changed, that is, controlled, it is worth exploring the meaning of these terms further.

Area of operation

Area of operation is easy to define. It is the markets the company operates in and the technologies or methods it uses to deliver to the market. Every company has, of course, an area of operation. At any one time that area may be appropriate in the sense that there is a match between customer requirements, the source of competitive advantage, and the ability of the company to satisfy those requirements at a profit: competitive capability. But even if that match exists now, continuous change will require continuing adaptation or testing.

Area of operation is tested by undertaking new ventures, promoting new products, entering new markets, changing existing products, investing in new technology or changing existing technology. The tests take the form of trial marketing, prototype designs, small-scale trial projects, a small acquisition, sending two executives to set up a trial operation in a new country, taking on one contract in a country before setting up a fully fledged operation, and so on. Generally companies first conduct a small-scale experiment. Or they may wait for a rival to try an experiment and learn from the rival's errors.

Occasionally the circumstances leave little scope for a small-scale experiment and the company has to play for large stakes — perhaps there is no alternative to a large acquisition or a major investment in order to get into a market or retain a position. Not surprisingly, such large-scale experiments have a high failure rate. For example, Imperial Tobacco made a carefully planned and thoroughly researched acquisition of Howard Johnson in the 1970s in order to enter the USA. It proved to be a costly failure. Usually moves on a large scale follow a series of successful experiments — they are really strategic moves, representing the backing the organization is giving to successful experiments. So, Hanson plc acquired Imperial Tobacco in the mid-1980s, applying its tried and tested acquisition formula.

Set of values

The set of values is somewhat harder to define, because it is more nebulous. It is all those attitudes and beliefs which condition the markets selected to operate in, and the methods which are used to deliver a product to those markets. It is the ideology or the culture of the business, its belief in quality, ways of treating employees, integrity. The value set can be clear and very strong or it can be a loose set of beliefs which is continuously adjusted to the circumstances. The value set may support and contribute to the control of the company or it may hinder that control. But it will frequently be subjected to the pressure of change.

The ideology is tested and changed by experiment. Many companies in the UK were founded by Christians whose beliefs conditioned much of the behaviour in their organizations long after they had retired. Such companies were permeated with a belief in integrity in the Christian sense of that word. But integrity, of course, is not an absolute and in the early 1970s it was difficult to be successful in the Middle East without adhering to local ways of doing business. The 'experiment' of exploring opportunities in the Middle East therefore involved testing the firm's values to do with integrity.

Direction

What we mean by direction is perhaps even harder to define. It is a word used frequently by managers and it has a number of meanings in a business context. Although frequently used in the futuristic sense of where one is going to, this meaning has little practical relevance in today's business world. But it does have another important meaning with three components: clarity, continuity and coherence. It means moving into the future from an existing area of operation and set of values in a clear, specific way, which has continuity and is also coherent.

Moving in a clear, specific way

This covers the kind of response which the company is making in the market place. It is the combination of quality, service levels and price which is being delivered to that market place. It is the way in which the company uses its technology, the performance levels it achieves, the safety and environmental respect it shows. A company has direction when it is clear what it is providing to the customers, how it is providing it, what it stands for. In other words it has direction when the existing area of operation is appropriate, the ideology is supportive and widely believed in, when it has a clear mission relating to what it is now.

It is easy to think of companies which move in a clear specific way — IBM, Marks & Spencer, John Laing which I am using so frequently as an example — their names spring to mind because what they stand for, what they deliver is clear. When managers and employees say that their company has no direction they frequently mean that it has no clear image in the market place, that it has no clear policies for treating and developing managers and employees.

Continuity of movement

This means that the organization is backing key activities with resources. It means that there is organizational energy and determination to succeed in core activities. There is a clearly visible intention to stay with the activity and the market. It is not a 'fly by night' or 'get rich quick' operation. It is going to be around as long as the demand lasts. There is confidence on the part of customers that the company can

and will supply product and service. When managers and employees say that their company has no direction they frequently mean that it has no commitment to the market. There is doubt as to how long it will stay. There is little determination. Managers are not backed with sufficient resources to deliver what existing customers want.

Moving in a coherent way

This means that the company is not pursuing a large number of mutually contradictory directions. It means focus, a limited number of comprehensible thrusts and positions in the markets. There is a core business clear to all. The balance between differentiation, low cost and focus is consistent and appropriate. Experiments at the boundaries of the business are not whimsical; they make sense. There is reasonable stability in roles and organizational structures and when they are changed people find it easy to understand why. When managers and employees say there is no direction you will find contradictions, the random taking of opportunities and structures which are always changing for poorly communicated reasons.

Lack of direction

In my consulting work, I frequently hear complaints from managers that their organization has no direction, that the top-level managers do not know what they are doing. This occurs even where there are written mission statements and formal communication sessions with top management. When I ask them what they mean they usually say that they 'do not know where the company is going'. However when one talks to them in greater depth, what emerges is a lack of clarity, continuity and coherence. When these are present in a company, in the 'now' sense, then there are no complaints about direction, even when there is no plan or idea of where the company is meant to be in five years' time.

Complaints about lack of direction will not be removed by publishing a plan of what is to be done over the next five years or holding a meeting. They will be removed by coherent experiments to change the boundaries, test direction. Clear, continuing, coherent direction is the same thing as vision. Vision integrates phenomena which are occurring now; it gives meaning and purpose to what people are doing and experiencing. The visionary is not some Delphic oracle. The visionary artist or business man or woman expresses the current or emerging mood in an innovative way and so gives the rest of us an understanding of what is happening around us, or to us, which we did not have before. It is not at all the same thing as clairvoyance.

Direction does not have to mean that you know where you are going. You are in an unfamiliar part of your city with no maps, so you do not know where you are

going — all you know is that you want to end up at home (make a profit). What do you do if you behave in a controlled way? You choose a specific street, you move continuously down it, you do it coherently, not taking random turnings all the time, until you come to a landmark which suggests that you are going in the right or in the wrong direction. If it is wrong you try another specific street. If it looks right you continue to travel in that direction.

If this is what successful managers are in reality doing when they manage strategically, how do they do it? They detect change and develop implicit, dynamic strategic issue agendas; they respond to those issues in an experimental way; and they build strategies on single issue responses when they have generated enough confidence from the experiment. Periodically they review the implicit agenda, making it explicit at a point in time; they review existing areas of operation, values, control systems and direction in the light of change occurring now. Each of these components of dynamic strategic management is considered in the sections which follow.

Developing strategic issue agendas

Detecting small changes

Potential strategies are conceived when someone in an organization detects a change in the market place or in the operational methods used to deliver product to that market place; when someone detects a mismatch between customer requirements and delivery capability; when someone detects inadequacies in the control system; when someone detects a change, mismatch, inadequacy with potential long-term consequences for a substantial part or the whole of the organization. It all starts when someone identifies a potentially widespread disturbance to the existing business, a problem or an opportunity, caused by the detected change. Such a change is usually one small change among many occurring all the time, and generally goes unnoticed by most other people in the organization and in rival businesses.

It is these small changes that are the really significant ones because they are so hard to detect; they seem so insignificant and yet they have profound consequences. For example, the arrival of a few Honda executives in the USA in the 1950s was a small change which led to the virtual demise of the US motor-cycle industry. The problem is that our whole educational background conditions us to ignore small changes — in traditional mathematical and scientific systems small changes have small consequences and we ignore them as 'noise' or estimating error. But we now know that there are many dynamic systems in science where small changes are magnified and escalate through the system with unpredictable consequences. It seems to me that business is one such system.[2]

Intuition and political processes

The meaning of the change and its potential implications are usually unclear and open to dispute because they are arising in an open-ended change situation. After the event, the significance of a change is of course quite clear — one business will have benefited while another will have suffered from it. But at the time the change is simply one among a large number which might or might not be significant, which might or might not be noticed, which could affect a number of functions or business units in the organization over the longer term.

Because the detected change could have long-term implications for more than one part of the organization, it cannot be handled alone by the individual who detected it. In all probability its full implications will not be understood by one individual alone and any significant response to it will require the agreement and cooperation of a number of managers in the organization. The one who detected it in the first place must secure management and organisational attention for it. An issue needs to be created and placed on the agenda of issues which are receiving management attention at the level where there is sufficient political power to progress it.

The kind of change we are talking about is generally small, its causes and its consequences are unclear and it is not adequately backed by information. Analytical processes consequently make a relatively small contribution to its detection and early structuring. It is the intuitive, judgemental processes of control which have most heavily to be called upon in this situation. Because intuitive reasoning is personal and subjective, it is open to far greater dispute than analytical reasoning. Persuasion and negotiation are the control processes required to get others to understand and back the issue. Turning a detected problem or opportunity into an issue is therefore a political process. A champion who believes in the relevance of the issue to the organization, a champion with political power, is essential if the issue is to be attended to at all.

The political process requires that the champion form a special interest group around the issue, a coalition with sufficient power to get the necessary attention in a situation where many potential issues are emerging all the time. The agenda is dynamic and changing all the time as a consequence of continuous change, the detecting of it and the manoeuvring to get issues on the agenda. Successful companies have active, dynamic, total-control systems where intuitive processes are allowed and encouraged to flourish and where effective political processes function. Where these are blocked by bureaucratic rules and highly authoritarian styles of leadership, the real strategy-making process is stillborn, no matter how elaborate the planning system.

For example — small changes and political processes in the building products market

To illustrate what I mean, consider the history of Laing's involvement in the manufacture of concrete building blocks. In the UK, the traditional method of constructing houses in the late 1940s was still that of outer cavity walls with two leaves of brick and room partitions also of brick. In the early 1950s concrete blocks began to be substituted for brick, in a small way, in the inner leaf of the outer wall and in the room partitions. The reason was the lower laid cost of blocks which are larger and cheaper than bricks. Initially the blocks were of the dense and therefore heavy, but cheap kind.

Top executives at Laing detected the change early on and identified the further savings in laid cost which could be secured with higher quality, lighter, but higher price blocks. In the early 1950s they set up a company, Thermalite, to manufacture blocks in one plant, using a licensed Swedish process and to develop the market for those blocks. Marketing activity was targeted at the architect and engineer specifiers of building materials, and by the early 1970s Thermalite, then operating from a number of factories, had a significant share of the market and yielded reasonable profits. An experiment, championed by a top executive, had shown signs of success and had been backed with resources. By the early 1970s it was a clear strategy.

Another products company in Laing's business portfolio was Lytag. Here Laing's research and development company had set out to develop a method of manufacturing synthetic lightweight aggregates by sintering waste ash from power stations. An effective manufacturing process had been developed and a factory set up. But it proved more difficult to persuade architects and engineers to specify this new product in the high-rise buildings for which it had been developed. Another experiment had been championed, but this time the outcome had so far been less successful.

Changes in thermal insulation regulations made it on to the agenda

In 1973 the massive increase in energy prices occurred and the managing director of Thermalite immediately identified the implications — building regulations would soon be changed to require the thermal insulation of houses. The higher quality lightweight blocks would be able to meet such regulations more cost effectively than the cheaper dense blocks. This change was judged to be far more important than the decline in housing demand which was occurring at the same time.

So in 1974, the managing director of Thermalite lobbied the Laing chief executive, the director of his division, the finance director and others to get attention for the issue of changing building regulations and the increased production capacity necessary to benefit from the opportunity. The issue rapidly took its place on the strategic agenda of Laing's top executives and before long

substantial investment to increase production capacity was made. The change in thermal regulations also created opportunities for Lytag which switched its emphasis from material for high-rise buildings to lightweight blocks. The Lytag manager also lobbied for and obtained funds for additional investment.

The switch to timber-frame housing did not make it on to the agenda
But other changes were also occurring — there were other solutions to the thermal insulation problem. One approach was timber-frame housing with outer walls of brick, insulation material and plasterboard, and partitions also of plasterboard. In the mid-1970s this method of construction was used in only a very small proportion of the new houses constructed. The block producers rejected it as a viable construction method for the UK on the grounds that it was unacceptable to house buyers and not suitable for UK weather conditions.

The small initial move towards the timber-frame method was barely noticed and decision makers in Thermalite and John Laing did not perceive its importance at the time of making the investment in additional Thermalite and Lytag capacity. The potential threat of timber-frame construction was dismissed at that time; the housing company and the building division were not using it and there was no champion or special interest group pushing it to the fore.

A major part of the importance of timber-frame construction lay in the fact that a dynamic new competitor was beginning to appear in the housing market. And this new competitor adopted the timber-frame method of construction for all its houses. At the time this competitor, Barratt Developments, represented a small, barely noticeable change. From small beginnings in the north of England, Barratt adopted an approach which had a major impact on the housing market within a few years.

Lawrie Barratt segmented the market in a way his competitors did not. Having detected the demographic changes which were causing rapid growth in first time buyers and single person households, coupled with house prices which made house purchase out of the question for many, he designed small, low-price housing specifically for this segment. He backed this with national advertising of a kind never seen in the conservative housing market and he added furniture and financial packages to his product. This innovative approach to the market led to very rapid growth and within a few years Barratt was the largest house builder in the country.

And he built his houses with timber frames, a practice which was soon adopted by many of his major competitors. By the end of the 1970s the top ten house builders had increased their market share to 45 per cent, from the 20 per cent of the early 1970s.

By the early 1980s the timber-frame method of construction accounted for one third of a very depressed market for new private houses in the UK. Thermalite, with

its recently built factories, faced considerable over-capacity. About this time, John Laing sold Thermalite in a management buyout. It also sold Lytag to another company.

Back in the mid-1970s, the changes in the composition of the population, upon which Barratt based his segmented approach to the market, had also been detected by head office planners at Laing, who recommended expansion of the housing activity and concentration on the small, low-price segment. But at that time no champion with enough political power took it up. At the time no one noticed the competitor from the north.

In 1978 the shareholders decided to split the company into separate property and construction companies. Responsibility for housing was put into new hands, a director who took on the champion's role for the timber-frame and housing expansion issues. These then attracted real organizational attention. John Laing boosted its housing activity towards the late 1970s, concentrating on the small-house, low-price segment. And in 1979-80 it established Superhomes to supply house packs of timber frame and other materials and components.

But small changes were still occurring

The block manufacturers were mounting a political and propaganda campaign against the timber-frame construction method. It was by no means clear what impact this would have. Many dismissed it as an ineffective rearguard action. Then the British public were treated to a television documentary which attacked timber-frame housing, raising doubts as to quality and longevity. The attack was specifically directed at Barratt.

At much the same time one could detect that the rapid expansion of the small, low-price housing segment was coming to an end. The sheltered housing segment for the elderly, developed by McCarthy and Stone, was expanding and the prospects for larger, more expensive homes improving. By the mid-1980s the level of Barratt's house building had declined and they and many others had largely abandoned timber frames. In an expanding housing market switching back to more traditional construction methods, the now privately owned Thermalite prospered again.

So throughout this story about mature, conservative markets, we have interconnected changes occurring in technology, customer requirements, population composition, government regulations, public debate, changes in the internal power structure of the company. Many were small, difficult to detect at the time and even harder to understand in terms of interconnections, implications and timing. Over the first 30 years of the story, the changes were rather gradual and predictable, but in the last ten years they were violent and very difficult to predict. None of the players got it right all of the time. All the organizations involved had to rely on someone detecting the change in the first place and then understanding

the implications and creating an issue which reached the agenda of those who had the power to decide.

Detecting small changes requires being close to the action

It was only possible to detect most of the changes by being close to the action, to the place where the change was occurring. Some of the changes could be detected from afar: the demographic changes were there to see in published statistics; the likelihood of higher energy prices and consequently the introduction of thermal insulation regulations was publicly discussed. But you had to be part of the industry and government negotiations to get any feel for exactly what the thermal insulation regulations would turn out to be.

And this was important because one form of the regulation would give a significant advantage to one type of block. You had to be in the market place to detect how timber-frame construction methods were being received, where Barratt was targeting its efforts and what construction methods it was using. You had to be in the market place to detect what a particular demographic change meant in terms of customer requirements and competitor responses.

Detecting small changes can therefore only be done by those close to the market place and to the operations which deliver product to that market place. It is they who detect the changes and they do so through informal contacts and discussions, by piecing bits of information together, drawing inferences and making judgements. Detection and understanding come from active observation, through asking questions and drawing intuitive conclusions. You cannot send market researchers out into a market with a general brief to find out what is happening, what is changing. You can send them out to find out how many houses are being built using timber frames and who is building them. But to do this you first have to have posed the question, noticed the change.

And this need to obtain information on small, significant changes from those right at the market and operational fronts creates real problems in companies of any size. Those who have to make the final decision are some way removed, but in the end it will be their intuition and judgement which will determine whether the change is accorded attention and responded to. Formal channels of communication are unlikely to rectify this: suggestion schemes or even formal planning reviews once a year are unlikely to give top executives the kind of feel which is necessary. A key to strategy-making therefore has to be the continuing, real, rather than ceremonial, contact between those at the very top of the company and those who operate at the 'coal face'. Top managers need to be detecting and understanding the small changes. And there is another very important reason for this — to become a real organizational issue the detected change and any response to it needs a champion.

The champion and the strategic agenda

The role of the champion is to turn any detected change, any identified opportunity or problem, into a strategic issue which receives the attention of that level of management having the power to progress it. The champion may have detected the change or may have been persuaded by those lower down in the organization. The champion must have power and unless he or she is an autocratic executive chairperson, others with power have to be persuaded that an issue has been identified and should be considered further. Since at any one time there are a large number of potential strategic issues, the champion has to fight to get the issue on to the agenda which is receiving real organizational attention at the time. He or she has to lobby others and obtain support — the issue's chances are greater if a special interest group can be formed around it.

And any issue will be one of a large number on the agenda, while the agenda itself will keep changing. The agenda is implicit and dynamic. Its shape at any one time is determined by what politically powerful champions and special interest groups are noticing, what is being brought to their attention, what they are trying to achieve personally and organizationally. An issue reaches the agenda, receives attention, through political processes. The political processes perform the function of a screening device to select important and relevant issues from the many. Politics take place within cultural constraints which restrict what is considered to be an issue.

The strategies which may eventually be pursued depend critically on this whole process of developing agendas. Simply putting matters into a formal plan does not make them issues. The issues are not detected in an analytically deterministic way and they rarely arise from formal market scanning. They can be detected low down or high up in the management hierarchy, but they get on to the agenda only when the top levels of management pay attention.

What happens to the issues, the way agendas develop, depends crucially on formal and informal management meetings. If these meetings waste time extensively reviewing the past or bickering about administrative matters then the strategic issues are unlikely to receive adequate attention.

The key points are:

- continuous change arising in open-ended situations, with all that this means in terms of lack of clarity;

- intuitive processes used to detect the change and the need for top levels of management to be close to those who operate where the change actually occurs;

- use of political processes to get the issues on to the agenda, that is, the activities of champions and special interest groups;

- a dynamic, changing-issue agenda, consisting of a number of single issues;

- the importance of formal and informal management meetings and the need for them to focus on strategic issues.

Consider now the nature of the experimenting which follows the arrival of the issues on the agenda.

Experimenting — trial and error responses to single issues

The political process of persuading colleagues and forming special interest groups to push an issue is necessary to attract sufficient management attention for that issue to take its place on the strategic agenda. It will then be discussed in the corridors, knocked about in car, train and aircraft journeys, surface at informal meetings in executives' offices, and at some stage appear on the written agendas of the regular, formal meetings of top management. This period of discussion could extend over months, even years, but sometimes a day or two suffices.

Sometimes a decision is taken rapidly and an experiment starts. On one occasion I remember, a powerful director briefly discussed an idea he had with the chief executive and then put it to a board meeting. The decision was taken there and then to proceed. The idea was to buy a disused hover barge, moored off the Saudi Arabian coast, and use it to off-load the cargo of ships waiting for many days to get into the port. That turned out to be an error — the obstacle was not a lack of physical off-loading capacity but a lack of staff to handle the mountains of paper work. In an earlier chapter I used the example of Company C,[3] where a major acquisition decision was made in a matter of days and the whole deal was concluded within a few weeks. So far that has proved to be a success.

But with greater frequency, we find that the progressing of an issue to the point of actual experiment takes much longer, often involving laborious checking, research and argument. So, the establishment of a house-building activity by John Laing in the USA was a live issue in 1982, market research was conducted in 1983, two executives were sent out to establish the activity in 1984, a small number of houses were built in 1985–86 and by 1989 the level of house building exceeded 800.

The role of the champion is central not only to getting the issue on to the agenda in the first place but also in progressing it thereafter. It is the champion and those colleagues whom he or she has persuaded to form the special interest group, who ensure that the issue is raised whenever appropriate, whenever the opportunity arises to keep the bandwagon rolling. The way in which formal meetings are run is also crucial to the attention which an issue gets.

Task forces

Once an issue has gained sufficient support we find that a task force emerges or is appointed. The task force is to be distinguished from the special interest group. The special interest group is a political coalition of those who have power to push issues, those who have the ear of the powerful, those who take part in decision-making on significant issues. Special interest groups are generally formed at the top levels of management. The task force is much more concerned with progressing the issue, with doing something about it. The task force and the special interest group could coincide but usually they do not. The champion could lead the task force, but someone else might be appointed to take on that role, while he or she retains a strong interest in progress and continues to provide political backing. The task force could consist of a formally appointed team of people, relieved of their everyday duties, or it could be a much more informal grouping of people who devote part of their time to progressing the issue.

Task forces, at their most effective, are usually multi-discipline and drawn from different business units where they have a common interest in the issue. Task forces may involve a large number of people or they may consist of two or three. And the task force could emerge even before any formal decision to progress the issue is taken.

What the task force does

The task force gathers information about the issue, asks questions about it, tries to structure it, applies analysis to it. This can mean conducting major pieces of soundly based market research. It can involve talking to a few people in the market place. It may need just a few telephone calls. The task force is trying to shape the experiment that might be conducted in response to the issue. It is trying to identify the risks and approaches to containing those risks. Members of the task force will identify and meet potential partners in any experiment that may be conducted, any joint venture that may be pursued. They will make personal visits to potential new areas of operation, hold discussions, negotiate with potential partners.

Much of what they do could be described as analytical, but even more important is the intuitive process of getting a feel for the potential new area, the potential new partners or customers. Personal judgement about markets and people play a vital part.

But even at the earliest stages, the focus is not entirely, often not even primarily, on the market and the competitors. Considerable, high-level attention is paid right from the beginning to implementation problems and possibilities. In my experience more time is taken up in discussions about and searches for competent managers to be entrusted with any venture or experiment, than is taken up with consideration of the markets and the competition. The focus is just as much on the potential

impact on the control system within the company, of which managers are clearly a part, as it is on the potential in the market. And this is not short-sightedness.

No matter how great the market potential, it will not be realized if the activity set up to reap it is not competently controlled. This concern with the control system is very much a part of trial and error response.

Adjusting the control system as change is accommodated

Day-to-day disturbance that arises in closed change situations is handled without any need to change the control system. The system is given and constant as far as any individual disturbance is concerned. You do not need to change anyone's role, or the organizational structure, or any other aspect of the total control system itself, just because a variance is produced. In conventional strategic management you prepare the plan and then design the systems, structures, roles and cultures necessary to implement it. The plan is supposed to have foreseen most of the disturbances. So when any change occurs, when any single strategic issues arises, it is handled within the plan framework and there should be no need to change structures, roles, cultures or systems.

But in open-ended situations the grand design falls apart and is ignored. The response is opportunistic and based on intuition. You cannot have designed the most appropriate systems, cultures, roles and structures in advance. Part of the opportunistic trial and error is therefore the adjusting of parts of the total control system as you handle the disturbance, the single strategic issue. The organization's total control system is no longer a given constant. It is like playing a Bach partita while continuously tuning the violin.

For example — a factory relocation

Among the businesses owned by a company which I will call Castings plc, there was one which manufactured ferrous castings and another, much smaller, which cast aluminium components. They operated from different sites and both were highly profitable. About two years ago, Castings plc had acquired another small company, on a third site, which produced more complex ferrous and aluminium castings than its existing businesses. The customers for all three businesses were in the aerospace and general engineering sectors. Their requirements were for high precision castings and they were pressing for price reductions. Over the first year the newly acquired company had incurred losses, recently stemmed but not reversed. Then the landlord of the site occupied by the acquisition gave notice that the premises should be vacated in nine months' time.

The board decided to review its whole position in the castings business as part of the relocation decision. The finance director developed 12 logical options covering various re-sitings and combinations of all the businesses. He rejected a

number on early analysis because they were clearly not viable. He then presented financial projections for seven options to the board, together with a number of judgemental factors: the original ferrous casting business would be disrupted by any move to a new site and any move of another business to its site would block its future growth; key personnel would be lost by any move; management at the newly acquired company was poor, productivity low, management took too technical a view of the business, resulting in over-engineered products, years spent on trying to get very difficult castings right, taking on business at prices which others would not touch; management at the other sites was good; impact of relocation or closures on customers was uncertain; impact of any closures on the investment community was uncertain.

The calculations showed that the highest financial returns could be obtained by relocating all activities to the site occupied by the original ferrous castings business. But the board in fact spent little time looking at the analysis. Most of the time was taken up by, most of the attention was focused on, key questions to do with the total control system of the organization. Would relocation at the original ferrous casting site overload management and damage a very profitable business? Would simply relocating the newly acquired business and redirecting it to less complex castings work, given the quality of management and the technology-orientated cultures of that business? How would organizational structures have to be changed to make any move or combination of businesses work? Would moves or combinations of the original profitable businesses divert top management from the main thrust of the business? What did colleagues think of closing down half of a recently acquired business?

The attention was being focused not on the future out in the market place, but on the existing capability of the organization's control system to accommodate the change: on changes to structures; on cultures; on management roles and the match of managers to those roles. And in my experience this is normally what happens when managers are confronted with strategic issues.

For example, consider what happened when Laing set about establishing a new house-building activity in the USA. The necessary information on markets and analysis of profit potential was carried out by staff functions and of course it was discussed by the board members; but they spent far more time on how the new venture would fit into the organizational structure, how it would be controlled, who would run it, what steps should be taken to test out the market before putting major investment into the venture.

Strategic management in reality

So, in reality, strategic management is not about a grand plan which predetermines everything. In reality there is planning, but it is the planning of experiments,

weighing the risks and limiting them as far as possible. And the risks lie within the total control system of the organization, with its control tensions, just as much as they lie out in the market place. What the experiments are doing is testing the boundaries of the business, those set by existing areas of operation, existing value sets, existing control system and existing directions.

Strategic management in practice is a dynamic game and ability to play, ability to form multi-disciplined task forces is a major factor in success. Organizations which do not encourage experimentation, do not allow the emergence of task forces, do not develop managers capable of operating in this mode, are organizations which do not possess the flexibility required to play business games. And business games are realistic strategic management.

But the game being played has to be clear, continuous and coherent; it has to have direction. The experiments have to be related to each other and to the business. The purpose is to explore and extend the boundaries of the existing business, not to dash here and there in entirely different areas trying to make a fast buck wherever one is to be had. Where top management allows this, you find people throughout the organization complaining of a lack of direction. Top management articulates direction, displays vision by the combination of experiments, of extensions to the boundaries which it actively encourages, and by the wild departures which it stops.

Building strategies from single issue responses

The prime role in progressing and actually conducting organizational experiments is filled by a task force. But whether any experiment is ever built into a strategy depends critically on the top management team.

The top management team

It is usually top management which decides whether there will be an experiment in the first place, whether management and employee time will be made available to progress it. The experiment may start without top team approval but it certainly cannot progress very far without that approval. The success with which the experiment is conducted will depend to a significant extent upon the continuing interest which the top management team displays in it. It is the top management role to ensure that milestones are set, points at which, and achievements against which, the conduct of the experiment is to be judged and decisions made as to its continuance.

This continuing involvement of the top management team is crucial because at various points during the progress of the experiment decisions have to be made about the allocation of resources to its conduct. And at some point it must be decided whether significant resource backing and management energy is to be put

into building on the experiment, so creating a new business or beginning to change the direction of an existing one. Building experiments into different directions for the organization creates its strategy.

Since the top management team is so crucial to the building of strategies from organizational experiments, successful organizations will pay particular attention to the manner in which that top team works together. If it does not meet regularly, both formally and informally, then experiments will not be monitored, the significance of early success will be missed and the competition may well take the opportunity. The manner in which the top management team conducts its meetings is just as important. If most of its valuable time together is used up in reviewing the past then once again the significance of experimental success or failure will be missed. If behavioural rules restrict open discussion and destructive political activity distracts attention from the issues, the same result occurs.

The leader

And the part which the head of that top management team plays is most crucial of all. How the leader views experimentation, accepts failure, rewards success, takes a personal interest in the conduct of experiments, has some vision of how the experiments relate to each other and the existing business, and uses the meetings of the top team, will all have a major bearing on the extent and consequences of experimentation in the organization. The leader sets many of the challenges, creates a sense of urgency to do something about them and expresses the determination to succeed.

Throughout, the processes utilized by the leadership and the top management team will be primarily political, intuitive and judgemental, backed by pieces of analysis. And the type and extent of the information gathered and the analysis performed will depend on the nature of the particular experiment being conducted.

Making agendas explicit, reviewing areas of operation, values, control systems and direction

Control by trial and error, accommodating open-ended change, is going on all the time in any thriving company. Thriving companies are always experimenting and pushing out the boundaries of their businesses. But there are points where top management has to take stock of this dynamic, organic activity and step back to look at the whole picture. In 1981 a large cash outflow and a small loss compelled Laing to do just this. Some companies, those with formal long-term planning systems, try to perform a strategic audit on a regular annual basis. Others do so when events come together to make it necessary and use rather more informal processes — top management holds special meetings in which it may involve those

lower down, or it may go off for a few days to some venue away from the office.

The fatal drawback of the annual long-term plan as the strategic stock-taking exercise is that it so soon becomes a ritual and, in practice, almost inevitably focuses on the projection of the existing business into the future. The stock-taking exercise is far more likely to succeed when it is prompted by some real need, some combination of events which create a distinct and real threat to, or a major opportunity for, the organization.

All that can be achieved by these events, be they plans or workshop meetings, is to make the current strategic agenda explicit. Since we are dealing with open-ended change, such events cannot identify tomorrow's strategic issues. If the stock taking exercise is to have any benefit then it has to be seen and used for what it is. It is an attempt to set out clearly what the existing issues are, how they relate to each other and whether they provide sufficient prospects for meeting the overall challenge which the organization faces now. Attempts to use this kind of occasion to decide upon 'the strategy for the future' simply lead to frustration. The strategy cannot be decided in advance in the face of open-ended change. It can only result from the issues which are being identified, progressed and backed.

Control by trial and error summarized

The appropriate response to open-ended situations is one of detecting change, conducting experiments and backing successful ones with resources. These responses are produced by the political system of the business, the components of which are leadership, the formal top management team, champions, special interest groups and task forces. This political system is illustrated in Figure 6, together with its key outputs of issue agendas and the backing of experiments.

The cutting edge of real strategy is determined by the manner in which this political system works, not by the sophistication of long-range planning procedures. Real strategic management is about improving the political system so that the organization is capable of playing dynamic business games to deal with the unknowable.

Political systems in business organizations

Any political system is fundamentally an established pattern within which power is exercised to make decisions which will be translated into action. And the decisions at the heart of political activity are those which cannot be made in purely logical, scientifically deductive ways commanding immediate, widespread support. They are decisions about matters of belief which affect the values and ambitions of people; matters which give rise to conflict and disagreement; matters where there

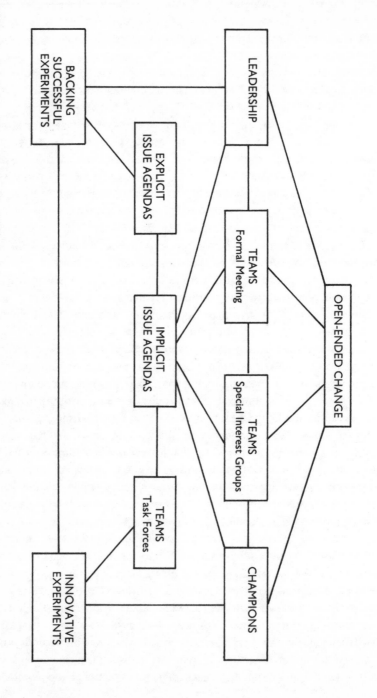

Figure 6 Political systems and control by trial and error

are no absolutes and where causes and consequences are uncertain.

In a national context such decisions have to do with matters such as fair ways of levying taxes, appropriate methods of national defence, effective means of deterring criminal activity. In a business context they have to do with entering a new market, acquiring another business, investing in a new plant, forming a joint venture with a competitor, balancing long-term profits against short-term profits and so on. Because there is uncertainty and there are no absolutes, because we are dealing to a large extent with beliefs and ambitions, decisions of this kind are made by the exercise of power within an established order.

The political system exists to control and to accommodate change; and it is that subset of the total control system of an organization which has to do with the exercise of power in making decisions on policy, in establishing the framework within which the activities of the organization are to be conducted. It may be contrasted with the administrative system, another subset of total control, within which the existing day-to-day activities of the organization are conducted. The political system of a business is no less important in controlling that business than the political system of the state is in controlling the nation.

Political systems are most easily described in terms of their formal bodies, rules and procedures and roles of people. So, in describing national political systems we talk about legislatures, government teams, committees, constitutions, prime ministers and presidents. The equivalent in business political systems are shareholder meetings, boards of directors, formal management team meetings, worker councils, articles of association, chairmen and women, and managing directors. These formal and visible aspects of the political system serve primarily as means of communication and obtaining formal approval of, and commitment to, decisions. They are primarily about legitimizing decisions. In some political systems this is all they are about, while in others they do provide some aspects of the really significant political activity. But the bulk of really significant political activity, the actual exercise of power, takes place outside the formal and visible.

Power is actually exercised in smaller, informal groupings — special interest groups, pressure groups and coalitions, all of which operate according to more informal rules and use informal modes of communication. The real political system, the actual exercise of power, has to do with leadership and team functioning. It has to do with the negotiated roles people fill, the way people in their roles relate to each other in team settings, the way people perceive their roles and those of others, the way in which roles and relationships are conditioned by the cultures within which they operate.

Three different political systems are commonly found in business, at least in the Western capitalist world. These are the oligarchic political system where power is concentrated in the hands of a small group; the pluralistic political system where

power is dispersed, allowing for a greater variety of principles and traditions; and the monarchic system where, of course, power is concentrated in the hands of one individual.

Oligarchic systems

In the oligarchic systems of the business world, the significant political activity, at least as far as strategic issues are concerned, is confined largely to a small group of managers right at the top of the organization. A few top corporate executives, a few divisional or business unit 'barons', often augmented by a very small number of close advisers or favourites, constitute the group within which important political activities take place. Only those issues which make it on to the strategic agenda of this small power group are ever progressed. The rest of the management hierarchy concentrates on the day-to-day and refers matters of strategic importance to the oligarchy at the top. It is the top power group who are supposed to perceive their roles in holistic terms and all others adopt parochial perceptions. Relationships between roles are clearly directing.

The advantage of this political system is that the concentration of power makes clear choices easier on control style and responses to strategic issues which have been identified. The disadvantage is that the perspectives and the ability to detect the many small changes occurring are both limited. The oligarchic political system is always accompanied by directing forms of personal relationships, almost inevitably by parochial role perceptions and by conservative, somewhat change-resistant cultures.

Pluralistic systems

In the pluralistic political systems of the business world, we find a much greater dispersion of political power through the organization. Significant political activity occurs at many levels in such organizations. Effective pressure groups and special interest groups can be formed at levels some way from the top. Experiment may be initiated and progressed some way before the involvement and approval of top managers is required. In the end that approval is of course required and there can be no strategy, no backing of successful experiments, without the involvement of the top team.

The advantage of this political system is its greater ability to detect small changes, it wider variety of perspectives and experiments. But the price is a less clear choice on how tensions of control are to be resolved and how identified strategic issues are to be dealt with.

Monarchic systems

The third political system found in the business world is that which is akin to

absolute monarchy. Political activity of any significance takes place right at the top of the organization and power is concentrated in the hands of one person. There is a 'court' of advisers and 'governors' but they do not really have the independent power of the divisional barons in the oligarchic system.

Each of these political systems can work. Each can secure sufficient commitment and agreement, or at least acquiescence, so that political decisions are actually taken and carried out. Each can be responsive to change, either successfully accommodating it or successfully blocking it. Each can generate the vision or direction which will carry the majority of the active, those who singly or in groups have enough power to determine what will happen. But success in all these senses requires leadership and appropriate team activities, opportunities and willingness to meet, to handle conflict and reach agreement.

The political system determines where the power is actually located and how it is actually used. This in turn determines which issues receive organizational attention and backing. So within the same institutional framework, the functioning of the political system differs markedly according to the style of leadership and the degree of actual participation. Whether champions emerge, whether issues are encouraged or blocked, all depend on the actual functioning of the political system.

Strategies are consequences, not determinants

The conventional view is that strategy, a predetermined road to be travelled to some fixed point in the future, is formulated first. The organizational structures and management roles, the control systems, management selection procedures, training and development programmes and reward packages are then all designed to fit the strategy, to implement it. The strategy provides the framework within which individual disturbances, tactics or single issues are then handled.

This chapter has argued that successful companies do not in practice use this deterministic approach. Instead they act opportunistically, experimentally reshaping and extending the boundaries of their businesses set by area of operation, values, control systems and direction. They play the business game which is appropriate to open-ended change situations. Strategy does not come first at all; it is the consequence of this opportunistic, experimental behaviour. Strategies are the direction from where we are now and are built on successful experiments or trials. The key is the organizational ability to detect change, develop and progress issues, experiment and back successful experiments. The ability to do all these things depends on the state of the organization's total control system — the organizational structures, cultures, set of management roles, instruments for matching people to roles and the processes which people in their roles utilize to control. Strategy does

not determine structure, systems and culture, it is determined by them. In a dynamic world they are of course interconnected, but the more useful way of looking at the chain of causation is that which sees strategy as being determined, by, not determining, the total control system.

This chapter has focused on how companies actually control in open-ended situations. But these are not the only situations they have to face. The next chapter turns to the implications of simultaneously controlling in both open-ended and closed situations at the same time.

Notes

[1] H Mintzberg, 'Strategy in Three Modes', in J Quinn, H Mintzberg and R James, *The Strategy Process*, Prentice-Hall (1988).
[2] J Gleick, *Chaos*, Cardinal (1987).
[3] See page 85.

7
Control Styles

Making choices between the requirements of control in closed and open-ended change situations

Chapter 3 reviewed the most effective way of controlling a business in closed change situations, that is, where the consequences of change affect the very short term only. And that way of controlling is based very clearly on detailed planning, regular monitoring and prompt corrective action. Control is secured by utilizing the Management Information and Control subsystem of the organization.

Chapters 4 and 5 examined the conventional strategic management approach to control outside closed change situations and some of the tensions which two forms of control give rise to. The conclusion is that this conventional approach cannot work as a form of control in the open-ended situations which companies nowadays increasingly face. In fact companies do not use it for control purposes at all. They use it mainly as a method of communicating and raising comfort levels.

Chapter 6 explored what successful companies actually do to control in open-ended situations, those where the consequences of change are unknowable and affect the long-term future of the business. Successful companies control in the only manner possible in such circumstances, through coherent, focused opportunism. And the organization's ability to pursue such opportunism depends critically on another subsystem of total control — the business political system. Opportunism is a team game for organizations of any size, and ability to play it successfully depends on a complex intertwining of individual initiative and intuition with group political processes.

In this chapter we look at how businesses simultaneously combine planning for the closed short term and opportunistic experimentation for the open-ended longer term. Since these control forms are so different and since they place diametrically opposed requirements on organization and behaviour, combining them creates the really fundamental strategic problem. The choice an organization makes to resolve this problem is its control style. Style in this sense is not some soft aspect of appearance, to be distinguished from systems, structures and processes. Style is a set of hard choices which have to be made continuously to sustain effective, balanced control: choices about structures, systems, roles, behaviour and processes.

We first review the principal tensions which the practice of two very different forms of control places on an organization and the people within it.[1] We then look at typical sets of choices which businesses make to resolve this tension — typical control styles.

Control tension

Consider first the requirements of each form of control in isolation from the other.

The requirements of control in closed change situations

Chapter 3 explored the requirements which control in closed change situations, at its most effective and in isolation from the needs of any other control form, place on organization and behaviour. In summary these are:

- applying formal, analytical, instructing processes to the elements of control;

- placing the prime emphasis on the planning element of control — monitoring and corrective action are made much easier because of comprehensive planning;

- setting objectives which are short-term and fixed — they have to be tightly constrained in that they are precise and taken literally;

- defining the roles of people carrying out the control tasks primarily in terms of authority and responsibility;

- constraining those roles by formal position in the hierarchy as well as by resource availability;

- developing role perceptions which are parochial in that people see their roles in terms of the part of the organization in which they are operating;

- fostering relationships between one role and another which are primarily of the directing kind. People are given objectives and instructed to take corrective action;

- matching people to roles using selection criteria to do with specific expertise, specific bodies of knowledge and a limited number of personal skills;

- matching people to roles by training and development programmes which are governed by the same criteria;

- using instruments of reward which closely relate individual short-term performance to rewards;

- designing organizational structures which are decentralized into market-related profit centres;

- developing cultures which are conservative with relatively unquestioning acceptance of objectives and instructions.

Now these are the requirements of the ideal short-interval control system being applied in a very orderly environment and in isolation from the need to practise any other form of control. The practice will never be that mechanistic, partly because of the human behaviour factor and partly because other forms of control have to be used at the same time.

The requirements of control in open-ended change situations

Control in open-ended situations, taken in isolation from the need to practise any other form of control, imposes the following requirements on organization and behaviour:

- Applying, to the elements of control, individual intervention based on intuition and judgement, as well as using informal rules, procedures and modes of communication.

- Focusing attention on the detection of small changes occurring now and having important long-term consequences. This is a form of monitoring and it becomes far more important than planning.

- Setting objectives which are long-term, tentative, changeable, loosely defined, because the future is unknowable.

- Defining roles in terms of attributes of collaboration and initiative to allow opportunistic experimentation.

- Constraining roles only through power, personality and organizational culture, not formal position. This is to avoid blocking trial and error.

- Developing role perceptions which are holistic in the sense that they are more concerned with the good of the whole organization than with the good of a part of it alone. We are looking for synergy and new ways of doing things, not more efficient ways of doing old things.

- Fostering relationships between roles which are facilitating. This is vital to allow the surfacing of whatever inadequate information is available and to allow the experimentation and innovation which is central to control in open-ended situations.

- Matching people to roles, using selection instruments where the criteria are personal competences, which are difficult to identify, rather than specific skills

and knowledge. It means using management development instruments which seek to develop intuitive, team-working competences above specific analytical and instructional skills. It means using reward instruments which are no longer related to short-term individual performance but to team performance and willingness to experiment.

● Designing organizational structures which reflect centralist tendencies. Complex structures are needed to bring issues and perspectives to the centre, to get people to take the holistic view and to provide a mechanism for directing the whole organization's attention and energy into important issues.

● Developing radical cultures which foster the questioning of objectives, perceptions and actions.

Meeting both sets of requirements at the same time
In every respect, therefore, control by variance taken in isolation, and control in open-ended situations taken in isolation, demand the diametric opposite of organization and behaviour. Of course they cannot be taken in isolation; both forms of control have to be applied simultaneously. Control in its total sense therefore imposes severe tension on a business and its management. Trying to do diametrically opposed things at the same time is bound to create tension. Control is not just about accommodating the impact of change on the basic business flows; in practical terms it is even more about resolving control tension.

And this is why the handling of strategic issues is always accompanied by even more attention to what needs to be done within the business than to what is likely to happen in the future out in the market place. Strategic issues, those generated by open-ended change situations, tend to disrupt any balance which management has struck between the extremes of the control tensions. New balances have to be struck.

And it has to be recognized that any move away from the demands of one control form will diminish the effectiveness of that control form. Improvement in one control form exacts a price in terms of diminished effectiveness of the other. Control style describes the choices which are being made, the balance that is being struck, the prices which are being paid. Control in the modern business world is a continuous balancing act; a continuous search for an appropriate way of relieving control tension.

These tensions are summarized in Figure 7. The left-hand side lists the ideal requirements of control in closed situations and the right-hand side lists those of control in open-ended situations. The lines joining them represent the tension. All organizations have to make choices between each of the extremes shown.

The first three control requirements shown in the Figure create method

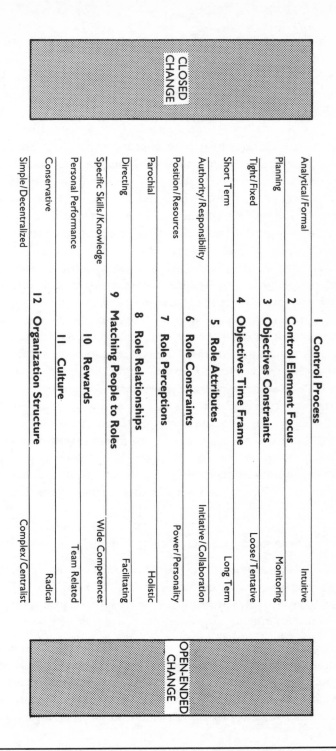

		CLOSED CHANGE
Analytical/Formal	1 Control Process	Intuitive
Planning	2 Control Element Focus	Monitoring
Tight/Fixed	3 Objectives Constraints	Loose/Tentative
Short Term	4 Objectives Time Frame	Long Term
Authority/Responsibility	5 Role Attributes	Initiative/Collaboration
Position/Resources	6 Role Constraints	Power/Personality
Parochial	7 Role Perceptions	Holistic
Directing	8 Role Relationships	Facilitating
Specific Skills/Knowledge	9 Matching People to Roles	Wide Competences
Personal Performance	10 Rewards	Team Related
Conservative	11 Culture	Radical
Simple/Decentralized	12 Organization Structure	Complex/Centralist
		OPEN-ENDED CHANGE

Figure 7 Control tensions

tensions — choices must be made on control process, control element focus and objectives constraints. These choices determine the method of control which is applied in given circumstances.

The requirements five to eleven create behavioural tensions: the way people are matched to roles; the manner in which roles are defined and determined; the perception people have of their roles; the relationships between people in their roles; and the culture which conditions the conduct of those roles. The manner in which behavioural tensions are resolved determines the nature of the political system to be found in the business.

Some organizations may choose to resolve behavioural tensions by always precisely defining roles in terms of authority, responsibility and formal position and then employing directing and instructing relationships between them, all within conservative cultures. Monarchic and oligarchic political systems then result. Other organizations consistently choose looser role definitions which stress collaboration, initiative and political power, with relationships which are facilitating in the sense that persuasion and negotiation are the major interpersonal processes employed. Such organizations tend to have more radical cultures. The result of these choices is a pluralistic political system.

The choice of method determines how the organization is controlled and the behavioural choices establish the kind of political system through which control is to be carried out.

Choices on structural form follow from those made on method and behaviour and they are only given meaning by those method and behaviour choices. So a business which uses a tight budgetary method of control will have to adopt some type of decentralized organizational structure with delegated power, if that budgetary method is to be effective. A highly authoritarian political system will have to be accompanied by some form of centralization, in parts at least, of the organizational structure if it is to work. A structure which is decentralized on paper is meaningless if the political system is such that all power is concentrated at the centre.

Choices on the time frame of objectives, long versus short term, are partly determined by the beliefs and predispositions of the managers at the top level of the corporation. These choices are part of the operation of the political system. Time-frame choices are also partly dictated by market conditions. Some companies will be predisposed to choose long-term objectives, but the actual choice will in the end depend greatly on circumstances. No matter how strong the predisposition, cash flow and short-term profit problems will cause an organization to refocus in order to survive. No matter how strong the focus on short-term profit, competitive pressures and market change will force an organization to undertake long-term investment if it is to survive.

Leadership, teams and control tension resolution

The control style of any business organization is simply a description of the choices it is making about the kind of political system it is to operate and the control methods it is to use. But how are the choices made?

Some, for example those relating to method, may be made explicitly and set out in formal documents, such as those specifying budgetary procedures. Other choices are made implicitly through negotiation between the people involved, for example many aspects of role definition and the interrelationships between them. Yet other organizational choices evolve in complex ways, for example the predominant culture of the organization. Choices may be made intentionally or by default. The control tension choices are made, or emerge, through personal choices conditioned by individual personalities and through group choices developed by political activity in the form of coalitions, pressure groups and the teams within which people work.

Control style is therefore not some once-for-all choice, but a dynamic, continuous process determined by the personalities of key people and the groupings which they form, the groupings within which they work. Change key people in the organization, change the way in which they form teams and coalitions, and you start to change the control style.

The most powerful impact on organizational choices between the control tensions extremes is in practice exerted by the leadership and the nature of team interaction right at the top of the organization. The personality, beliefs and philosophy of the central figure, or leader, of the organization is a principal determinant of control style. So a central figure who has a strongly held, clear 'theoretical' framework within which he or she operates, will make definite personal choices about structural forms, interpersonal relationships and control processes. If the views and beliefs of the leader on control are ably articulated by word and deed, such beliefs will permeate through the organization. Part of the vision of the effective leader relates to control style. The leader's vision is what clarifies the situation for those around him or her, and a major part of the situation is the manner in which the organization is to be controlled.

But of course no leader can operate in a vacuum. No leader can realize any vision without a team which shares that vision and has the ability to put it into practice. Control style will therefore be determined by the ability and cohesiveness of those around the central figure in the organization. Each member of this top team is in turn a leader of his or her own team and so the impact of choices made about control style at the top spreads through the organization.

It follows that when the central leadership of the organization is weak or confused, where the top team lacks ability and cohesion, the control tension choices are likely to be confused and inconsistent throughout the organization. The role of

top management in the determination of control style is therefore of major importance.

Classifying control styles

So control style is a pattern of method and political system choices. Since these choices depend heavily on the personalities and beliefs of leaders and the nature of team working, the pattern of choices is dynamic and changing. In principle, therefore, there are a very large number of possible styles of both the successful and unsuccessful kind and the practice of any one of them need not last for very long. In practice, however, leaders and their teams cannot change styles overnight — they face inertia created by the style which already exists. And in practice there are distinctive patterns of choice, or style, into which most organizations fit — typical control styles do exist and we can identify them by setting out typical combinations of method and political system choices.

Control methods range over a spectrum. At one end there are formal, analytical processes focusing on planning with fixed objectives, which are applied in all change situations. Further along the spectrum there are companies which apply formal planning/fixed objective methods in closed change situations and informal,

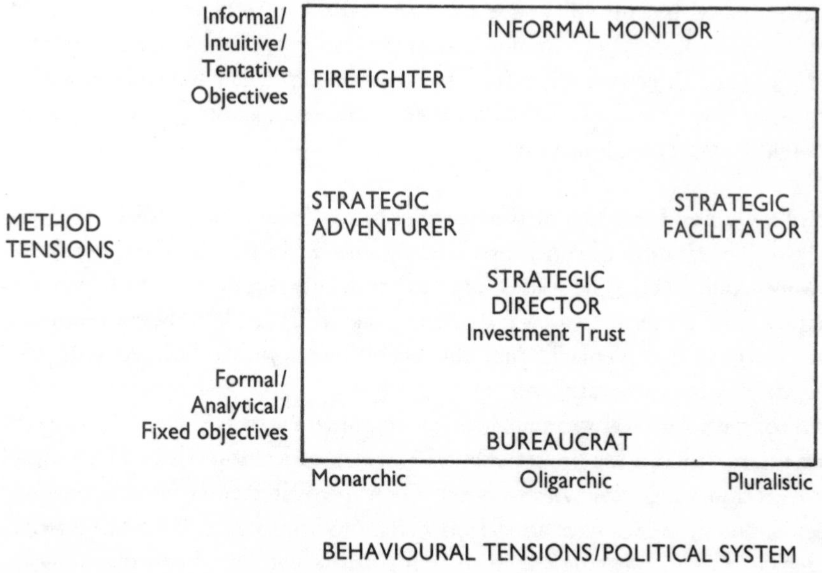

Figure 8 Classification of control styles

intuitive processes focusing on monitoring/action with tentative objectives in open-ended situations. At the other end of the spectrum there are companies which apply informal processes with tentative objectives in all change situations. This spectrum of control method choices is depicted along the vertical axis of Figure 8.

The political systems which organizations commonly operate are the monarchic, the oligarchic and the pluralistic.[2] That spectrum of choices is depicted along the horizontal axis of Figure 8.

This two-way classification can be used to locate the six typical control styles shown in Figure 8. I have found that all of the two dozen or so companies with whom I have worked fall into one of these six categories.

Six major styles of control

Two styles, the Firefighter and the Informal Monitor, always use informal, intuitive methods to control the business no matter what the change situation. They differ in that the former has a monarchic political system which functions reasonably well, while the latter employs an oligarchic system, but one which does not function all that well. Another style, the Bureaucrat, always employs formal methods no matter what the change situation and it operates with an oligarchic political system.

The remaining styles all adapt the method of control to the change situation and they differ only because they use different political systems. The Strategic Adventurer has a monarchic system, the Strategic Facilitator has a pluralistic system and the Strategic Director an oligarchic political system. There is also a variant of the Director style which I have called the Investment Trust Control style — it is the style found in most conglomerates.

Control style and the roles of the corporate and business unit levels

The above classification of control styles draws no distinction between corporate and business unit levels. The style applies to the whole corporation. In Chapter 3 a classification of strategic styles was described, one which fits into the conventional view of strategic management. And this classification was concerned with the control style of the corporate level.

Since conventional strategic management sees things in terms of plans, both short and long term, it looks for the contributions which different levels make to those plans; to formulating, reviewing and acting on them. It focuses on structures to support planning, and resource allocation systems to implement plans. The style of management or control is described in terms of the pattern of contributions to planning. It is based on the view that there is a distinctive specialization between corporate (business portfolio and synergies) and business unit (securing competitive advantage) levels in terms of contributions to planning, monitoring and action.

But a rather different view of the roles of the corporate and business unit levels emerges if one thinks in terms of two different forms of control — one which is control by variance in closed change situations and the other which is control by trial and error in open-ended change situations.

In control by trial and error, the shape of the corporation's business portfolio, the restructuring of its business units, the cooperation and transfer of skills between them, is a consequence of the experiments which are conducted at the corporate level, or business unit level, or through cooperation of both. The business portfolio, restructuring and skills transfer are not the consequence of some corporate grand design within which the business unit prepares a competitive advantage grand design. Instead, the competitive thrusts which occur at business unit level, the transfer of skills between one unit and another are all consequences of the experiments which are being conducted.

And to conduct the experiments you have to go through the whole process of detecting change, building issue agendas, progressing the issues, conducting the experiment and backing successful experiments with organizational energy. This is a political process which involves management at corporate and business unit level throughout in ways which vary from experiment to experiment. The sharp distinction between the role of the corporate level and the business unit level falls away. If you think in these terms you start asking what contributions different levels of management are making to the experiment process. Detecting change in the first place requires contributions at both levels. Developing any issue and getting it on to the agenda, the activities of champions and special interest groups, involves both levels, although this activity is particularly important at the corporate level. Forming task forces to conduct experiments may well require contributions from the business unit level. Backing successful experiments with organizational energy and resource calls for major contributions from the corporate level.

Throughout, both levels are involved in a complex political process, with patterns which vary from experiment to experiment. And at the same time, short-term objectives are being negotiated between the two levels and short-term performance is being monitored.

The form which the trial and error contribution of different levels takes depends on how the tensions of control are resolved. It depends on whether facilitating relationships are the norm or whether directing relationships predominate. It depends on whether analytical processes are utilized more than intuitive processes. It depends on the emphasis placed on long-term rather than short-term objectives. How these tensions are resolved constitutes the style of control. And it is leadership and the nature of team formation and functioning at the corporate level which exerts a powerful impact on the choices made throughout the organization.

It is therefore not all that productive to talk about the style of the corporate level

as something distinct from that of the business unit level. They are both involved together in one process. Style will permeate the whole organization. The corporate level cannot somehow detach itself from competitive advantage in the market places of its business units and deal in the abstract with portfolios and restructuring. Business units will find it difficult to adopt styles of management and control which do not fit into those of the whole corporation.

Style relates to the corporation as a whole rather than to a particular level in that corporation, and sharp distinctions between their contributions to planning processes provide a misleading starting point for the exploration of control style. Style has much more to do with dynamic political interaction. The discussion on control styles in this chapter therefore draws no distinction between corporate and business unit levels. Instead it focuses on the overall pattern of choice made to resolve the tensions created by the need to apply different forms of control simultaneously.

The rest of this chapter briefly examines each of the control styles identified above.

Control styles which cannot meet the challenge of the 1990s

Practising one control form in all change situations

Styles which cannot meet the challenge of the 1990s, styles which are quite clearly failing even now, are those which make no distinction between one change situation and another. These are styles where the tensions of control are hardly recognized, let alone resolved. The choices made on method tensions are too simple; they are appropriate for only one of the important change situations.

Two of these styles, the Informal Monitor and the Firefighter, make the method choices which are appropriate only for trial and error control and consequently fail to cope effectively with closed change.

The third inadequate style makes most choices appropriate to closed change situations and therefore lacks the flexibility to deal with the open-ended. That is the Bureaucrat style of control.

This section looks at the key features and consequences of these three styles.

The Informal Monitor style — little planning and less opportunism

Companies which practise this form of control have chosen, usually by default, not to use effective analytical and formal processes of control, even when dealing with change arising in closed situations. They focus on longer-term objectives and all objectives tend to be loose and tentative in the sense that there are no clear goals on what they are trying to achieve in the market place. Inadequate short-term profits

are accepted over lengthy periods for a whole variety of reasons, some of which may have to do with benevolent attitudes towards the people in the organization, to safety or environmental concerns, but mostly to do with a rather vague belief that the long term will bring greater profit.

Because of the choices which have emerged on processes and objectives, the company has to fall back on informal and intuitive processes to deal with all kinds of change. But in fact the informal processes do not function well either in this type of company, due to the nature and functioning of its political system. In Informal Monitor companies, the political system is an oligarchy. A small number of people hold all the power, delegating little to those below them. This powerful group does not work together as a team. Individuals in it conflict unproductively and avoid contact with each other to cut down on the conflict. There are consequently few formal meetings. The lack of formal meetings is not compensated for by informal meetings — managers meet only infrequently across functional and business unit divides.

The informal and intuitive processes do not work well because of the way in which the behavioural tensions are resolved. Managers in this type of company have highly parochial perceptions of their roles and the predominant relationships between roles are of the directing kind — you reluctantly do what you are told to. Structure may be decentralized on paper but top management does not in fact delegate — top managers try to direct even in matters of detail.

The consequence of these method and behavioural choices is a focus, by default, on monitoring in the sense of detecting change. Processes for planning do not function and relationships inhibit action. This focus on monitoring and informal processes gives the style its name — the Informal Monitor. It is a style, unfortunately practised by many companies in the UK, which leads to control paralysis. It may get along for years on end but as soon as it is confronted with more onerous customer requirements and more rapid change, it ceases to cope.

A failure of leadership

Why does this happen? It happens because of a failure of leadership. The central figures in the organization have no coherent control philosophy or clear perception of their roles. It happens because of the absence of any effective teamwork. Typically, the leader in such a company devotes his or her attention either to outside interests or to an excessive regard to detail and fails to develop an effective, committed top management team. Teams are built only if people meet each other, work together and develop some kind of consensus. This does not happen in companies practising the Informal Monitor style of control. The leader either does not appreciate the need for analytical detail in controlling closed change or lacks the drive to ensure that such processes are put in place. He or she also does not

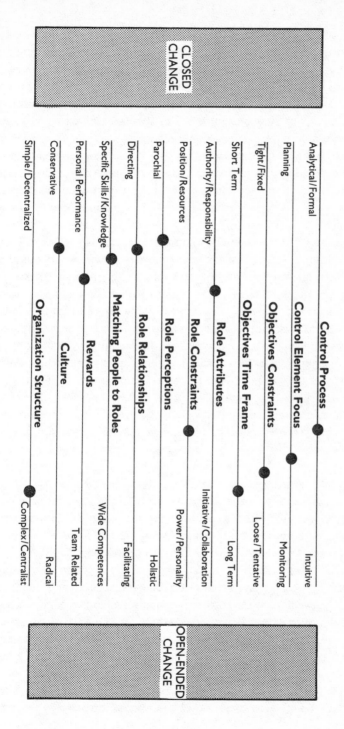

Figure 9 Informal Monitor control style

appreciate the need to develop a political system in the company which enables the building of teams.

In such companies you will find a great deal of disjointed discussion on what is wrong with its management and organizational structure. You will detect an awareness of the market and often coherent descriptions of how it is changing. Typically the views on what is wrong with the company and how and why its markets are changing are based on informal observations; informal, although often astute. But all this awareness and knowledge rarely finds expression in any corrective action.

The typical choices which the Informal Monitor makes to resolve the control tensions are shown in Figure 9 — the circles on the line (here and in later Figures) indicate how those choices veer to one or other of the change situations.

Where the Informal Monitor style is found

This style of control tends to be found in the smaller companies, where it is blocking further growth. Or it may be found in medium sized and even larger companies which were once competitive but have now lost their way. Management consultants are certainly familiar with this style — those companies which experience it provide fertile hunting grounds for them.

Consequences of the Informal Monitor style of control

The first consequence of this style of control is a volume of disturbance which top management cannot handle. All disturbances have to be referred up the hierarchy, top management becomes overloaded and many disturbances are not dealt with at all. And in particular it is the major strategic issues which are ignored.

There is consequently a lack of strategic direction or accepted values and beliefs. The almost complete lack of teamwork means that agreed direction and agreed values are impossible to develop. Instead there is continual conflict with no resolution. There are no processes or forums in which strategic agendas can be developed. There are no task force procedures where they can be progressed. Major strategic issues do not therefore receive organizational attention.

In this style there is no clear focus on objective time frames. Tight short-term or financial control is lacking and so is strategic direction. Both categories of disturbance are simply observed with little coordinated planning or effective action being taken to handle them. The consequence is an inability to deliver low-cost, high-quality, timely delivery and all those other essential customer requirements.

The Firefighter style of control — much opportunism and little planning

At first sight companies falling into this category are very much like those who have slipped into the Informal Monitor style. Here too managers draw little distinction

between the day-to-day and open-ended changes which continuously disrupt their long workday lives. And long workdays are one of the first signs that you are dealing with a Firefighter. Managers arrive early in the morning and take pride in staying well into the night. These managers also employ predominantly informal and intuitive processes in controlling their business. But there are major differences — the element of control which receives all the attention in these organizations is action and the political system enables this action to be taken. These are the 'action men' of the business world. Car telephones are an essential accompaniment to importance and while executives dash around the country, those car telephones are always fully employed.

The Firefighter company chooses not to use the formal or analytical processes to control the business even if such processes do exist. And this is an active choice, not one made by default. Managers in such companies prize informality and fast action. They consciously and proudly choose short-term profit about which there is nothing tentative or loose. Failure to produce profit is not tolerated for long and consideration for people, safety or the environment is not an acceptable excuse. These are the 'get rich quick' companies. The culture is radical in the sense that rapid change is actually sought out. The different emphasis on objectives constraints and the different culture is a major factor distinguishing this style from the Informal Monitor.

As a consequence of the method choices made, the Firefighter has to rely on intuitive and informal processes. But in the Firefighter companies these processes do work. The political system of the Firefighter company is monarchic. Considerable power is concentrated in the hands of one person who is very heavily involved in the affairs of the company. But leadership here does at times enthuse and excite the managers of the business, while at other times it frustrates and even infuriates them.

Managers are continually involved in informal meetings and the team process of persuasion and negotiation are much in evidence. Role perceptions tend to be more holistic than they are in the Informal Monitor companies and there is collaboration and personal initiative. But relationships between the roles are as directing as they are in the Informal Monitor companies and while there may be evident team functioning there is also considerable conflict and dissatisfaction. Apart from a small, dedicated and well rewarded core, staff turnover tends to be high. The result of the control tension choices made by the Firefighter is an intense focus on the action element of control. Planning is despised and there is no time for much monitoring.

Authoritarian leaders
Once again the pattern of choice can be traced back to leadership. Firefighters have strong, rather authoritarian leaders with 'bulldozer' personalities. They generate

excitement and apply considerable pressure on those around them. They do build teams. The result is a mixture of loyalty and resentment. All works well in rapid growth situations but higher customer requirements, rapid growth above a size threshold, or market decline all spell trouble. The concentration of power in the hands of one person at the top, a person who does not delegate much and will not use formal systems to deal with the day-to-day, creates a significant barrier to the growth of the company above a particular size.

You will find that such companies have poor and somewhat confusing organizational structures. Role clarity is not their strong point and there is a tendency for managers to turn their hands to anything that comes up. When you call on the chief executive officer your conversation will be interrupted continually by telephone calls and people knocking on the door. He will revel in these interruptions, believing them to be signs of his importance. He will feel that the business is humming. He will keep cancelling meetings as something else more important crops up and disaffected middle managers will wait into the late evening to catch up with him. Meetings will rarely start on time.

Other signs are poor delegation and lack of staff resources. Senior managers will spend their time analysing long computer printouts — there are few staff available to do it and there are no resources in the systems department to enable them to get the information out in the form they need. So they proudly stay until one in the morning to have the figures ready for tomorrow's meeting with the client.

But the Firefighter companies do hum. They are innovative. All is action, but uncoordinated and unplanned action. Such companies either never think about structures or roles, or they change them every few months or even every few weeks. The way in which people perceive their roles and the way in which they relate to each other does mean that political processes work; there is teamwork and evident leadership. Enthusiasm and cooperation, sometimes grudging, does go some way to make up for other deficiencies in the control system.

The typical choices which Firefighters make between the extremes demanded by the two control forms are shown in Figure 10. Once again they tend to be those most appropriate for open-ended change. The difference from the Informal Monitor lies in the behavioural choices which determine the political system.

Where the Firefighter style is found
The Firefighters are, in my experience, always companies of small to medium size. The lack of structure and role definition is a barrier to growth. You will always find that the Firefighter company's activities are very much focused on one individual. Everyone in the organization talks about that person; most decisions are referred to him or her. When you ask the Firefighter why there is not more delegation, the answer will be that people of the right calibre are not available. The Firefighter

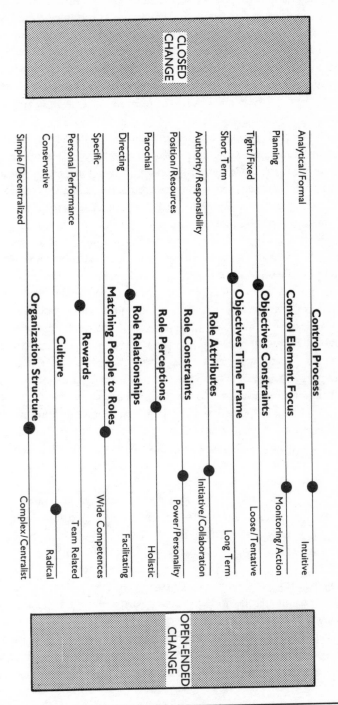

Figure 10 Firefighter control style

rarely listens to colleagues, and even less to subordinates, and categorizes criticism they make or problems they raise as 'negative' behaviour. But despite all this they do cooperate and while they complain frequently they join in the frenzied activity.

Apparent use of formal systems
It should be pointed out that many companies qualify for the Firefighter control style description even though they do have formal systems for handling day-to-day disturbance. I know of one company which does have computerized control systems and regular meetings. Appearance alone therefore suggests that it would be inappropriate to label it as a Firefighter. But actual management behaviour indicates otherwise. In this particular company the formal systems do not readily produce the information managers require for effective control. Behaviour is therefore not conditioned by the systems.

Apparent decentralization
The same applies to apparent decentralization. Other companies I am familiar with do have clear structures set out in organization charts and even job descriptions. But one or two managers at the top behave as if this structure and those job definitions do not in fact exist — all matters of any significance still have to be referred right to the top. They are always changing the formal structure, often trying out one complex structure after another.

The key point is not therefore what appears on paper but what happens in actual control terms. The key point is whether the people in the organization actually behave in the way indicated by the formal structures or in fact ignore them to a significant extent. Whatever the formal or informal structure of the Firefighter, a key distinguishing feature is that one manager at the top holds on to all decision making of any significance.

Consequences of the Firefighter style of control
An inevitable consequence of adopting this style is a high level of disturbance which is fed to the top of the hierarchy. The result is that many disturbances are not dealt with at all; it is the exciting new ventures which receive the attention. Those in charge of servicing the new business when it arrives and keeping the existing customers satisfied experience considerable pressure and frustration. They do not have much power to handle the disturbances themselves. They tend to be starved of the necessary resources and have to rush around 'putting out fires' as best they can.

Another consequence is a lack of strategic direction and clear area of operation which is widely understood in the organization. Direction tends to be at the enthusiastic whim of one powerful executive at the top.

There is usually a contradictory atmosphere of enthusiasm and loyalty side by side with complaints and frustration. The rather confused state of the control

system and the behaviour of the top management require the management team to work long hours. Those at the top tend not to 'hear' the complaints raised by management lower down. The culture allows expression of views on problems but top management generally tends to blame difficulties on the lack of competence of those lower down, rather than on resource constraints or any behaviour patterns of their own. Infighting and unproductive conflict occur side by side with cooperation when the need is really pressing.

There is innovation and an ability to handle change but an inability to cope with size. Companies adopting this style of control seem to bump into a size barrier at sales levels of about £10-£20 million per annum. New business is always arriving but pushing the existing business aside.

Compared to the Informal Monitor, the Firefighter style of control does have a functioning political process and can actually do something about change. But the lack of short-interval control systems makes lasting and continuing progress impossible. The Firefighter and the Informal Monitor both fail to deal adequately with the day-to-day because they lack effectively functioning Management Information and Control Systems.

The Bureaucrat — some planning but no opportunism

The third inadequate style treats all change as if it arises in closed situations. Here control tension is resolved by always adopting the requirements of control in closed change situations. A company that actually uses formal long-range planning systems to control in open-ended situations falls into this category.

You will recognize the Bureaucrat by the considerable emphasis which is placed on the application of formal processes to the monitoring element of control. There may also be some emphasis placed on planning, but it will never occupy the same importance as monitoring. The one element of control which you will notice little in the Bureaucratic organization is action. Much stress is placed on formally written down rules and laborious, but ineffective review meetings. Managers in these organizations spend much time arguing about the precise meaning of the rules. They arrive at meetings with a bundle of files to which they refer on being questioned. They answer questions put to them by the person chairing the meeting within their area of responsibility and competence. They do not initiate wide-ranging discussions.

The organizational structure of the Bureaucrat is elaborate and well documented, but usually overlapping and not always clear, despite the formal descriptions. These structures are almost always difficult to understand — Bureaucrats love matrix structures. Roles are usually carefully, even pedantically defined and written down, but nevertheless overlap and are often far from clear — job descriptions tend to be conceptual rather than task related.

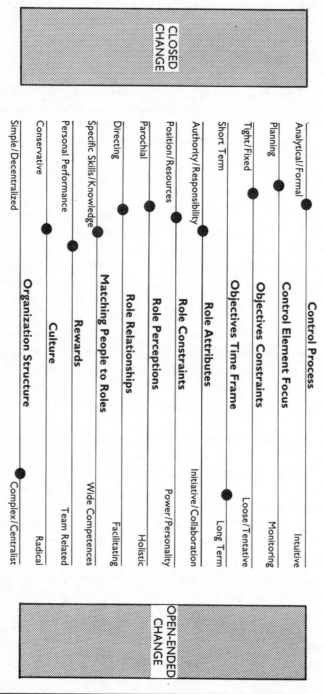

Figure 11 Bureaucrat control style

In the autocratic bureaucracy the predominant pattern of management relationships is directing. Just about every disturbance, day-to-day or strategic, has to be
referred up at least a few rungs in the hierarchy and any significant change can be
made only by those at the top. Then there is the supposedly participative
bureaucracy. Here just about every disturbance has to be handled by a committee
meeting. This generally turns out to be something of a fantasy — the disturbance
is handled by a manager in fact, but it has to be endorsed, usually after lengthy
discussion, by some committee. This is the form of control perfected by the Doges
of Venice whose elaborate structure of usually large committees provided the
perfect cover for the ruling families to do what they wished. In the modern world
this style of control has been developed into a fine art by higher education
institutions in the UK. Bureaucrats have oligarchic political systems.

The typical choices made by the Bureaucrat are shown in Figure 11. They
indicate a strong tendency always to make choices appropriate to closed change
situations.

Where the bureaucratic style of control is practised in the business world you will
usually find that the business is a publicly owned corporation. This style of control
is so slow to change that there are probably few good examples left in privately
owned businesses — change and competition have already led to the disappearance
of all but the recently privatized public corporations.

Consequences of the Bureaucrat style

A major consequence of this control style is a poor ability to build and progress
strategic agendas. The conservative culture tends to block recognition of significant
change until its consequences are almost disastrously apparent. This leads to a lack
of strategic direction despite the emphasis on formal planning; a lack of swift action
to deal with defects in operations revealed by the extensive focus on monitoring; an
inability, despite careful planning, to deal rapidly with day-to-day disturbance
because procedures are so cumbersome.

Control styles which can meet the challenge of the 1990s

Matching control form to change situation

A key feature which distinguishes successful from unsuccessful styles of control is
that successful styles match the form of control to the nature of the change situation
in which control has to be practised. This means that successful styles operate
simultaneously at both ends of the method-control tensions. They choose to utilize
formal, analytical and quantification processes to plan for the day-to-day
disturbances arising in closed change situations. At the same time they use intuitive
and negotiation processes within an effective political system to handle open-ended

change situations. And handle here means detecting change, developing strategic issue agendas, acting in the sense of experimenting, then backing successful experiments and so building strategies.

All successful companies resolve the role definition tensions, to some extent at least, by a form of control specialization. Roles of the lower levels in the management hierarchy are defined primarily in the way required by day-to-day control and the concerns of managers at these levels are primarily those of handling day-to-day disturbance. Other disturbances are referred up the hierarchy to a point which tends to specialize in handling the bigger open-ended issues.

But at some point in the hierarchy, roles have to encompass both definitions; at some point, managers have to deal with both types of disturbance and in a sense, therefore, they have dual roles. At these levels managers personally have to resolve the tensions created by role duality and the need to apply formal processes in one situation and intuitive processes in another.

While managers have to resolve these tensions personally, they cannot resolve them in isolation. Each manager has to do so in a way which is compatible with, and therefore involves, other managers. He or she has to do so within a team, or political context, so resolving not only method but also behavioural tensions. The manner in which these tensions are resolved depends upon the political system which exists within the company. One successful style can be distinguished from another primarily in terms of the political system which it employs.

The style which employs an oligarchic political system is called the Strategic Director. Within this style there is a distinctive variant called the Investment Trust style of control. Yet another style has a pluralistic political system and I have called this the Strategic Facilitator. Finally there is the company which uses a monarchic political system and I call this the Strategic Adventurer. The rest of this section explores the key features and consequences of each of these four potentially successful styles of control.

The Strategic Director style of control — short-term planning and centralized opportunism

Managers in companies which practise this style of control distinguish between the day-to-day, closed change situation and the disturbances to the business which arise in open-ended change situations. Of course they do not spend the day consciously deciding whether one disturbance is day-to-day and another open-ended. But they do show by their behaviour that they recognize the difference.

The day-to-day is dealt with largely in a localized manner, any referral up the management hierarchy normally being minimal. Such disturbances relate to the existing business and are handled within scheduling or budgetary frameworks.

The oligarchy

When it comes to the open-ended, the essential disturbance detection, issue agenda development, experimenting and strategy building are confined largely to a small oligarchy at the top of the organization. The real power group usually consists of two to three holding company executives, and a small number of top divisional executives. It is this group which deals with matters of any strategic significance. There would also normally be about four or five senior managers just below this group who would from time to time be brought into the inner circle, depending on the particular issues being dealt with. It is here that special interest groups form around particular issues. Issues only ever get on to the agenda if one of the most powerful four or five in this group supports them. It is within this group that the intuitive processes are applied to handling open-ended change. The procedures and communication are largely informal, the regular formal meetings being used to report on the progress of strategic issues and secure formal commitment and approval of the whole group.

Typically, few new ventures are undertaken or investments made without first being subjected to formal market research. But this is essentially a checking procedure on issues to which there is already some commitment, or it is used as a blocking mechanism by one or more of the powerful who disagree with progressing the issue. There is then a clear top team and effectively functioning political processes within that team.

Directing may take the form of pushing and prodding a business unit to develop in a particular direction. Or it may take the form of blocking developments the business units wish to undertake unless they can provide an extremely good case. The key characteristic is not what they do but how they do it, where the power lies to do it. Strategic Directors go in for a sharp hierarchical specialization between control in closed and control in open-ended change situations.

Roles

Role perceptions tend to focus on role in relation to parts of the organization. There is considerable loyalty to and identification with the particular part of the organization in which a manager or staff member works. It is consequently often difficult to deploy resources from one business unit to another. These parochial role perceptions are particularly noticeable at top management levels and lead to power exercised by divisional 'barons'.

Structure

Some Strategic Directors may adopt complex centralist organizational structures and others may go for simpler decentralized structures. But whatever the structure,

relationships between managers in their roles are directing in the sense that the overall framework within which they are to operate, the direction in which they are to go is fed down from the top. Some Strategic Directors have formal long-range planning systems and others do not. But in reality these systems provide comfort and support capital allocation procedures — they have very little to do indeed with the real activity of strategy-making. Strategy-making occurs within the political system.

Objectives

Many practitioners of the Strategic Director style set rather fixed long-term objectives for market share, new product development and research and development spending. Loss-making activities may be tolerated for quite some time if it is believed that they hold the seeds of long-term growth and a move to higher technology. But this position depends very much on the circumstances. In difficult times, the emphasis shifts firmly and effectively to short-term, financial control. In other companies practising the style it may be the short-term objectives which usually receive most emphasis. But whether the emphasis is short-term or long-term, objectives in this style are usually focused and fairly fixed. They have to do with well defined areas of operation, with synergy, competitive advantage in clearly specified areas.

Culture

Such companies tend to be characterized by a strong conservative culture of benevolent paternalism, for most of the time anyway. It is a culture which prizes personal integrity and requires controlled behaviour. Conflict is taboo and outbreaks of anger are remembered for a very long time. Disagreements are generally not expressed at formal, regular meetings. Conflict and disagreement are matters to be resolved in private and not aired in public. Practical experience in the industry is highly valued. The whole culture tends to be very much conditioned by the markets in which the core businesses operate. Usually, only those with their roots firmly in those markets, and with a track record within the company, achieve real power for any length of time. It is consequently extremely difficult for any outsider to exercise much influence on the future direction of the company. The few who enter the business at very senior levels tend to leave within a short space of time without ever having made much impact. It is this conservative culture and the resistance to outsiders at the top which leads to the persistence of the same control style even when the top team changes.

The manner in which tensions are resolved by the Strategic Director is summarized in Figure 12.

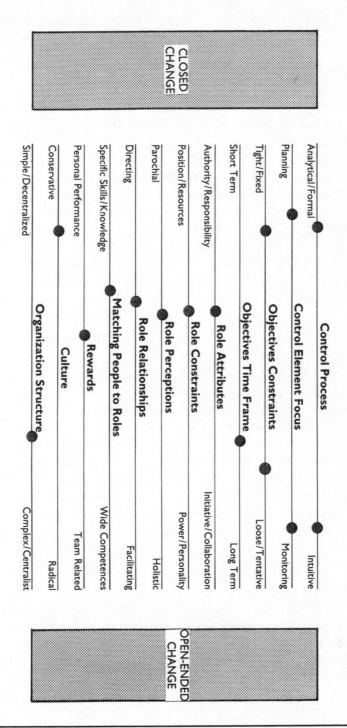

Figure 12 Strategic Director control style

CLOSED CHANGE		

Control Process	Analytical/Formal	Intuitive
Control Element Focus	Planning	Monitoring
Objectives Constraints	Tight/Fixed	Loose/Tentative
Objectives Time Frame	Short Term	Long Term
Role Attributes	Authority/Responsibility	Initiative/Collaboration
Role Constraints	Position/Resources	Power/Personality
Role Perceptions	Parochial	Holistic
Role Relationships	Directing	Facilitating
Matching People to Roles	Specific Skills/Knowledge	Wide Competences
Rewards	Personal Performance	Team Related
Culture	Conservative	Radical
Organization Structure	Simple/Decentralized	Complex/Centralist

OPEN-ENDED CHANGE		

Consequences of the Strategic Director control style

The mechanism is there to deal with day-to-day disturbances in an effective manner, to deliver consistently the sources of competitive advantage in the core market places — on-time delivery, quality and low cost.

The effectiveness with which the day-to-day is handled cuts down on the volume of disturbance with which senior and top-level management has to deal. But the oligarchic political system and directing approach adopted to the big issues impedes strategic item agenda building. A small, like-minded group of top managers rarely involves those below in strategic matters. Small changes occurring in open-ended situations may therefore take a long time to detect. Task forces to progress individual strategic items are not frequently formed and when they are, they involve only the same small group right at the top of the organization. Of perhaps greatest importance, the cohesive culture, no doubt an important contributor to the effectiveness with which the day-to-day is handled, acts as a block to significant change.

Strategic Directors tend to be rather secretive and do not communicate or consult widely when it comes to the key issues. The whole political system leads to slower detection of change and fewer innovative experiments. Strategic Directors tend consequently to stick much closer to well defined core activities, to particular recipes for growth and acquisition. They also tend to have fewer business units with much less overlap than other styles. Where there are the inevitable overlaps, they tend to be managed by the centre.

The Strategic Director style is most appropriate in markets which are reasonably stable; where synergy and integration are important; where large investments in research and development or facilities are required; where an overall competitive advantage is needed. They tend to go for market share and low-cost competitive advantage. The style also becomes appropriate when the organization faces some major threat which requires the focused and coordinated energy of the organization in a short time period.

There is a distinctive variant of the Strategic Director style, practised by a number of conglomerates in the UK. I have called this the Investment Trust style of control. It has the same kind of oligarchic political system in which strategic issues of any significance are all dealt with by a small top management team. This style is always accompanied by extremely effective short-interval control systems.

The Investment Trust control style

The distinctive feature of this style of control is what we might call strategy specialization. By this I mean that the corporate management level specializes in a particular type of strategy which is pursued from the centre — the acquisition of other companies, the building of a portfolio of 100 per cent owned investments.

Management at the corporate level also focuses on the short-term control of companies already in the portfolio. Companies already in the portfolio manage both strategic and day-to-day aspects of their own businesses without corporate level interference, subject only to achieving agreed short-term performance targets and securing approval for all capital expenditure above generally very low limits.

The corporate level therefore operates as an industrial management company or an extension of the Investment Trust type of operation. While investment trusts proper hold portfolios of small minority investments in companies and exert little impact on their management, companies practising an Investment Trust style of control hold controlling interests and do apply control in carefully defined areas. They tend to choose an area of operation where open-ended change is less important.

Consequences of the Investment Trust control style

The consequence of this very clear-cut style of control, when practised effectively, is rapid growth in corporate terms. But the growth comes mainly from acquisition rather than from the organic growth of the business units. This is probably a consequence of pushing the difficulties of strategy-making down to the business units, while sharply focusing management attention on short-term performance. However, it is clearly a very successful style of control when allied to the kinds of strategy specialization which companies such as Hanson and BTR adopt.

The Strategic Facilitator style of control — short-term planning and participative opportunism

As in Strategic Director companies, managers in the Strategic Facilitator companies distinguish between the day-to-day and the disturbances which arise in open-ended change situations. They utilize effective Management Information and Control Systems in much the same way as the Strategic Directors. The difference between them lies in the political system they employ to handle open-ended change. The pluralist political systems found in these companies mean that special interest groups form around strategic issues at both top and lower management levels, at least the level just below the top. They are characterized by wider strategic agendas and more experimentation. This political system depends upon facilitating relationships.

Strategic Facilitators generally have decentralized organizations and they may or may not have formal planning systems for the longer term. Once again the existence of a formal planning system makes little difference to the manner in which strategic issues are handled. It is the political system resulting from the way in which behavioural control tensions are resolved that determines how strategic issues are handled.

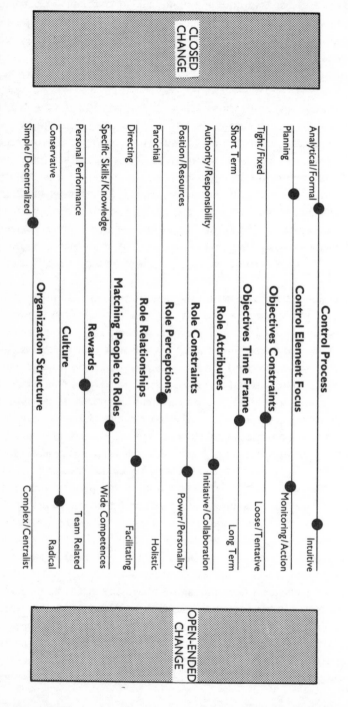

Figure 13   Strategic Facilitator control style

In these companies, the big issues are managed through processes of informal discussion between executives at the top level and those lower down, usually subsidiary company managing directors and their senior managers most directly concerned with the matter. Issues of strategic importance are frequently raised and identified by a number of champions who form special interest groups. The future direction of the subsidiaries, acquisitions and other investment projects are mainly the consequences of initiatives taken by individual executives below the top level, driven more by their own experience and intuition than by much formal analysis. The relationships between profit-responsible executives is governed by informal rules and actual power rather than hierarchical position. The culture of these companies tends to be characterized by an almost fierce belief in independence, freedom and personal responsibility. Managers prize informality.

With regard to the objectives time frame managers usually take a position closer to the long-term end of the spectrum than to the short-term end. Constraints on the pursuit of profit tend to be rather loose: a long-term, socially responsible attitude is adopted to safety and the environment; overlaps between the subsidiaries themselves are managed through processes of persuasion and negotiation. Role perceptions tend to be parochial; managers see themselves, in strong terms, as part of their own subsidiary rather than as part of the company as a whole.

Interpersonal relationships, particularly at top and senior management level, are very much of the facilitating rather than the directing kind. The cultural tension is resolved by taking a position close to the radical, flexible end of the spectrum.

Figure 13 illustrates the typical choices made in this style of control.

Consequences of the Strategic Facilitator control style

The first consequence is that the day-to-day disturbance is effectively handled. Variances in quality, cost and profitability are usually detected in an orderly fashion and in time to do something about them. But there may be confusion as to the part the top management committee is playing in the control process and some inadequacy in the information passed up to it. The approach to short-term financial control may suffer. Meetings between the chief executive and the managing directors may tend to concern themselves with administrative matters on the one hand and big issues, such as acquisitions, on the other. The one-to-one contact which is so vital to effective day-to-day control may therefore not be strongly applied.

The second consequence of the style is that smaller volumes of disturbance are fed up the hierarchy, thus allowing those at the top to devote more time to the open-ended. The pluralistic political system leads to fairly rapid detection of change and the development of wide-ranging strategic issue agendas. The political system encourages the emergence of champions and multiple perspectives. Strategic issues

do receive organizational attention and are progressed by task forces.

A major problem may be a lack of group cohesion and sense of direction. Each of the subsidiaries may be clear about where it is going, but there may not be much clarity on the future direction of the group of companies as a whole.

Another problem, closely related to the first, is that the strategic agenda may never be made explicit. This means that interconnection between one issue and another may never be examined. Members of the top management team may also feel some dissatisfaction with the purpose or role of that team. Since strategy decisions are being taken largely by specific groupings of managing directors and head office executives depending on the nature of the problem or opportunity, what is the purpose of top management as a group? Strong parochial role perceptions may also develop and indeed are likely to be even more of a problem than they are in most Strategic Director companies. Developments of this kind are dangers of this style, but they have more to do with the way in which it is conducted than with the style itself. Better utilization of formal management meetings to focus on strategic issues and develop a team responsibility for strategic decisions, as well as the use of periodic workshops to develop a sense of direction and review the strategic agenda, would overcome these problems.

The Strategic Facilitator style leads to diversity in the total business portfolio and a less strong focus on a few core activities. It is an appropriate style of control in conditions of very rapid change, where markets are highly unstable and more fragmented.

The Strategic Adventurer control style — short-term planning and individual opportunism

This is found where there is one dominant individual at the top of the company. This dominant individual is frequently the entrepreneurial founder of that company. But that individual does delegate on day-to-day matters and the company does use effective short-interval control. It is this more than anything else that distinguishes it from the Firefighter style. The following paragraphs describe this style through a number of quotations from prominent practitioners. Entrepreneurial behaviour is possible in large companies if it is accompanied by short-interval control.

Amstrad

Let us consider some extracts from articles on Alan Sugar.

> Amstrad, the company which he [Alan Sugar] founded [20 years ago], runs and still half owns, has helped to turn technological novelties of the early 1980s, such as word processors and personal computers, into high street goods to be found in many of the

studies and spare bedrooms of Britain ... Amstrad consistently doubled in size each year in the mid 1980s before notching up £90m profits on sales of £351m in the first half of this financial year ... He has been busy this past year setting up Amstrad subsidiaries in Spain, Italy, West Germany, Belgium and the Netherlands. Already successful in France and Spain, Sugar predicts that within three years he will be generating more sales in West Germany than in Britain ... Alan Sugar is now trying to apply his winning formula to satellite television ... in joint venture with Rupert Murdoch ...

He operates with a small team of close advisers ... All the ideas for new products — their design, pricing and marketing — are kicked around by this team, though participants say that Mr Sugar is the dominant force in almost all stages in the process ... he is unimpressed with formal qualifications when choosing his lieutenants ... refusal to stick with the conventional is one of the most refreshing strands running through Amstrad ... None of the company's core group is shielded by layers of secretaries and public relations people.[3]

Some further insight into the Amstrad approach to control can be gleaned from reports on a speech which Alan Sugar made at the City Business School.

One of the first lessons I learned in business is that I believed too much in my advisers ... In our company we attract people who either catch on very quickly or they last two minutes. When they catch on, they understand the entrepreneurial flair of the company and see their colleagues using innovative ways and methods to achieve their tasks. Not conforming to the standards that are written down in books, but by cutting corners, taking a few risks, assuming the rest of the team will accept what they are up to when they have finalised their projects, not needing to stop step by step in their thought pattern to see if the group agrees before they proceed ... Amstrad culture is all about realism, swift thinking and decision-making without committees. Rise or fall by your own decision or get out. A sense of urgency to get to the point. It is essential to retain a strong corporate culture and philosophy, otherwise the business can drift and become confused and lost in direction. We have trained our staff to stand up and be counted. We don't want any corporate wimps. There are so many people in companies who shy away from confrontation ... One of the things I have learnt from the Japanese is to pay attention to detail.[4]

Virgin Group

Finally, consider some quotations about another of those conspicuously successful entrepreneurs of the 1980s in the UK, this time Richard Branson. He started his business career in the mid 1960s at the age of 16, launching a national student magazine, developing a mail order discount record business, retail record business and then a record label. The Virgin Group which encompasses these business interests now has a sales level of £300m and profits in the £15–£20m range. In addition he runs Voyager, the holding company for his airline and tourism

businesses; the charitable Virgin Health Foundation which markets Mates condoms; and a number of other business interests. The following quotes relate to the Virgin Group.

> Branson in fact runs Virgin almost at arms length ... he has remarkably little input at operational level. Physically separated from even his senior colleagues ... the three operating divisions of music, communications and retail/property, are all run independently with their own chairmen or managing directors ... Virgin is a well managed, professionally run company, not dependent purely on the talents of one man. Branson's major skill ... is his ability to delegate responsibility, and let go of projects once they are up and running ... Says Branson, '... My skills are finding the right people to run the companies and coming up with ideas for new ventures.' ... communications at the top [of Virgin group] remain remarkably informal and bureaucracy free. Apart from regular board meetings ... the directors have an easy-come, easy-go relationship. The group's organisational structure reflects the decentralised arrangements at the top. Virgin's 2,500 employees worldwide work in small units of up to 80 people, each with its own director ... Branson is keen on promoting insiders, and encouraging company loyalty with incentive and share option schemes ... Branson realised he must systematise the business, and in summer 1984 he appointed Don Cruickshank as managing director ... to create a proper head office. Cruickshank recalls that when he arrived 'everything was very jumbled together, there was one accounts department for everything.' He set about divisionalising the group in a sensible way to match the company's growth in different fields, established a central treasury function to look after funding and appointed a finance director ...[5]

Key features

A number of points stand out about approaches to control in both cases. Control in open-ended situations is clearly practised by all of them in a manner which emphasizes informal, intuitive processes. The strategy actually pursued is not in fact part of some grand, well thought out design based on careful forecasts. Strategy here has more to do with sharply attuned opportunism and a determination not to fail. No formal planning systems or carefully conducted market research are apparent. In each case the central figure stands out as a strong directing force, but nevertheless one which recognizes the importance of teams, cultures, training, the use of confrontation, disagreement and political processes. The political system though is clearly monarchic. They fiercely reject formality and formal expertise. But they do delegate, they do trust other people, they do pay attention to detail where it matters, they do utilize clear organizational structures where they matter. They therefore do apply more formal and structured approaches to dealing with the day-to-day.

Typical choices made by Strategic Adventurers to resolve control tension are marked in Figure 14.

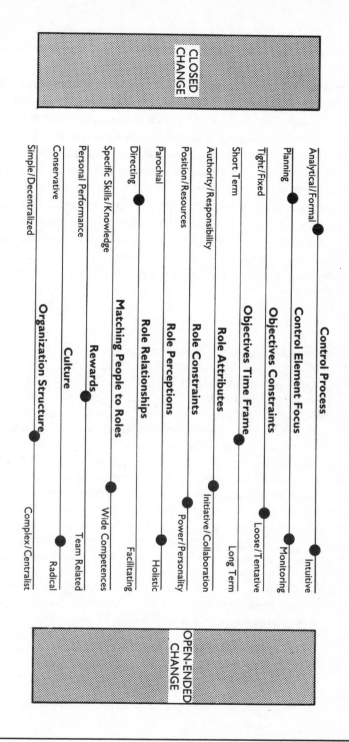

Figure 14 Strategic Adventurer control style

The diagram shows a control style profile with the following dimensions, ranging from CLOSED CHANGE (left) to OPEN-ENDED CHANGE (right):

Control Element Focus	Control Process: Analytical/Formal — Intuitive
Objectives Constraints	Planning — Monitoring
Objectives Constraints	Tight/Fixed — Loose/Tentative
Objectives Time Frame	Short Term — Long Term
Role Attributes	Authority/Responsibility — Initiative/Collaboration
Role Constraints	Position/Resources — Power/Personality
Role Perceptions	Parochial — Holistic
Role Relationships	Directing — Facilitating
Matching People to Roles	Specific Skills/Knowledge — Wide Competences
Rewards	Personal Performance — Team Related
Culture	Conservative — Radical
Organization Structure	Simple/Decentralized — Complex/Centralist

The personalities and statements made by the people in these examples remind me very much of the entrepreneurs whom I have worked with and classified as Firefighters. The essential difference is that the former do delegate and do apply more formal approaches to handling day-to-day disturbances, thus overcoming the blockages to growth which those practising the Firefighter style seem inevitably to experience.

The Strategic Adventurer style fits fast-moving markets but it does rely very heavily on one charismatic leader.

Which style?

This chapter has described six styles of controlling a business into which I have found that most companies can be classified. Three of these styles are quite clearly inadequate for the 1990s. More stringent customer requirements demand the effective application and use of modern Management Information and Control Systems in handling day-to-day disturbance to the business, in delivering competitive advantage. Without this approach to control, it is impossible to deliver customer requirements for higher quality and service levels, for timely delivery and low cost. The Informal Monitor and Firefighter styles of control must therefore be changed by those practising them if they are to survive. And fortunately that is a relatively simple matter. All it requires is the investment in analysis, training, communication and participation which are well documented and in which many firms of management consultants excel.

But this is not enough. Most businesses in the 1990s will have to deal with more and more open-ended change as competitor groupings change, environmental concerns increase, markets either fragment or globalize. To deal with this unforeseeable change, which impacts on personal beliefs and ambitions, companies must have effective political systems in which issues are detected, given attention, progressed and built into strategies. And this requires the application of intuitive and negotiation processes. The political system is a consequence of the manner in which the behavioural control tensions are resolved. One control style, the Bureaucrat, drowns the innovative processes in a lake of rules and regulations and promotes political activity of a pointless sort which focuses on arguments about the rules. Organizations practising this control style in a competitive environment will have to change if they are to survive.

Potentially successful styles are those which adapt control form to change situation. They have effective Management Information and Control Systems for closed change and effective political systems for open-ended change. How do we judge whether a political system is effective or not? The answer depends on what you think it should achieve. If you believe it should block change then dictatorial

leadership, rigid institutions, few special interest groups and champions, and the suppression of issues, are all signs of success. If the aim is to deal with a clear major threat such as a war, you would use much the same criteria to judge success. If you are seeking adaptation to change, a process of learning, then an effective system is one which secures enough consensus for action; special interest groups and champions thrive; direction, vision, motivation, clarity on area of operation and values are generated.

One of the three political systems, the monarchic, depends heavily on one individual for its success. Since such individuals seem to be relatively rare, the Strategic Adventurer style has limited application. The Investment Trust style which applies a standard recipe to acquisition must also have limited scope. For the great majority of companies the important choice is that between the Strategic Director and the Strategic Facilitator styles, ie, the choice is between oligarchic and pluralistic political systems.

These common practical alternatives each have advantages and disadvantages. The Director, with its more contained political processes, is more likely to produce clear focus and overall direction. It is more likely to take the benefits of synergy and secure competitive advantage where a major thrust is required in one area. But the range of issues it can deal with, the scope of change which it actually detects, is inevitably lower. It is a style which is probably most appropriate in the more stable markets, where there is a dominating core business, with high interconnections between business units, large investments in equipment or research and development, or a need to dominate markets.

The Facilitator, with its more open political processes, will inevitably be better at detecting more change, raising a wider range of issues, getting more commitment. But the need to resolve the continuing tensions are more widespread through management levels. It is harder to get a sharp focus on what should be done. This style is more appropriate for diversified portfolios, markets where differentiation is important, for niche markets and more rapid change.

Whatever the style adopted, and successful companies may well shift from more Directing to more Facilitating styles and back again, the key question is how total control is to be improved. The next two chapters address this problem.

Notes
1 Some of these tensions were discussed in Chapter 3.
2 These were discussed in Chapter 6.
3 *Financial Times*, 4 July 1988.
4 *Sunday Times*, 3 May 1987.
5 *Management Today*, March 1988.

8
Dynamic Strategic Management for the 1990s

Recommendations on developing an appropriate control style

A business survives and is consistently profitable when it continuously and creatively matches its competitive capability to changing customer requirements. And this continuous and creative match can only be achieved through the effective control of the business. The central proposition of this book is that if the control of a business organization is to be effective, then the form of control adopted, that is, the manner in which change is accommodated or created, must be appropriate to the nature of that change.

This is a simple common-sense proposition. If change is such that it can be easily understood and foreseen then it makes sense to use a form of control which is based on detailed planning. If on the other hand change is ill structured and inherently unpredictable then there is no realistic alternative to control by trial and error; to conducting experiments in a manner which contains the risks of the unknown as much as possible; to a process of organizational, creative learning.

It is now commonly accepted that as we go through the 1990s change will be even faster than that to which we have become accustomed in the 1980s. But that is not all. The nature of change is likely to continue polarizing at two extremes: closed change, with easily understood and predictable short-term consequences at one extreme, created by customer requirements for higher quality, better service, faster delivery and lower cost; and open-ended change, with ill-structured and unforeseeable long-term consequences at the other extreme, created by factors such as intense competitive pressure, changing competitor groupings, changing regulatory policies, changing demographic patterns and life styles.

And closed and open-ended change require different forms of control which place conflicting demands on people, structures and systems. Control style is how these conflicting demands, or tensions, are resolved. Strategic management is all about developing a control style which is appropriate to conditions of increasingly rapid change, which can cope simultaneously with increasingly polarized change.

The view developed in previous chapters is that strategic management is about:

- Delivering what the customer wants today and doing it better than the competition. This means tight short-interval control.

- Continuously, consistently, creatively delivering what the customer requires tomorrow and thereafter and doing it better than the competition. This means detecting even the smallest of the key changes occurring now, experimenting in a coherent manner to find appropriate responses and building strategies from successful experiments, all faster and better than the competition. And this requires a responsive business political system.

Strategic management is about continually improving both short-interval control systems and business political systems, so that the organization is a fitter and more skilful player in the market place than its rivals. The emphasis is on developing organizational ability to make dynamic moves in the market place, accommodating change, reacting to it, creating it so that competitors will be forced into reacting.

On this view, strategic management is not a separate kind of management which has to do with the long term and what is to be done tomorrow. It is not about fixing long-term objectives and drawing up plans to achieve them. It is not about installing strategic management styles which focus on procedures for formulating and reviewing long-term plans.[1] It is not about deciding in advance how you are going to play market games. That is static management. The dynamic management required for the 1990s involves two things. First, it involves getting the organization fit and flexible enough to take the initiative or respond to unexpected turns in the market game. Second, it involves actually playing the game, innovating, experimenting, making organizational and market moves, devoting attention to the detail of execution.

The traditional analogy used to illustrate strategic management is that of the general tactically deploying his troops within the framework of a well thought out battle plan. The picture is one of orderly, focused activity. The more appropriate analogy is that of the game player, fit and disciplined but nimble, flexible and coping with each uncertain move in the game as it becomes necessary. The tactics are what count and strategy emerges only from successful tactics. A strategically managed company in this view is something of a contradiction in terms. It is one which is vital and flexible; it is alive and bubbles with many new ways of doing things. But at the same time it controls its existing business in a disciplined, clearly structured manner and pays attention to detail where detail matters.

Recommendation 1

Stop thinking that you can deal with the uncertainties facing your business by writing down future mission statements, setting fixed long-term objectives and preparing formal long-term plans; or by developing grand designs for the future which will take you into greener pastures.

Abandon any intention to install formal long-term planning systems and procedures. Scrap them if you already possess them; they are by now a waste of valuable time. They are a waste of time because they do not take account of, or deal with, the inherent difficulties of managing open-ended change. And it is this kind of change which you will face more and more in the 1990s. Even more seriously, managers whose thinking is conditioned by conventional strategic management tend to focus on the likely and miss the creative; they play games which are simple and transparent to more cunning competitors. Grand designs cannot provide the dynamic instrument with which you can play market games in conditions of true uncertainty.

Do not hire strategy consultants who promise to apply rigid planning techniques and write your corporate strategy for you. The product you buy will have a very short shelf-life indeed. What you need to do instead is improve your company's ability to innovate, experiment, be opportunistic, play dynamic business games. And consultants can help in this longer lasting endeavour.

But do not take this recommendation to mean that there is no need to think coherently. This is not a recommendation to abandon all rigour and simply swim with opportunistic looseness. It does not mean rejecting the questions and insights which conventional strategic management has to offer; it can help you to ask the right questions and it does provide approaches to indicating whether your proposed responses to strategic issues make sense or not.

But in the end you have to deal effectively with open-ended change and this means systematically developing strategic issue agendas, experimenting coherently in a manner which limits risks, and consistently backing successful experiments. You will have to develop agreed areas of operation and values as well as a sense of direction, all from a process of creative learning and experimenting. The instrument for doing this is the political system of your business. The whole process, intuitive and political, is far more difficult than a formal planning approach would have you believe.

And it is not only effective control in open-ended change situations which matters. At the same time, even tighter short-interval control systems are required.

The rest of this chapter lists some of the most common problems for, and obstacles to, effective short-term control and to the effective functioning of political systems in companies today. These matters have already been discussed in previous chapters. Here they are briefly summarized and 12 recommendations are made to overcome them and develop total control styles which are appropriate for the 1990s.

Improving short-interval control of the business

Effectively handling day-to-day disturbance in closed change situations

The first step in dynamic strategic management, in developing an appropriate control style, is to install and continually improve short-interval control. This means continually improving the Management Information and Control Systems required to handle day-to-day disturbance. It means setting precise, time-definite objectives, reviewing progress at short intervals and taking immediate action. If this is not done then there will be no time for the strategic and there will be no implementation tool. The cards, the basic skills for playing business games, will be lacking. Delivery of competitive advantage will be impossible.

But there is a fundamental problem. It is argued by some that it is inappropriate to apply a system of control, whose distinctive characteristics lie in stability and precision, to an environment characterized by turbulent and even chaotic change. Some would have it that businesses in today's chaotic world should avoid clearly defining the roles and responsibilities of managers and should involve everyone in everything.[2] This view presses for the scrapping of rule books and manuals. It calls for self-managing groups of workers, smaller numbers of managers and supervisors with much larger spans of control. Managers are pressed to see their roles in facilitating terms. Only in this way will the organization be able to attain the degree of flexibility and openness which will enable it to innovate and change in tune with the turbulent environment.

The argument is that while the benefits of Management Information and Control Systems, clarity, precision and tight control, are very clear in stable environments, these very benefits become disadvantages in rapidly changing environments. Of their very nature they encourage insularity on the part of workers and managers, and by focusing with such precision on foreseeable patterns they cut down on the ability to see change as it occurs. New and different ways of doing things are of necessity discouraged by well specified Management Information and Control Systems.

It is true that today's business world sharpens a fundamental dilemma — how to preserve the undoubted benefits of sophisticated Management Information and Control Systems, while at the same time avoiding the inherent ossification which such sophistication brings. But this book firmly rejects any suggestion that the dilemma can be resolved by weakening short-interval control as a tool for handling day-to-day disturbance and delivering competitive advantage. Sloppy role definition and unclear responsibilities will certainly do this. Management Information and Control Systems require clear roles and responsibilities. They require analysis, measurement, precision and comprehensiveness. All of this is vital to the delivery of competitive advantage.

The dilemma has to be resolved in some other way; by clearly seeing, and behaving according to that insight, that Management Information and Control Systems are only a subsystem of total control, suited for dealing with one category of disturbance, the day-to-day. The rest of the total control system, its political subsystem, must be deployed to deal with other types of change, including continuing change to the Management Information and Control System itself. Managers have to become even more adapted to dealing with balance, to judging when one subset of control is to be applied and when another is more appropriate.

The first obstacle to effective short-interval control encountered in practice is therefore one of fundamental philosophy — some managers believe that tight short-interval control is incompatible with truly entrepreneurial behaviour. That there is a sharp tension cannot be denied — it arises from two different change situations which place conflicting demands on the organization. But simply ignoring it is no way to deal with the tension and that is what you do when you satisfy none of the demands of control in closed change situations.

Recommendation 2

Do not be persuaded that a turbulent and rapidly changing environment makes the application of tight short-interval control to the day-to-day less relevant. It is even more vital. But you have to recognize that this kind of environment will require frequent changes to Management Information and Control Systems to maintain your ability to deliver what customers want more effectively than your rivals. It will also require more and more managers in the business to develop the ability to judge when to apply tight short-interval control and when it is more appropriate to utilize substantially different parts of the total control system of the business, to recognize when they are dealing with disturbances which demand flexible, innovative responses.

The second major obstacle to effective short-interval control follows from the first. Control styles are chosen, or develop, which treat all change in the same way. Either such companies have no Management Information and Control Systems, or management, especially top management, does not actually use those which do exist as a mechanism for control. Managers may define roles of subordinates but in practice they may not actually delegate authority. They keep interfering in matters of detail; they do not observe hierarchical relationships; they do not allow their subordinates to manage within budgetary limits and require instead that all expenditure be authorized by them. They set objectives but never review them or hold managers responsible for achieving them. They do not trust those lower down and make complaints about the quality of management, but they never take action to provide training or to recruit competent staff.

The consequence is either a great deal of rushing around, making conflicting and disruptive decisions, or there is much discussion and complaining which leads to little action. These are the Firefighter and Informal Monitor styles of control. Bureaucrats often suffer in similar ways — short-interval control becomes ineffective because roles are defined in conceptual rather than task-related ways; because roles are so heavily prescribed by rules and procedures; because even small changes usually require extensive committee procedures to deal with them.

Recommendation 3

If you recognize your organizational control style as that of the Informal Monitor, Firefighter or Bureaucrat, then you must, without delay, install modern Management Information and Control Systems. You must do this to secure the benefits of consistent quality, reliability, flexibility, high service levels and tight cost control. A more detailed, hard to copy Management Information and Control System than your rivals' is a major source of competitive advantage.

So invest in the comprehensive, precise definition and measurement of work tasks and their interconnections. Allocate clear responsibilities and sharply define roles in relation to the work flows of the existing business and the handling of day-to-day disturbances which affect them. Apply appropriate technology to deal with the increased detail and greater flows of information. Set short-term, time-specific and detailed performance objectives. Emphasize short-interval, one-to-one reviewing and action.

If you have a detailed, hard to copy Management Information and Control System, use it. Resist the temptation to interfere with the day-to-day decisions of your subordinates. Set objectives and then make sure you review them. But do not try to review them and generate action on them in a committee — this is a matter for one-to-one executive control.

If you have installed a Management Information Control System and believe it to be adequate, think again. Review the system. Improve it and make it appropriate to deal with the environment of the 1990s. Do not let management pride, some short-sighted 'macho' concern, block the identification of weaknesses in your short-interval control. Identify the weaknesses and correct them.

Never lose sight of the fact that the Management Information and Control System is only part of the total control system. It cannot operate in a vacuum. It needs to be supported by, to coexist and not conflict with, the culture of the organization and with the other processes of control, the intuitive and political processes required to generate innovative behaviour. Installing Management Information and Control Systems and significantly changing them are strategic issues. Changes to short-interval control methods have widespread consequences throughout the organization — they affect the way people work and relate to

each other. Sensitive application of political processes, consultation, involvement and training of those involved is required in this strategic issue as much as in any other.

Even when companies have comprehensive, modern short-interval control systems and managers do use them, there are still frequently found obstacles to their most effective use. The budget is the centrepiece of the Management Information and Control System and problems in its effective use are particularly important. Chapter 3 listed some of the common problems experienced by companies in the application of budgetary control. One problem is a lack of clarity on the purpose of the budget. The budget may be simply a standard against which to check progress; or it may be a target which people believe in and strive for; or it may be a realistic projection of what is likely to happen. Long-winded annual budget procedures, tied to the preparation of three-year, five-year and ten-year plans, are rituals which may satisfy the performance standard criterion but are likely to achieve less in motivation terms and even less as realistic projections.

Recommendation 4

Clarify the purpose of your budget and make sure that all who are using it as a control instrument are involved in its preparation and have a common understanding of its purpose. Its fundamental purpose must be to motivate management in the short-term control of the business by providing a realistic projection of what can be achieved. Management must therefore believe it and be committed to it.

This means that its preparation must not be dictated by laborious reporting requirements of top management. It must be prepared within a time frame, and extend over a time frame, which makes it believable to those who will have to use it as a control device. Especially do not get it all tied up with the preparation of long-term plans. This will simply drag out the process and make it less useful for its prime purpose — the short-term control of the business.

Scrap that intensive annual budget ritual and move to much tighter short-interval control with five quarterly, rolling budgets. Regularly updated budgets for shorter time periods will provide a more reliable picture of what is likely to happen in the short term. Set a small number of realistic budget and other targets to be achieved by each manager in the next three months. Review them regularly and hold managers accountable for achieving them.

When reviewing budgets, focus on the issues which variances are identifying, not on lengthy discussions of, and excuses for, past performance. And do not focus only on negative variances, on unexpected failure. Look for unexpected success as well and how you can benefit from it.

Tighter budgets, with a sharper, shorter-term focus, which are more frequently updated, have implications for performance appraisal. The current widespread practice is the annual performance appraisal to which salaries and bonuses are often tied. This is another modern business ritual. Rituals are meant to reinforce belief, but few annual performance appraisals achieve that purpose. They tend to become bureaucratic form-filling exercises which few take all that seriously. It is far more effective to combine individual performance appraisal with the regular three-monthly reviews of performance against budget and other targets. The personal performance of managers and the determination of their rewards is then more regular and much more focused on what they are required to achieve.

It is no excuse to say that there is not enough time for quarterly performance reviews — the essence of management and control in closed change is to ensure that objectives are achieved. Frequent reviews of performance against objectives give a strong message that the objectives are serious.

Recommendation 5

Tie performance appraisal firmly to a rolling five-quarterly budget. Set a small number of performance targets for the next three months. Agree them. Review them at the end of the three months. Reward the achievers. But you have to remember that this is only part of control, part of performance. Control and performance in the long term are just as important. You have to make judgements about the weight to be attached to these different types of performance. No one has yet succeeded in setting up a mechanistic system for doing this.

Another obstacle to the effective use of Management Information and Control Systems relates to the quality of information flows and the way in which they are tailored to the needs of different levels in the management hierarchy. Chapter 3 discussed five important requirements. Information flows must be related to the markets in which the business operates and demonstrate where profits are being made or money is being lost. Information flows should produce measures of what really counts, not just financial variables. Key indicators on quality, service levels, delivery times, complaints and any other source of competitive advantage are essential. 'Flash' measures on volume, order books and prices, even if they are not precise, are needed to indicate what is happening to profit now. Information flows should be tailored to the needs of each level in the hierarchy. Each level of management should receive well thought out key indicators on a daily, weekly, monthly and quarterly basis; not vast quantities of information, but a page or two of really key information which gives a real 'flavour' of what is going on.

Recommendation 6

Focus your monitoring processes on variables which measure what is really important to your business, variables which also direct your attention to the future rather than to the past. The normal accounting variables of profit earned two months ago are not adequate. Develop a set of key indicators appropriate to each level of management. Concentrate on a few of the most vital indicators — order books, order flows, quickly obtainable volume measures of activity, indicators on quality, responsiveness, adaptability and so on. Present them in a form which allows genuine and rapid comparisons. These measures may not be as accurate as the normal accounting variables, but what you lose in accuracy you will gain in early warning of disturbance. Ensure that you measure and monitor all the key aspects of competitive capability. Ensure that the information generated by your Management Information and Control Systems, the information on which you focus for control purposes, relates directly to the market segments you operate in. You must be able to answer the question of where you are making money and where you are losing it. But focus on this question should not generate vast quantities of information which managers will never have the time to look at, let alone the time to act on.

These recommendations have stressed the more mechanistic aspects of short-interval control. But this is only a subset of the total control system. Short-interval control needs to be supported by training and development, culture and ideology. These matters are dealt with in Chapter 9.

Improving the political system of the business

Handling strategic disturbance in open-ended change situations

At the same time as the management of any business is handling the day-to-day disturbances to basic flows of orders/requisitions, inputs/outputs and money, it has also to handle strategic issues generated by open-ended change. Management has to attend simultaneously to the control which ensures that customers are satisfied cost effectively today, and to the control which will produce a continuing match of competitive capability to unpredictably changing customer requirements and competitor pressures.

And what is required in that dynamic situation is the continuous generation of a stream of innovative ideas for repackaging and re-presenting existing products; developing new ones; rearranging alliances with customers, suppliers and competitors; improving day-to-day controls. What is required is some effective system for screening and setting priorities for these new ideas; for reaching a consensus on

which to pursue and progress; for actually progressing new ideas and trying them out. And there has to be some means of selecting successful new innovations and giving them organizational backing so that they produce a significant increase in profit.

In the dynamic situation we are talking about, conflicting personal ambitions, values and judgements will all be aroused at each stage. The systems and mechanisms have to be able to resolve such differences effectively so that successful innovations come to the surface, make progress and are built into strategies. And this is what political systems do. Political systems are all about establishing enough consensus on central values, philosophy of control and broad approaches to issues to enable action to be taken. Political systems are all about resolving differences and implementing responses to change through the application of power and persuasion to issues where judgement, based on values and intuition, must be exercised; where the response to the issues itself affects power and belief.

To improve the dynamic games which a business plays, we have to ask what needs to be done to improve the functioning of the political system of the business so that changes are detected, issues are brought to the surface and attended to, failures are terminated and successes are backed. We have to look at how the obstacles to effective political functioning can be overcome. A flexible business political system enables a continuous stream of innovative ideas to reach fruition. And the way to cope with true uncertainty, with open-ended change, is through a continuous process of learning by innovation.

The environment of the 1990s demands political systems in businesses which accommodate, adapt to, learn from and even create change; systems which promote growth. The political system has to be responsive to change and this means a system which, through appropriate behavioural rules, encourages innovation, the emergence of champions and the formation of special interest groups. It means using formally constituted teams and their meetings for more than legitimization, using them to raise, explore and address the issues. It means actually doing things, experimenting and learning.

And this requires action teams or task forces. It means leadership which is determined, obsessed with success and which generates vision and direction. The prime requirements of the kind of political system we need for the 1990s are:

- leadership which presents challenges, focuses attention, creates understanding, articulates direction, shares power;

- champions who promote innovation in many parts of the business, who are alive to the changes, who are determined and flexible, who accept that the outcome of the experiment could be quite different from the original intention;

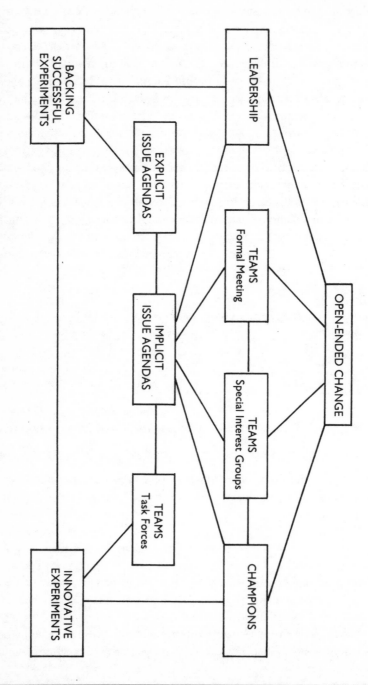

Figure 15 Political systems and control by trial and error

- teams forming around special interests, management teams who use the more formal occasions for more than legitimization, task forces which do things.

The principal components of the business political system necessary to respond to open-ended change and the output of that system are summarized in Figure 15, reproduced from Chapter 6.

The key questions which need to be asked in relation to effective business political systems are:

- How do you get changes detected and issues formulated into a dynamic strategic issue agenda, a stream of new ideas leading to experiments?

- How do you ensure that the issues attract sufficient organizational attention?

- How do you ensure that issues become coherent experiments which are actively progressed with determination?

- How do you ensure that successful experiments are backed and built into strategic direction?

Let us now consider each of these questions in turn, identifying the obstacles to answering them effectively and making recommendations to overcome these obstacles.

Teams: champions and special interest groups
The champions of a business are those managers who detect a disturbance caused by change and develop an emotional commitment to doing something about it. They are in touch with the market place and the shop floor; they have multiple perspectives; they are able to draw intuitive conclusions from inadequate information. Champions have the determination required to fight for and push their ideas to fruition. But they are also realistic and flexible — they know that they are dealing with uncertainty and the outcome may well be the unexpected success. They have the personal stature and leadership skills to persuade others and to form coalitions or special interest groups. They are the effective source of innovation. They are key to the agenda-building process.

But if champions are to have any impact, they must have power and influence; they must be close enough to the top of the hierarchy to get organizational attention for their ideas. Champions may be found at the top of the hierarchy or lower down, but they always require the support and encouragement of the top. It is only when those at the top pay attention that the issues makes it on to the agenda.

The strategic issue agenda consists of ill-structured problems and opportunities

extracted from a large number of such potential problems and opportunities. The really important changes are usually small and the prize goes to those who notice and respond to them in time. The information about these changes is inadequate, unreliable, constantly changing and dispersed throughout the organization. One or two people in the organization, unless they are exceptionally capable, cannot be relied upon in these circumstances to develop an appropriate strategic issue agenda. No one level in the hierarchy will, on its own, be able to gain access to sufficient information or be able to see enough of the total picture.

Detecting small changes, developing issues agendas, cannot be left to some specialist staff function; it is impossible for a group of people not in direct contact with the many facets of the business to be well informed enough to be entrusted with this task. No staff function will be able to secure the necessary political support for an item to receive adequate line management attention; agendas built by staff functions cannot then be real. Effective agenda development flows, in the first instance, from the efforts of champions and special interest groups at a number of levels in the hierarchy. Open-ended change impacts on the business at all levels in the hierarchy. In fact it may well be noticed first at the lowest levels of management. It is therefore of vital importance that managers at the top of the hierarchy are in touch with levels much lower down.

What are the obstacles to the emergence and operation of champions and the special interest groups which form around them to promote innovation?

Excessive concentration of power

The first and perhaps the most frequently encountered obstacle, in my experience, is an excessive concentration of power at the top of the management hierarchy. Typically, monarchic and oligarchic political systems in businesses, with their heavy concentration of power right at the top of a corporation, do not provide an encouraging environment for the widespread emergence of champions. In these political systems, champions can only emerge at the top. Where there are one or more highly talented figures at the top, innovative entrepreneurs, this will not matter. But in the absence of exceptional figures, rigid hierarchies and over-powerful executives who block discussion and stifle ideas which are not their own, lead directly to organizations which are incapable of innovation. You will hear those lower down saying, 'I did not express my opinion because they keep telling me I am negative', or 'There is no point in putting that idea forward because they never listen.' You will hear the powerful few saying, 'Those below us are not good enough.'

In a rapidly changing and complex environment, it is of major importance to utilize the perceptions of middle management. Many important agenda items arise at this level and only succeed in reaching the strategic agenda if the middle managers

can persuade their superiors to take it up. Pluralistic political systems encourage this upward flow of issues.

Isolation of top executives

A second, and related, obstacle to an effectively functioning political system is the isolation of those at the top of the management hierarchy from the market place and the shop floor. This occurs where the most senior levels of managers form a tight, closed circle, the members of which rely largely on the more formal methods of communication — budget reviews, market research reports and 'state' visits to the subsidiaries. They call for detailed, analytical justifications for every new proposal because they no longer receive any direct input from areas where those important small changes are actually occurring. They have no basis on which to exercise any intuitive skills they may possess. They do not listen to those lower down in the hierarchy or to their customers.

Composition of the top team

A third significant obstacle to the emergence of champions espousing a wide range of issues relates to the composition of the most senior management teams in the organization. Where power is heavily concentrated right at the top of a corporation there is a noticeable tendency for the powerful to promote into their ranks only those who have closely similar views and approaches to business. The result is a form of management inbreeding which cuts down on the range of issues which emerge. In such organizations one tends to find top teams composed of a narrow range of personality types. Conflict may be reduced but multiple perspectives are sacrificed.

Inadequate management resources

Other obstacles to the effective operation of champions and special interest groups are to be found in a lack of time and management resources for such activities to occur. All people in positions of any power are overloaded with responsibilities for the existing day-to-day business, despite adequate systems, because there are quite simply too few of them. Or the quality of management in general is not high enough to produce the wider-thinking champions and that in turn is a consequence of inadequate training and development. Predominant cultures which do not allow conflict or permit failure are other blockages to effective political systems.

Recommendation 7

Strategy is about innovation. So set targets for numbers of innovations — you cannot set targets relating to what the innovations will be, but you can focus on the number which are emerging and make everyone aware of this. Regularly

monitor the number of innovative ideas which reach your strategic agenda; not just major new products or technologies but any small idea for doing things differently. If the number is disappointingly small:

- Consider where these ideas come from. Do they always come from a small number of people at the top? If they do then find out why. What is blocking the emergence of a wider range of champions? Explicitly examine the manner in which political power in your business is concentrated or dispersed. And seriously ask whether too much power is concentrated in the hands of a few at the top. Look at the backgrounds of your colleagues in the most senior management teams. Have you all been with the company for many years? What happened whenever newcomers were introduced into the team from outside the company? Did they simply merge in, or did they keep making proposals which were rejected until they left? If you answer 'yes' to these questions you need to consider seriously whether the business is suffering from inbreeding and therefore blocking the identification of innovation issues. Explicitly examine the personality balance of the top management team. Do you all belong to a small number of personality types? Could this be why innovations are always blocked?

- Consider how the most senior managers stay in touch with the market place and the shop floor. List the numbers and types of contact for a selected period of time and discuss them at one of your meetings. Are they purely formal contacts which are unlikely to give much fresh insight into what is going on? If they are, rearrange your duties to allow more purposeful contact so that you become more responsive to the innovative suggestions of subordinates.

- Instead of continually shelving potentially important strategic items because you have insufficient time, set up middle management groups to develop them and to suggest items which they think should be commanding attention. Do not turn these into formal committees, but make sure that a number of meetings are held each year. Change the composition from time to time. Working groups of middle managers can be an important tool in building more effective strategic agendas.

- Review the support you give to champions. Do managers perceive that you value the suggestions they make or do they know that you find such suggestions irritating or even arrogant. Examine the typical reaction to the failure of a new idea — whether it terminates a career or whether imagination and determination are encouraged even if it fails.

- Appoint one of the organization's most senior managers to a position where

the main duties relate to the promotion of new ideas; a business development director who trawls the organization for suggestions on how to do things more effectively.

Teams: multi-discipline task forces

A business which is really being managed strategically is one which is alive with new ideas, small ways of doing things better, arising at many levels of the organization. It is one in which these new ideas are fed up a receptive hierarchy to the levels where there is the power to do something about them. It is an organization with a dynamic strategic issue agenda, one which is continuously according organizational attention to strategic issues. It is one in which champions and special interest groups thrive. But that is not enough. There must also be in place the mechanisms to progress issues which have been accorded attention. A strategically managed organization is one in which task forces are easily formed and managers know how to manage multi-discipline projects.

The purpose of task forces, or project teams, is to identify further the nature of a specific strategic issue; to apply analytical checks to possible ways of dealing with it; to specify tentative objectives in dealing with it, and to try out different approaches. Task forces conduct the strategic experiments of the organization. It is a learning process, one of trial and error, which requires multi-discipline and multi-business-unit inputs. It requires project management skills and it is vital if issues are to be progressed, rather than just talked about. Are effective task forces a noticeable feature of your organization? If they are not it is unlikely that you have an effective strategic management capability. If this is so, what are the obstacles to task force formation and management?

Failure to appreciate the need for task forces

The first obstacle is that the top management team does not appreciate when there is the need for a task force. A company which I am working with at the time of writing this chapter is in the process of a major reorganization. The top management team spent months developing its ideas on what the new organization should be. It took some soundings from the next level in the hierarchy and then announced the new structure. This was a major restructuring which created new divisions, involving the transfer of assets, management, product lines and customers between subsidiary companies. It had major implications for accounting processes, invoicing, production scheduling, transfer pricing and many other details of the business. But the top management team simply left all this to be sorted out by newly appointed divisional managing directors and their staffs, many of whom were also coping with personal moves from one subsidiary to another.

These are clearly occasions where a properly constituted task force is required,

composed of managers from different business units and different functions, to work out the details before they are implemented. But top management did not perceive the need. The result was a chaotic implementation period and significant management dissatisfaction.

No encouragement for task forces

A second obstacle to effective task force functioning is a lack of monitoring, control and encouragement from the top management team. Another company I have worked with did set up small task forces to progress new business ventures. But unless they were headed by one of the main board directors they were simply left to two or three managers lower down to get on with. The top management team did not attach much importance to such new ventures at its meetings and they were hardly ever referred to — they were too small. All the top-level attention had gone into formally approving the new idea and then it was largely ignored. None of these small new activities ever succeeded in this company during the period I worked there.

Composition of task forces

A third important obstacle is that task forces are not set up properly. They are almost always composed of the 'great and the good' in the organization. Members are always drawn from the same list of people and consequently their approaches to every project are necessarily similar and run the risk of missing more innovative ways of dealing with the issue. There is little to shake the received wisdom. Are the task forces applied to important strategic issues always composed of the senior managers working in cloak and dagger secrecy? If they are, you really need to question objectively the need for that secrecy. The price you may be paying for excessive secrecy may well be narrow views and lost innovative approaches.

Functional and business unit barriers

A fourth obstacle to effective task force functioning is also perhaps the most widespread obstacle. It arises directly from the functional and business unit barriers which are inevitably created by the need for effective day-to-day control of the business. Most managers are conditioned by approaches to day-to-day controls, with their focus on precise objectives and swift action. They are far less comfortable with tentative objectives, with the need to abandon initial objectives when unexpected success stares them in the face. They are inevitably conditioned by functional approaches and business unit loyalties and have difficulty in crossing those boundaries to get different perspectives on a problem or opportunity.

Roles are perceived very often in parochial functional and business unit terms, all too tied up with the existing business. The result is that too few members of the task

force look at the dynamics of the business game which has to be played, at what the competitors will do. Many companies simply lack the project management skills which are necessary to run effective task forces.

Finally a major obstacle to effective task force management lies in insufficient management resources to constitute task forces and provide sufficient analytical support to back them. These are matters which are discussed in Chapter 9.

Recommendation 8

Use task forces to progress the key issues facing your business. Do not leave major reorganizations, product developments, technology changes or even small new ideas to the uncontrolled cooperation of those most affected by the change. Simply announcing a change will not make it happen effectively — trial and error need to be carefully controlled if the organization is to learn anything from it, and creative learning is the essence of strategy. The way to control trial and error is through multi-discipline task forces across functions and business units. What you are looking for in an uncertain situation is multiple perspectives. You cannot achieve this by always appointing members of a small clique of the 'great and the good' to your task forces. Bring in people from lower down the hierarchy. Task forces are outside the hierarchy and should be treated as such. Do not cloak the operation of task forces in unnecessary secrecy.

Having set up the task force, take a strong and continuing interest in it. Set milestones and keep reviewing them.

Your management development programme must pay particular attention to 'growing' managers capable of managing multi-discipline projects.

Teams: senior management teams and their meetings

The real, dynamic, strategy-building process is one of continuously detecting change and bringing issues to the surface through the activities of champions and special interest groups, and then progressing them by checking, exploration, trial and error, using multifaceted task forces. Champions, special interest groups and task forces will all, at one time or another, draw members from the most senior management teams in the whole organization as well as from other levels in the management hierarchy. So one set of contributions made by the top management team to the dynamic strategic management process lies in its membership of these often much less formal groupings.

But the key contributions which the formal top management team itself makes to the whole strategy-building process is first to accord attention to a particular issue, then to support task forces in the conduct of coherent experiments and finally to direct organizational resources and energy into successful experiments so that they become the strategy or direction of the enterprise. These contributions have two aspects.

The first aspect is that of legitimization. It is top management, acting as a team, which formally acknowledges the importance of an issue, gives authority and resources to task forces and officially recognizes the strategic direction which their experiments may give rise to. Many top management teams, when they meet as a team, focus almost entirely on this legitimization aspect. The formal meetings are all about demonstrating consensus and rubber stamping what is happening.

But there is another aspect to the contributions which the formal top management team can make. It can, in a real sense, oversee and monitor the strategic issue agenda and provide a useful forum for its actual development. And it can take an active interest in what task forces are doing; it can monitor their progress and establish priorities in what they are doing. It can ensure that the experiments which are conducted are coherent in the sense that they have some connection to each other and to the existing business. This continuing real, as opposed to simply legalistic, involvement will mean that a sense of direction is generated and that successful experiments are recognized earlier on and backed more effectively.

Over-emphasis on legitimization

Perhaps the main obstacle to the effective utilization of the formal top management team in the strategic management process is an over-emphasis on the legitimization aspects of its contribution.

Look at all your regular, formal management meetings — the board meetings, the weekly or monthly meetings of senior managers. Look at the agendas for these meetings and the way in which the time is spent. These meetings are very expensive in opportunity cost terms — the executives concerned could be meeting customers or sorting out organizational and production problems instead of holding long discussions. But they are worth the high opportunity cost if they are being used to pool the information about rapidly changing situations which those executives are carrying in their heads; if they are being used to identify the really important issues with which the business has to contend. All too often this is not the case. The meetings are frequently run to rigid agendas concerned with reporting on the past. You no longer have time for expensive history lessons or self-indulgent trips down memory lane — the 1990s will be too tough for you to spend your time telling entertaining anecdotes.

Obstructive informal rules

The informal unwritten rules governing behaviour at board and management meetings are often totally inappropriate for constructive agenda building. Properly managed conflict, the purpose of which is understood, can be a highly valuable way of clarifying the nature of strategic disturbance, provided it is not abused by the

participants. But all too often conflict is implicitly forbidden. A common unwritten rule at formal meetings is: 'Don't rock the boat'. Each executive refrains from any questioning, comment on, or constructive criticism of, the activities of a colleague on the understanding that he too will receive an easy ride.

Or take another frequent rule: 'There is no point in making any suggestion the chairman is against, check it with him first.' These rules will make the meetings so sterile that they are a complete waste of time. And it tends to happen that the higher up the hierarchy you go the more counterproductive the behavioural rules governing formal meetings become. Look particularly at your board meetings; they may well be the biggest waste of very valuable time in the organization.

Composition of the top team

The composition of senior management meetings in terms of personalities is also an aspect which must receive explicit attention. If the business world is now so complex that one person, or one small power clique, cannot be expected to cope adequately, then one or two powerful personalities who dominate the meetings are performing a positive disservice to the organization.

If executive meetings are to have a positive impact in terms of building agendas and then progressing them, they must have some balance of personalities. You need the aggressive pusher of new ideas. You need the more cautious checker of new ideas. You need people who are not totally caught up with the existing state of received wisdom; even those with a bizarre approach. You need the quiet 'observer' who is capable of interpreting what others are saying, voicing the areas of agreement, giving shape or structure to the discussion. A positive act of design is required for management teams, an act based not simply on business and functional responsibilities, not just on expertise, but on personalities.[3]

Recommendation 9

Examine all your regular, formal management meetings. Are you wasting valuable management time in highly formalized reporting and information exchange? Are your meetings simply rituals to sanctify decisions which have already been taken by a powerful few? What about the unwritten rules of behaviour? Is conflict of any kind forbidden? Is constructive criticism studiously avoided? If you answer 'yes' to these questions then you need to change. You will not be building effective strategic agendas. Carry out the following programme for each of the senior management meetings which takes place in your organization:

- Appoint one person to listen to what goes on and measure the time spent on simple information exchanges, on minor administrative and policy matters,

and on issues which are of real significance to the business. Get that person to list the important issues which were raised and then given no further attention.

- Then hold a special meeting of that group to hammer out the purpose of the meetings they hold. Confront them with the evidence of time spent on different categories of business and particularly on the issues raised and not progressed.

- Get team members at this special meeting to write out their view of the informal rules which govern their behaviour at the meetings. Get them to discuss whether these are helpful or not. Get them to put forward the rules which ought to govern behaviour. In particular they should consider the importance of allowing strong differences of opinion and even conflict.

- Get team members to consider their personality differences explicitly and what distinctive contributions such differences make. Are they different enough? Or is the group a cosy club of like-minded people who will not provoke each other into seeing the important disturbances?

Use the above programme of analysis of meetings to change their format and composition so that they become relevant to building the necessary strategic agendas. Scrap those lengthy formal agendas which focus all your attention on the recent past and develop different agendas for each meeting, agendas which focus on specific strategic issues. Do not continue to waste valuable management time. Deal with administrative and minor policy matters outside the meeting. Recognize that day-to-day control is best exercised on a one-to-one basis and do not use valuable meeting time to keep reviewing the past. Start your meetings with the important issues and keep the day-to-day review items for the last places on the agenda. Above all develop behavioural rules which allow real issues to be explored in a frank and constructive manner, rather than polite information exchange. Scrap those meetings which do not serve this purpose — they are a waste of time.

Teams: strategy workshops

Strategy-making is about continuously developing dynamic, implicit strategic issue agendas, giving priority to and progressing selected issues by experimentation, so that they become strategic direction. It is about continuous innovation. But from time to time events do come together in a way which makes it necessary to make the strategic issue agenda explicit and review it. It may be a dramatic decline in profits, a major cash outflow, a change in the top management team, an innovative experiment which calls for a significant gamble. Whatever the prompt, top

managers will experience the need to take stock of the situation, structure the issues and clarify the direction.

It is at this point that companies without long-term planning systems set off for two-day retreats away from the office. For those companies with formal long-term planning systems, the need for such a retreat should never arise. After all, the planning system is supposed to take stock of the situation annually. But in fact even in these companies, special stocktaking exercises are found to be necessary. Managers from these companies also go off for long weekends at expensive country hotels. Either before (or more usually after) these retreats, the consultants are called in. What happens at these get-togethers? Take an example, which in my experience is typical.

The weekend planning retreat

The background is one where a team of competent and intelligent managers had recently taken control of an ailing instrumentation company. They had installed the necessary Management Information and Control Systems and were running a tightly controlled business in the short-term sense. But profitability was still not adequate and to them this was a pressing strategic issue. Having rationalized the business and attended to the day-to-day, they now wanted to establish a more integrated approach to the strategic and to identify new opportunities. They had no formal long-term planning system or any market research and planning staff, but they understood and spoke the language of conventional strategic management. They were well informed and understood their markets; they listened to their customers and talked quite comfortably about the structure of the market and the sources of competitive advantage.

This team of managers held two one-day meetings away from the office, the objective being to develop a strategy for the future. They conducted a SWOT (strengths, weaknesses, opportunities and threats) analysis and produced the first draft of a strategic plan. That plan set out profit targets, a desired growth rate, a percentage return on capital. There were also statements on the market segments they were operating in and broad strategies for acquisition. The rest of the document consisted of SWOTs. This plan was predominantly a description of the existing business with a few precise long-term profit targets and a few vague suggestions on what they might do in the future.

The management team felt somewhat disappointed with the result of their deliberations. It was too vague. The SWOT list did not seem to lead them anywhere. When they described what had been happening at their day-long events, they used phrases such as 'going around in circles' or 'not seeing the wood for the trees'. The results of their deliberations were nevertheless communicated to middle

managers who were asked to roll the communication down to the rest of the organization.

They then called in consultants who conducted a survey of middle and lower management opinions and concerns. The message came back that managers did not believe that the company had a sense of direction; they did not think that those at the top knew where they were going. This added to the frustration which some members of the top management team felt with the whole process. They had, after all, communicated; but those lower down had not heard. On questioning top management itself, the consultants discovered different perceptions of the outcome of the strategy exercise. Some people thought it was a reasonable strategic framework, others thought it was not. Far from bringing about agreement, the disagreement and confusion persisted.

It would be easy to dismiss this story as an example of poor strategic planning. Two points make me uneasy about reaching such a conclusion. The first is that the members of this particular management team are highly intelligent and clearly competent. They knew what they were doing in day-to-day terms and they understood discussion of strategy in its conventional meaning — they had been trying to do what the conventional approach prescribed. The second point is that, in my experience, this example is typical. And I have seen it repeated, many times, even in companies with rather sophisticated annual long-term planning procedures and large corporate planning staffs.

The reason why so many of these expensive weekend jaunts produce so little in terms of a plan for the future and in terms of clarity on the part of the participants lies in the way in which members of the management team think. Their whole approach is conditioned by conventional strategic management, by dealing with contained change situations. But they do not face contained change. They face open-ended change. They are looking for the probable and the likely in change situations where these terms have little meaning. They are trying to do the impossible, namely, deciding in advance how they are going to deal with future open-ended change. They are trying to prepare a strategic issue agenda for the future and there can only be one outcome to such an attempt — disappointment.

Focus on what the agenda is now
It is far more realistic to focus on what the agenda is now, what the issues are now and how the organization's control system needs to be adapted so that issues of this kind can be dealt with as they occur in the future. The focus should not be on what might happen in the future and on decisions as to how they will be dealt with if they occur. The focus should not be, as it is with formal planning, on detailed objectives and routes to those objectives. It should be on the nature of the problems and the opportunities and what organizational changes are required to allow them to be

handled effectively. The real purpose of a special stock-taking exercise is to clarify the existing situation, make the existing issue agenda explicit and generate commitment and clarity. The process of exploration and discussion is far more important than the outcome itself.

Formal planning focuses on the quality of the outcome — stock-taking exercises focus on the process for generating clarity and commitment and this is more important. What is required is some set of events which are outside the normal hierarchy, outside the normal timetable and outside the formal organizational procedures. These conditions can be met by setting up a special set of events or workshops. The purpose of these workshops will be to clarify and make explicit the strategic agenda at that point in time. The purpose will be to identify what the problems and opportunities actually are; to give them structure and make them explicit. The purpose will be to clarify area of operation, values and direction from where we are now. And all this in a way which engenders belief and commitment. A realistic focus for these workshops is totally different from that of formal strategic planning, and attempts to conduct them with a view to producing conventional long-term plans is unlikely to succeed.

Lack of common understanding

The first obstacle to effective strategy workshops is the lack of common understanding of the purpose of such workshops, common expectations of the outcome, common understanding of the meaning of direction and vision. Different levels of satisfaction therefore result from a particular outcome. The first step must be to agree explicitly on what the workshop process itself can and cannot achieve. It cannot achieve a plan or grand design for the future. It can achieve clarity on what the situation is now and commitment on what to do about it. But the obstacles are more numerous than simply misunderstanding the workshop purpose.

Received wisdom

A second obstacle to effective workshops arises when the management team is too involved in the business situation to view it in a new or dispassionate way. All of us become culturally conditioned to any environment in which we have spent any time. We are all victims of received wisdom of one sort or another. Ironically, the more cohesive and well informed the team, the more easily it is constrained in its thinking. What it is trying to achieve — agreement and well informed judgement — can actually be a hindrance if it is present too early on.

What is needed is first an opening out, a wide exploration, a new perspective, before the later stage of homing in and cohesion. And this is needed because we are dealing with the open-ended and the ill-structured. Managers are constrained by their own functional specialisms, by their narrow business unit interests, by their

relationships with each other, by their own power ambitions, by personal desires which have little to do with the business situation, often by their very personalities, from performing this opening-out step. Furthermore the opening-out step is accompanied by confusion and stress and is therefore often avoided. Most of a manager's time is spent in handling day-to-day disturbance and the whole approach required for this is at odds with that required in a well functioning workshop situation. Effective handling of day-to-day disturbance requires quickly establishing specific objectives and clear action plans. Early application of analytical techniques is called for. The direct opposite is what is required, initially anyway, in the kind of workshop situation we are discussing. We are therefore requiring a considerable act of flexibility on the part of the manager. This is a major obstacle to the type of open-ended process required in a workshop environment.

Lack of tenacity

Another obstacle lies in a lack of tenacity. Managers work under severe time pressures and the strategy workshop is the easiest item to abandon. Quite frequently one workshop will be held but will end in some confusion or with what most feel is a trivial result, and later workshops will then be postponed, perhaps never to be held, under the pressure of day-to-day events.

Difficulty in persuading others

The major obstacles, however, lie in the 'group' processes themselves. Managers are gathered together in the strategy workshop situation because the most up-to-date information, the most pertinent judgements, are locked in their heads. You will not find this information on the latest market changes and competitive moves in market research reports or on computer screens. Most of the judgements are intuitive. And it is difficult to make intuitively reached judgements explicit in a way which will convince colleagues. It is extremely difficult for any of us to set out clearly what steps we followed in reaching an intuitive judgement. The whole essence of intuitive judgement is that it is based on a complex set of observations and past experience that we ourselves are only dimly aware of — it does not have clear steps. But to persuade others there has to be some explicit argument. We have to be able to take others through a series of steps which will lead them to the same conclusion. Because we are not making all our assumptions clear, there is great scope for misunderstanding and differences of view.

The key is to have someone in the group who listens and tries to impose some structure on what the others are saying, someone we may call the voice of the group or the 'shaper'.

Composition of the workshop

The composition of the group and the personal relationships between those in it is

all-important. Take some common problems. If the chairman or woman, or the chief executive of the company runs the workshop, a subtle message is immediately conveyed. All see it in hierarchical terms. What is said, how you say it, even where you sit round the table will be dictated by the hierarchical relationships. And if the person in the chair has a powerful personality, the message will not even be subtle. You will then have the usual board or executive committee meeting. There will be no opening out of the discussion.

For the same reasons an effective strategy workshop should not replicate an existing board or committee — the relationships are already fixed; the members are already very familiar with each others' positions. What you need is people close to the market place and the shop floor. You need some outspoken, even eccentric, members who are not overawed by the hierarchy. You need some who are more imaginative, perhaps even unrealistic. You need others who are more restraining, even pedantic, who will pour some analytical cold water on ideas, thus testing them. Above all you need someone who is skilled in detecting and articulating areas of agreement, someone who can act as the voice of the meeting. This is an extremely difficult role because it requires a degree of detachment and independence — a tall order for one who is also a participant, a manager in the business itself, who has much to gain or lose as a result of the discussion. It is therefore in this role that outside consultants have much to contribute.

Lack of follow-up

A further obstacle is a lack of follow-up in a form which creates progress in the deliberations of the workshop. It is vital to set out in writing what the arguments were and where they led to; what agreement was established. If this is not effectively done then the next meeting will simply go round in the same circles as the last one and there will be no progression. Without progression the workshop approach will simply be abandoned. The write-up of the meeting then provides the basis for later review and follow-up. Follow-up should also include passing down what is being considered to lower levels in the hierarchy.

Recommendation 10

Make your strategic agenda explicit, check its relevance and comprehensiveness in a manner which recognizes the inherent difficulties of handling open-ended change — ill-structured problems and opportunities which are difficult to identify; which by their very nature cannot be foreseen; which call for up-to-date information locked in managers' heads. Do this by setting up a series of workshops to accomplish the following:

● Identification of the key problems and opportunities, the issues and challenges, which face the business now.

- Clarification of the broad areas of operation, the sets of values within which issues are to be dealt with, the direction in which the business is moving.

- Establishment of task forces, to progress each of the key issues within the overall sense of direction, areas of operation and values.

Be clear on the purpose of these workshops. You are using them to promote understanding and commitment, to utilize information and perceptions which you cannot get at in any other way. The purpose is to clarify direction and to raise comfort levels, not to forecast the future and decide what to do about it. Do not turn these workshops into regular and eventually boring affairs. Use them when events come together to require an explicit look at the strategic agenda.

To overcome the obstacles to using the workshop approach effectively you should:

- Clarify the purpose of the workshops at the very first meeting.

- Establish the right atmosphere of informality and open-mindedness. The workshop must be perceived to lie outside the normal hierarchy. Different rules of behaviour apply during workshop meetings. The most powerful executive should not chair it, or at least not chair the first few sessions.

- Attend carefully to the composition of the workshop. Of particular importance is the need to include one who can act as the voice of the meeting, the 'shaper'. This person may or may not be the leader of the organization. He or she may be someone from outside the organization. A challenger of accepted wisdom is also a vitally important member.

- Use and manage conflict and encourage the devil's advocate.

- Do not give up after the first one or two workshops.

- Use conventional strategic management to provide insights and raise questions which may help to structure the discussion, not to reach rapid, facile prescriptions on what to do.

- Avoid degeneration into detail.

- Ensure progression by interesting and understandable write-ups of progress.

- Follow up and review.

Recognize that while the output you require is consensus and clarity, the process will necessarily be characterized by conflict and some confusion in the early stages. But the outcome will be a clarification of where you are now and what coherent experiments you should be progressing now.

Leadership and direction

Leadership is to the political system of the business what gravity is to the solar system — successful leadership holds the political system together and ensures that it functions in an effective, coherent manner. A failure of leadership leads to disjointed operation of the political system in which change is either not detected at all or responses to it are never progressed and built into strategies. Leadership makes a number of distinct contributions to the whole process of handling the disturbance caused by open-ended change.

Effective leaders build teams

A leader contributes to the control of the organization through other people. Competence in selecting the right people and motivating them to work together is the key to successful leadership in business. A leader establishes, through his or her own conduct, the predominant form of relationships between managers in their roles. A leader has a significant impact on the way in which managers perceive their roles and the manner in which they actually carry them out.

Leaders may give strong messages on these matters or the messages may be weak and confused. We all know of companies where the person at the top of the organization adopts a strongly authoritarian, or directing, style of relationship with those who report to him or her. Such leaders will hold the reigns of power very tightly and select the issues on which they will involve their immediate subordinates in ones and twos, depending on their own judgement of the issues' relevance to other people. Others will be excluded from participating in the discussion and progression of issues and meetings of the wider management 'team' will be used for legitimization only. As a direct consequence, the real teamwork right at the top of the organization will be almost non-existent and managers will perceive their roles in parochial terms. This strongly directing style of relationship between people and parochial role perceptions will spread downwards through the entire organization.

The leader's approach to work spreads through the organization

It is striking how a leader's personal approach to his or her own work will spread through the organization. In one company I know of, the leader arrives early and stays late, he rushes about with frenetic energy, postponing one meeting after another. When he does arrive at the meeting, he does all the talking, strongly criticizing anyone who disagrees with him, and imposes his will. All the senior managers in the company behave in the same way and this applies even to those who are not comfortable with the style and keep complaining about it.

In the parcel delivery company which I used as an example in an earlier chapter, the leadership style was much more facilitating. Issues were frequently put to the whole of the formal management team and open discussion was encouraged. The

managing director of that company listened and tried to promote consensus before summing up and deciding what should be done. The result was noticeable teamwork throughout the organization. In other companies the leadership style is weak and confused, and the inevitable consequence is an almost complete lack of teamwork, with confusion and endless unproductive conflict.

Leadership, then, plays a prime part in resolving the behavioural tensions of control, in making the organizational choices between directing and facilitating forms of interpersonal relationship and between parochial and holistic role perceptions. Leaders have a major impact on how roles are defined in terms of the attributes that are called on and the constraints that are imposed on those roles. Leaders play a vital part in selecting, developing and rewarding managers. These choices determine how champions, special interest groups, task forces and formal management meetings actually operate. And the choices are not made by formal announcement, but by conduct, example and personal contact. They are intimately tied up with the personality and competences of the leader.

Vision

A second and interrelated contribution which leadership makes to the control of the organization is through what is called vision. Leaders clarify situations, they articulate what is not all that clear to those around them, they reduce uncertainty and increase comfort levels. They express values and beliefs which challenge and excite those around them. They create a sense of urgency, presenting issues and challenges. They embody the determination and persistence required to win. But they do all this with the flexibility required in open-ended situations. Vision, in the sense in which I am using it, is the same thing as direction. And direction is clear, coherent, continuing movement from the existing situation. It is easy to see why vision and direction are so important. The essence of handling disturbances arising in open-ended change situations is experimentation, trial and error. It is about being flexible and open to innovative ideas, trying things out without being all that clear about where they will lead. This essentially involves a lack of clarity, consistency and continuity which could become so extreme as to be confusing, demoralizing and highly disruptive to the existing business.

The kinds of experiment which are encouraged must therefore have some perceived connection with each other and with the existing business. The experiments must not be wild and unconnected — some perceived logic in what is being done is required. And above all, the experiments so essential to the building of strategies must not unduly disrupt the existing business. Strategic experimentation must not mean arbitrarily changing short-term objectives, rendering short-interval control ineffective.

Managers in a chemical company I recently worked with complained about a

lack of direction, and the examples they gave of what they meant all referred to top management decisions to try out new products in what seemed like a random manner, one which kept disrupting existing production schedules. Effective leaders create a sense of direction by finding ways of conducting experiments which are perceived to be connected, which are related to the existing business, which do not disrupt it. Vision is not clairvoyance, it is a practical matter.

What are the obstacles in practice to these vital contributions of leadership, building teams and creating direction or vision?

Obstacles to effective leadership

The first is a personal work style which leaves no time for the really important contributions of leadership. This happens where the chairman or woman or the chief executive does not really understand the role and so becomes too involved in detail and the day-to-day. Such managers do not trust subordinates or delegate to them. They keep interfering with those below them. Or they have such wide spans of control that they cannot effectively keep track of what is going on.

Second is an inability or unwillingness to listen. Such leaders surround themselves with 'yes men' and consequently lose touch with the market place and the shop floor.

A third obstacle is where leaders lack the personality and the competences required to clarify, structure, summarize, draw conclusions, motivate, enthuse and push people to achieve what they are capable of. Or they may lack the necessary determination, commitment and involvement.

A fourth obstacle to effective leadership is an inability to strike an appropriate balance between directing and facilitating personal relationships. The former is appropriate where the objectives can be made clear or where there is some clear threat or well identified opportunity. The latter is appropriate in open-ended situations. People tend to adopt fixed styles, but different change situations require some alteration in personal style. For example rapidly changing markets require facilitating relationships to enable champions and task forces to operate. But an immediate threat, such as a significant cash outflow, may demand a directing approach. Because so many leaders find it difficult to match personal style to the change situation, the only effective response may be to change the leader to fit the most pressing change situation.

Recommendation 11

Explicitly examine the key features of the top leadership of your business. How it operates and the impact it has on the extent of innovative response throughout the organization is even more important than computerized systems or long-term objectives. But while systems, objectives and markets are subjected to analyses

and examination, the nature, quality and impact of leadership style and practice rarely are. An explicit examination of leadership means a personal questioning by the leader:

- His or her style of interpersonal relationships. Is the balance between directing and facilitating relationships appropriate to the kind of change which the organization faces? Do you listen to subordinates or are you always telling them what to do? Is the style blocking or encouraging the surfacing and progression of issues? You will only find out by an independent survey of management perceptions.

- His or her personal work style. Do you trust subordinates and delegate sufficiently? If you keep saying they are no good you are failing in your job because you are not selecting and developing real management teams. Do you have the time to attend to the really key issues or are you always rushing around? Are you in touch with the market place and the shop floor or do you sit on the executive floor cocooned by senior executives and personal assistants? Do you keep injecting new ideas in a disruptive way or do you create direction? Once again you need a perception survey.

Review your understanding of the role of the chief executive and the chairman or woman. Be aware of your personality and the impact it is having. Many regard this as Organization and Behaviour rubbish. But an intensive examination of the impact you are having, feedback on your style, is in reality more vital than the manner in which the more visible and 'practical' systems are operating.

The rapidly changing competitive environment of the 1990s, and the inherent difficulty of handling strategic issues, point strongly to strategic facilitation as the appropriate role for the top levels of management in the processes of strategic control. This means using the knowledge and skills of those close to the market place in a constructive and purposeful way. It means quality control of the processes which management levels lower down the hierarchy are using to handle strategic issues. It means guiding and suggesting and where necessary intervening and taking the initiative.

Perhaps competitive advantage and the need for centralized functions push you to the strategic directing end of the spectrum. But question the need for this before you pay the price of failing to detect some of the major strategic disturbances which may hit your business.

The 'intelligence service': information gathering and analytical support

Strategies are the consequences of many competitive moves, some of which succeed

and others of which do not. The emphasis is on the word competitive. In order to make these moves in the first place and then build them into strategies, the business organization must be a fit, flexible, adaptive and imaginative player of business games.

And this means an effectively functioning internal political system which has a number of distinctive characteristics. The first is visionary leadership, where vision means reducing uncertainty which others in the organisation perceive, articulating beliefs and values which are challenging and exciting, giving shape or direction to the competitive moves made, illuminating and making sense of what is happening now, presenting and reinforcing the competitive challenge, generating an urgent determination to win in the open-ended game and building teams to play the game. The second is the wider distribution of power so that champions emerge and special interest groups form to detect change and passionately push issues. The third is multi-discipline task forces which progress experimental responses to issues. The fourth is periodic 'workshop events' which develop consensus, commitment and clarity.

But political systems operate within an administrative framework, the tool for implementing successful political experiments — in a business this is the Management Information and Control or short-interval control system. And political systems also need the backing of intelligence services — those who gather and analyse information on the environment within which political games are played, as well as the behaviour and thought patterns of rivals, which in turn condition the moves they might make.

Business enterprises also need 'intelligence services' if they are to win at business games. And the prime contribution which information gathering and analysis should be making is that of providing some insight into the competition. Insight and understanding of the competitors will not be developed by simply listing their resources, describing their facilities, analysing their current product offerings and market positions. This may help, but more is required. The key to competitor intelligence is insight into the personalities and mind sets of the leaders and key managers in competitor companies. It is surprising how much can be put together by systematically searching published material and extracting bits of information from employees who used to work for competitors, as well as from top management contacts with opposite numbers in rival companies at trade association and other meetings.

Business games are not played in a simple environment and it makes sense to know as much as possible about the environment — it will affect the outcome of the game. The structuring of issues, the effectiveness of experimental responses will be powerfully aided by pertinent information on and analysis of market, technological and government policy trends. Even on a longer-term view, most

companies face change situations which are a complex mixture of the closed, the contained and the open-ended.

Information gathering and analysis make contributions to identifying and structuring significant aspects of key issues as well as to persuading others of the importance of the issue. And once specific issues are given shape, command agreement and are being progressed, then information gathering and analysis become even more vital.

Many companies today are not providing enough resources to enable adequate application of the necessary analytical processes. The trend to lean management structures and cost-conscious decentralized business units has, in many cases, been taken so far that the business has been stripped of information gathering and analytical support.

Time after time I attend management meetings which identify potentially serious problems or interesting opportunities. But intelligent progress on those matters requires further information, sometimes just a few hours of time to assemble and set out in a coherent way what is already available. But there are no resources to do it. So it is not done and the decision is made on unnecessarily inadequate information, or it is not made at all.

Most companies also do not recognize that the 'intelligence services' are part of the political system. They do not give those providing analytical input enough power actually to apply sufficient influence. It is no use having a group of analysts and information gatherers run by a manager who is disregarded and, as someone recently put it to me, 'would never dare to suggest that one of the subsidiaries is doing something wrong'. A resource which is as weak as this, politically, is indeed a waste of money.

Strategic management is a political process in which the major players are the line management. But they always need information and analytical support and to be effective they must accord some political power to those who provide the support. Analysis is not the final presiding function, it is not the director of line management — it is one of the political inputs to the whole process. In the trend to reduce staff functions and give strategic decision-making to managers, the political contribution of analysis has been weakened too far in many companies. You do need, in a business of any size, a manager with political clout, who is responsible for providing the analytical and information gathering functions. This manager needs to temper analysis with knowledge and judgement; he or she needs to understand the part analysis can and cannot play.

Recommendation 12
Ensure that you do have resources to gather sensible and practical information and to provide analytical support for effective strategic management. See this

support not as some form of staff usurpation of management roles, but as a support and a serious contributor to the political process. Your political processes require the effective representation of the analytical voice. This does not necessarily mean a large market research or corporate planning department. It does mean a politically important figure who can see that adequate information and analytical inputs are made.

Recognize where analysis is important. It makes some, but not the most important, contribution to identifying change and to necessary consensus building. But, much more important, ideas developed in intuitive ways will need to be tested. When issues are clarified and some agreement secured, analysis comes into its own. Some way down the process of managing open-ended change it is a key contributor.

Walking the management tightrope

This chapter has presented 12 recommendations for improving the dynamic strategic management of business in the change environment of the 1990s. These are recommendations to improve the total control system of the business organization: to remove the obstacles to effective short-interval control over the day-to-day changes which impact on the business; to overcome the obstacles to control in open-ended situations, by innovation, through the political system of the business.

Both aspects of control have to be practised simultaneously if the business is to succeed. But each imposes quite different demands on the total control system and this creates control tension. Control styles which resolve this tension by largely ignoring the demands of either cannot succeed in the 1990s. The effective style choice for the majority of businesses lies between strategic direction and strategic facilitation and that choice is unlikely to be a once-for-all one. Successful organizations will shift the balance to meet the pressures of change.

This continuing attempt to resolve the tensions created by the short-term planning and opportunistic forms of control is the tightrope managers have to walk. The task will be even more difficult in the 1990s as change polarizes at the closed and open-ended ends of the spectrum.

Strategy is conventionally seen as primarily about anticipating and responding to changing market requirements. It is certainly that. But this book has argued that it is not possible to decide in advance what will be done to anticipate or respond to changes; how the market game is to be played cannot be predetermined by some grand design. It is more useful to think in terms of making the organization and its management fit and flexible enough to play the game as it unfolds. And that means improving the total control system of the business in both the precise short-interval sense and the much more fluid innovative, political sense.

Strategic management is all about matching competitive capability to customer requirements, but not in a predetermined way for specific points in future time. The game is too dynamic for that. In a dynamic setting strategic management is about making individual moves in the market, responding to single issues, accommodating, reacting, making moves which force competitors to react. And it is about changing the total control system, re-balancing control tensions, as the game is played.

Some recommendations on how to deal with the tensions which this dynamic game places on the structure, cultures and management resources of business organizations are discussed in the next chapter.

Notes

[1] See the British Aerospace example quoted in Chapter 2.

[2] T Peters, *Thriving on Chaos*, Macmillan (1988).

[3] R Meredith Belbin, *Management Teams*, Heinemann (1981).

9
Resolving Control Tension

Recommendations on organizational structure, culture and management resources

Dynamically sustaining short-interval control and political systems, both of which are superior to those of rivals, and which generate innovative experiments, is no easy matter. Both systems have to operate simultaneously but they make conflicting demands on organizational structures, cultures and management. The dynamics of effective strategic management require a continuing resolution of these conflicting demands — a tightrope walk.

Structure and culture enshrine the existing and even the old. Of their very nature they are obstacles to the effective handling of open-ended change. Continuing dynamic experimentation demands the unconventional approach which goes round existing structures, questions current cultural rules and attitudes, and does not stick rigidly to clearly defined roles. All this is required to generate imaginative and innovative responses to intense competition and other external pressures. But, the unconventional — going round structures, cutting across roles and radically questioning cultures — is positively harmful to the disciplined day-to-day control of the business.

How do we resolve this dilemma? What structural forms are required? What kind of culture is needed? How can the potentially stifling effect on innovation be overcome?

Organizational structures to implement strategies

Structures and short-interval control
Since effective strategic management is built upon the ability to implement, consider first the structures which will enable implementation; that is, structures to support tight, short-interval control and the ability to deliver competitive advantage. In the absence of any other requirement, short-interval control at its most effective requires of organizational structure:

- **Rigidity.** Clearly defined roles and responsibilities as well as pre-programmed

rules are required and this means fixed and inevitably rigid organizational structures. Looseness and flexibility will not do the job.

- **Compartmentalization.** This follows from the clearly defined roles and is aimed at breaking down opportunities and problems into easily manageable and monitored parts. It points to decentralized profit centres where objectives can be specific and motivation to achieve them high. It means management focus on specific parts of the organization and specific responsibilities.

- **Separation.** Overlaps between the largely self-contained profit centres are designed out in the structure, or they are governed by clear policy rules, or they are simply ignored.

- **Restriction of top level management to monitoring and intermittent directing.** Decisions on how to handle the day-to-day disturbances are made largely at profit centre level and the top or corporate levels of management are confined to the monitoring element of control with occasional directing interventions when things start going wrong.

Structure and competitive advantage
Rigidity, compartmentalization, separation and restriction of top management roles do lead to the most effective Management Information and Control Systems in a technical sense. But technical perfection is not the ultimate aim. Delivery of competitive advantage is. This may mean that inevitable overlaps cannot be ignored or always governed by policy rules. It may be vital to profitability that products and services are transferred from one profit centre to another. Some form of transfer pricing or dual accounting and performance monitoring will then be essential. This is a problem which crops up time and again and presents a stark choice between retaining profit centres with all their inter-trading problems or combining them into one activity and losing tight control and motivation benefits.

The delivery of competitive advantage may also demand some degree of centralization, thus conflicting with the requirements of effective short-interval control in a technical sense. So, pooling research and development expenditure, centralizing purchasing and inventory control, and global control of product policy over otherwise independent national profit centres may all enhance competitive capability but render tight, short-interval control more difficult.

Structure and open-ended change
The conflicting demands on structure are magnified when the dynamics of changing competitive advantage are taken into account. Rapidly changing and increasingly fragmenting markets are making differentiation a more and more important source

of competitive advantage. Differentiation calls for flexibility, decentralization, ignoring the overlaps which the fragmenting markets are creating, and for decision-making to be devolved down the organization. The price to pay is higher cost but the market will pay it. However, there are other powerful trends as well. There is increasing globalization in some important markets. Some technological developments destroy established differentiation. These developments call for low cost as the source of competitive advantage, spreading vast research and development as well as marketing expenditure, sharing distribution outlets, taking buying gains. In structural terms this means centralization, designing out the overlaps and greater top-level involvement in decision making.

So, the conflicting requirements placed on structures by short-interval control and competitive advantage sharpens when one considers what innovative experimentation requires in structural terms:

- **Flexibility.** The rapidly changing environment of the 1990s, with its rising volumes of disturbance arising from open-ended change, means looking for the new and the innovative. In structural terms this calls for looseness and flexibility.

- **Integration.** Effective handling of the open-ended calls for the overview, for synthesis and integration. It means pulling things together and focusing on the whole rather than the parts. It means involving people across business unit and functional divides. In purely structural terms it points to complex centralism.

- **Synergy.** Strategic control calls for the creative use of overlaps between units, for taking the benefits afforded by synergies. It means looking for new ways of managing interfaces between units. It means communication across boundaries and cross-fertilization. It is not clear that centralization will achieve this, but decentralisation all on its own certainly will not.

- **Wide top-level participation.** Integration and synergy, in conjunction with rising volumes of disturbance and the inherent difficulties of handling it, point to top-level or corporate management as a participant in all the elements of control in open-ended situations. And these factors suggest that this participation should take the form of facilitation rather than direction. Simply acting as a monitor is not sufficient. This points to decision making at profit centre levels with strong influence from the centre of the organization.

Closed and open-ended change are therefore pulling organizational structure design in different directions. Consider the conflict viewed from a purely structural point of view. Rigid on the one hand and flexible on the other. Decentralized on the one hand and centralized on the other. Ignoring overlaps on the one hand and building

on them on the other. The top level specializing in the monitoring element of control, with an intermittent directing style on the one hand, but participating more fully in a facilitating mode on the other.

Resolving the structural dilemma

One approach to resolving the structural dilemma created by the conflicting needs of control might be to install separate formal structures to handle day-to-day and open-ended change. An example of this approach is provided by the structures used by Texas Instruments a few years ago.[1] Quite apart from the normal organizational structure, Texas Instruments set up a parallel organization based on strategic business units. The latter formal organizational structure formulated strategies, while the more normal hierarchy implemented them.

But this approach is doomed to failure. As soon as you set it up it too becomes characterized by rigidity. It adds a high degree of complexity and even confusion. It cuts across the responsibilities required for the day-to-day. It does not recognize the inherent difficulties of managing open-ended change.

Other structural solutions to the problem are to use matrices to deal with overlaps and interconnections. This form is found particularly in companies trying to deal with complex international and global markets. But matrix structures are notoriously difficult to operate. You will notice that those adopting this approach are continually changing structures. Changing structure as the first response to a problem represents a failure to think the whole thing through.

We cannot reasonably expect organizational structure alone to accommodate all the tensions of control. As usual in a management situation we have to find a way of balancing diametrically opposed forces and each balance imposes its own costs and reaps its own benefits. My firm conviction is that attempts to design structures which simultaneously meet all the opposing requirements placed on them lead to confusion and destructive conflict, wasteful of resources.

Structures should be designed first with day-to-day control needs in mind. Without clear structure, Management Information and Control Systems cannot be utilized. If they are not used, the total volume of disturbance referred up to high levels of management will be so high that there will never be time to handle the open-ended. Clear structures are based on present or recent past patterns. They are inevitably characterized by rigidity, overlaps, compartmentalization, separation and devolved decision-making. These are obstacles to handling open-ended change.

But they are obstacles which can be countered by the operation of the political system, the very processes required to handle the open-ended.[2] Rigidity can be softened by people talking to each other and taking the wider view when it is necessary. Purposefully used workshops and task forces can be used to obtain integrated perspectives and action. So what we end up with are two subsystems

operating in parallel. One is formal and the other is informal and the danger of their cutting across and confusing each other is therefore minimized.

The organizational structure should be designed to implement the strategy, to deliver the competitive advantage, not to identify change and conduct experiments. This is a point of major importance. You do not design organizational structures with particular strategies in mind. All you can do is design the structure to deliver competitive advantage, that is, control the day-to-day, in a way which causes minimum obstruction to the processes required for strategy building.

Day-to-day control will be more effective the more decentralized it is into profit centres, the flatter and the more closely the organizational structure corresponds to distinctive market segments. In this way you can more clearly define roles and establish responsibility. In this way you can locate control as close as possible to the market place and the operational response. Profit centres as close as possible to the market place are called for in order to achieve the most effective day-to-day control.

Fortunately this structure design rule also has some benefits when it comes to open-ended situations. The application, at this profit centre level, of informal, flexible political processes will also lead to more effective identification of open-ended change and the building of strategies. But the inevitably parochial focus is going to be an obstacle which must be dealt with by processes of political cooperation between business units.

The rule then has to be to decentralize as far as is consistent with the delivery of competitive advantage, when the obstacles to that delivery cannot be removed by political processes. Having done this, the rule is to use the informal, political processes to soften any resulting rigidity and deal with the overlaps which could act as an obstacle to competitive advantage.

But, enthusiasm for decentralized, flat, simple, formal organizations must be tempered by two important considerations.

First, by flat we mean organizational structures with as few hierarchical levels as possible, with spans of control as wide as possible. But the political processes which must accompany flat organizations are not low-cost operations; they are resource intensive. Cut out too many levels of management and you may well find that there is no management depth, no management time, to operate the political processes and handle open-ended change.

Second, devolving responsibility and decision making down the line does not mean stripping managers down that line of support. Resources will be required to support the informal intuitive and political processes required to deal with the open-ended. Although much of the information required is in the heads of the managers, much of it is not. Although analytical processes can make little contribution to identifying and securing agreement on the nature of open-ended change, it becomes vital as experimental responses are progressed. Resources to

provide information and analytical support in a time of rapid change are vital.

Recommendation I

Ensure that your formal organizational structure is as simple as possible. Push decentralization to profit centres, related to market segments, as far as is consistent with delivering competitive advantage to those segments. Question whether you need to stop the decentralization process for these competitive advantage reasons. Try to achieve the same result through purposeful use of informal, political processes to promote cooperation. If this is not possible question it again before you move away from the decentralized profit centre concept. Keep your organization structure as flat as possible, but not so flat that you remove the management resources you will require for the political processes demanded by effective handling of open-ended change.

Organizational cultures to encourage innovative experiment and competitive ideology

Decentralization down to profit centres, with their focus on profit objectives and with their inevitable overlaps between activities, typically lead to certain types of behaviour by managers. We can classify these types of behaviour as:

- **Narrow objective focus.** The behaviour of managers appears often to be governed by rules which are encapsulated by such sayings as: 'Only the bottom line counts', 'All I need to do is achieve the profit targets for my unit', 'You cannot tell me to achieve the profit target and then tell me I must trade with a sister company or buy my materials through a central purchasing organisation'.

- **Parochialism.** Managers may well adopt a narrow focus on their own part of the organization to the detriment of the whole. You will then find that competition with sister companies comes to occupy more importance than competition with those outside the group. Much time is wasted in conflict over shadow pricing. Opportunities which require collaboration between units are never taken up.

- **Them and us.** Here we find conflict between the business unit and the head office. The former regard the latter as expensive and unproductive overheads. The units avoid using the services available at the centre as much as possible.

This behaviour is not conducive to open political activity, to innovative experimentation. The corporate level plays a major part in sending out messages on which attitudes are acceptable and which are not. It must be made clear to managers that the narrow objective focus and the parochial perceptions are unacceptable and

based on a serious misunderstanding of management roles, even in a decentralized situation. Management is never about 'either or' choices. It is always about balance. So when managers are given profit responsibility for profit units they are being totally unrealistic if they think that this is all that counts. There are always constraints on the manner in which that profit can be obtained. It must be made clear that the good of the whole, the policy set by the corporate level, provides constraints within which they must operate.

But how do you get people to behave in this way? How do you get these messages embedded in the culture, in the attitudes and behaviour of the managers in the organization? The group processes which are necessary for handling open-ended change make some contribution. Managers who are meeting to deal with open-ended change will develop attitudes which take the whole organization into account. That is the purpose of the meeting. They will be subjected to peer pressure to do so. Another way is to educate and develop managers so that they will adopt helpful rather than harmful approaches. Selecting those with the right personal qualities and attitudes in the first place is also important.

Recommendation 2
Develop attitudes and behavioural rules, that is, an organizational culture, which supports decentralized structures operating in the interests of the whole corporation. Do this by more widespread use of the group processes required to handle open-ended change, by involving more people in an orderly way in the 'big issues'. Bring antagonists together and manage the conflict by allowing the application of peer pressure.

An appropriate response to the environment which is already with us places very onerous requirements on management. And the requirements are more onerous than they were, not just at the top levels, but all the way down to the supervisory levels. It is not too strong to say that it demands a revolution in management. What is, and will increasingly be, demanded is higher quality of management at all levels and adequate quantities of management resource at all levels.

More open-ended change requires higher quality management at many levels

Consider what happens once you realize that the business world is now far too complex for a small corporate management clique to handle on their own. You use political processes which include senior managers below the corporate level. You also decentralize further into smaller profit centres and find that you have to apply the political processes to these newly profit-responsible managers in order to

provide the necessary degree of integration and manage the overlaps which decentralization creates. These profit-responsible managers now have to collaborate with other colleagues more than ever before and they find they have to promote team working among the middle and supervisory levels below them.

What you have done is to take significant numbers of managers trained and developed in narrow functional traditions and required them to manage in a significantly different way. Overnight you have turned numbers of middle managers into senior managers required to take much wider perspectives and manage in a far more collaborative way than before. Will they cope? The answer is definitely not, unless they are provided with the right kind of support. Where that support is not provided you will hear constant complaints about the poor quality of management. What was adequate or appropriate quality becomes poor quality because you have changed the requirements without providing the support. And that support is the training and the development which will fit managers to occupy their new and significantly different roles.

Changing the roles of managers

These problems were all encapsulated in a one-day meeting between the directors and senior managers of a provincial bus company which I attended a little while ago. The three directors had bought this company on privatization about 18 months earlier and had proceeded in a professional manner to rationalize and introduce the systems required for adequate control. They had converted a major loss into a modest profit. The organization had been decentralized into district profit centres. Three managers who had previously run bus depots or planned traffic routes and timetables had become profit responsible district managers. They were required to prepare and agree budgets. The purpose of the meeting was to establish budget policies and strategies for the following year.

We went through a sensible process of establishing what the target profit should be and what the budgets so far prepared indicated could be achieved. There was a significant shortfall from target and the discussion focused on what could be done to close the gap. The results of the discussions were then compared with a similar discussion last year. The action points identified for this year coincided closely with those identified last year, but the most significant of those had never been implemented. Why?

The reasons given all centred around the quality of management. The directors implied that the senior profit-responsible managers had not pushed implementation far enough. The senior managers complained that their middle and supervisory managers were not capable enough; that both the senior managers and those below them had been too busy. The need for training was identified and the reasons why enough of it had not been forthcoming were inconclusively explored. But another

point also emerged. This was the first time the directors had produced last year's list and complained about non-delivery. The directors had not regularly reviewed budgets with the senior managers who reported to them. In turn the senior managers had not reviewed budgets effectively with those below them. There had not been the time and anyway the managers below them were not of suitable quality, so it was said.

These problems and complaints are by no means unique. I hear them repeatedly. And they are always due to the same cause. The significance of changing managers' roles from traditional, functional responsibilities to wider, profit responsibilities, with cross-functional, strategic, project management aspects, is simply not clearly enough identified and adequately dealt with. When management roles are changed in this way it is essential to use political processes as a management development tool; to change management selection criteria; and provide appropriate training and development for managers.

Political processes as a management development tool

First, from the directors down, each level had misgivings about the quality and ability of those below. They used this, together with inadequate quantity of management time, to justify the lack of control review meetings with their teams. All were operating on the misguided view that it is sufficient to set objectives, communicate them and then leave the review until next year. The message conveyed by this behaviour is clear — the level above you does not attach much importance to the objectives. But more important, the lack of control review meetings means that an important training and development experience is being lost.

Monthly meetings at which they all reviewed the budget but, far more important, discussed the problems and opportunities facing the business, would have conveyed many messages to the senior managers and given them experience in the kind of more open-ended thinking that their new roles required. Similarly if these senior managers had made the time to review budgets and discuss problems and opportunities with their managers, the messages and the development experience would have been spread more widely throughout the organization. The application, throughout the organization, of the team processes which are so important for handling open-ended change, are in themselves a management development experience of major importance. You cannot afford to say that the time is not available or that the quality of the managers is too poor. The application of group processes will themselves improve the quality of managers.

Management selection

The second point about the bus company discussion described above relates to management selection. All the participants in that discussion recognized that if the

quality of their managers was too poor to meet the demands, then there was something wrong with their methods of selection. You cannot decentralize your organization, you cannot apply the vital political processes, if you do not have managers capable of filling the roles, of meeting the attributes and operating within the constraints of those roles.

Decentralized structures which purposefully use political processes place different attribute requirements on roles from those placed on them by centralized structures which utilize formal, directing approaches to the strategic. The attributes of collaboration and initiative become far more important. You are looking now for people with intuitive competence, with flexible approaches and the ability to think widely. You are looking for broader attitudes, for people who have collaborative skills and who do not think and behave within narrow functional or business unit boundaries. Above all you are looking for people who are capable of balancing opposing forces, flexible thinkers who are not dogmatic but can change their minds and approaches as the circumstances change.

Since you have to rely more on team working you are looking for a balance of personalities. It is not just the personality of one individual that counts, but how that personality fits in with, complements and compensates for, the personalities of others in the team. The whole management selection process becomes much more difficult and requires non traditional approaches.

Recommendation 3
Review your management selection procedures. Recognize that you are looking for attributes which must fit different roles. Recognize that you are looking for people who will fit in with the team and who will provide the necessary balance of personalities within it.

Management training and development
The third point that stands out from the bus company discussion is the importance of management development and training at all levels. You will not be able to go out and select all the managers you need for the 1990s. There are not enough of them and anyway the selection processes available are not sophisticated enough to enable you to make the right choices consistently the first time round. You have to train and develop the managers you need for the 1990s. And you have to do it now.

There is ample evidence that companies are not taking this requirement seriously enough. You cannot identify or deliver competitive advantage if you do not have an appropriate total control system. You cannot operate an appropriate control system without management which possesses the right attributes to fit the roles required by the control system. Proper training and development of your managers is the most fundamental source of competitive advantage. And yet few companies

accord it the importance they do to technology or marketing. Management development in your company cannot be left to a clerk who arranges conference and training programmes which managers themselves identify. Management development requires expertise and it requires political clout in your organization. It should become a part of all your review processes. It should be a regular item on your agendas. It should attract considerable organizational attention.

Recommendation 4

Review your management development policies. Give one of the politically most powerful figures in your organization specific responsibility for management development. Accord it high organizational attention. Put it on the agenda of your regular meetings. Monitor what is being done. Make sure you have the expertise to do it. Above all specifically tie your management development programmes to the attributes which your control system requires of management roles.

If management development programmes are to be designed to fit people to the attributes of required roles then it has to be recognized that roles differ as one moves up the management hierarchy. As we move up the hierarchy from supervisory through middle to senior and corporate levels, the balance of the attributes and constraints on the roles changes. It is not that role attributes and constraints are different; it is their relative importance which changes.

As we move up the hierarchy, initiative and collaboration become relatively more important attributes of the role. As we move up the hierarchy the constraints of power and culture become relatively more important. As we move up the hierarchy the role is less concerned with the day-to-day and more concerned, relatively, with the open-ended. This description of change is in relative terms, the balance changes, the focus changes. The open-ended is not just a matter for the top. Group processes, demanding collaboration and initiative, are important for control throughout the organization. It is simply that these aspects rise in relative importance with movement up the hierarchy.

Since time and capacity to learn at given stages are limited, since development should focus on immediate rather than far distant needs, it follows that development programmes should be designed around these relative changes in attributes and constraints as we move up the hierarchy. There should be clear programmes to fit managers for their existing roles and clear programmes to assist them to make the difficult transition to the next level up.

In-house versus external development programmes

Meeting the challenge means developing cadres of managers who are capable of

open-ended, widespread thinking. We require managers who are able to question conventional wisdom; who are capable of questioning company and industry recipes. And this becomes more important the higher up the hierarchy they move.

In-house training runs a serious risk of propagating company and industry recipes. It has the great strength of being more able to relate the development experience directly to the work place. But it has the serious drawback of parochialism. Development programmes, particularly those designed for the higher levels of the hierarchy, should therefore contain significant components of training which occur outside the company and outside the industry. Managers must be exposed to colleagues from other industries and other companies if they are to develop wider perspectives.

The trend to developing MBA programmes for senior managers which are dedicated to one company and run in-house by Business Schools is therefore highly questionable. The greatest benefit a participant in an MBA programme receives is the discussion, the mind-broadening experience of contact, with managers from many diverse areas.

This need to provide development experiences for managers away from their work place, not just as an opportunity for a few but as a matter of course, places a heavy burden on outside training organizations and in particular on Business Schools. If Business Schools are to provide the training and development for practising managers which is appropriate to their hierarchical level and to their roles in relation to their company's control systems, then the emphasis has to be on skills, particularly the skills of unstructured thinking. Providing learning experiences of this kind requires a 'training' orientated approach and a reasonably high proportion of staff who have experienced these problems themselves, staff who are in touch with current business conditions.

Most Business Schools have indeed recognized these requirements and many have made significant moves to meet them. But many still face significant obstacles in making the necessary adjustments. Business Schools are usually part of higher education establishments and these are quite properly conditioned by academic cultures which emphasize broadly-based education. But the academic culture does sometimes look down on the kind of 'training', as opposed to 'education', which is vital to practising managers. The result of this cultural attitude is that management education is viewed in some Business Schools as a collection of academic disciplines.

Business Schools firmly lodged in higher education institutions find it increasingly difficult to pay for teaching staff who have the necessary understanding of the requirements of business in the 1990s. Promotion in many of these institutions is often not geared to teaching skill; it may depend more on quantities of refereed research and administrative contributions. Recruitment policies

sometimes discriminate against those in their fifties because they are too close to retirement. But these are often managers with considerable experience to share. Social attitudes are such that teaching is no longer a high status activity.

The need for management development in a setting wider than one company or one industry is vital to competitive advantage. But the institutions which exist to provide it are hindered in their current attempts to adapt by cultures and policies presenting obstacles to meeting the need.

The answer seems simple and it is the one embodied in current government policies on higher education, which aim to change academic cultures and practices so that the educational establishments, of which Business Schools are a part, become entrepreneurial businesses. The aim is to foster close contact with industry, produce directly practical and relevant education in industrial and commercial terms and generate income from sources other than the public purse. Will all this produce the educated managers that the the business world of the 1990s will need? The answer is most probably not, for a number of reasons.

First, while the practical, relevant 'training' type approach now being propagated is appropriate for post-experience development of managers, it is not appropriate for the bulk of the activities of Universities and Polytechnics and for a significant part of the work of most Business Schools. The major part of what they do is the education of undergraduates who have no experience. 'Training' type approaches build upon past experience and there is therefore little foundation for such an approach with undergraduates. What they need is broadly-based education, that which develops wide perspectives and the ability to think, the foundation without which later post-experience management training cannot easily be built.

Initiatives to propagate enterprise throughout social science, arts, history and fundamental science departments seem absurd in this context. Traditional academic cultures and practices with their concern for thinking ability rather than immediate relevance, are far more appropriate for undergraduate education. There is little reason why teachers of undergraduates should have business experience or even contact with business — they are teaching fundamental, vital skills which do not require such experience or contact. The danger of imposing what seems right in one area, practical relevance for post-experience management development, on all aspects of higher education could well undermine the fundamental education upon which later development has to depend.

The second reason for pessimism regarding the current direction of higher education in the UK relates to the diversion of the time and energy of academic staff away from their core activities. The pressure being applied to academics to generate income from selling services such as consultancy and short courses can only dilute their efforts and reduce their effectiveness in the core teaching areas. Just when businesses are being advised to 'stick to the knitting' and concentrate on improving

their competitiveness in core business areas, doing what they are best at, educational establishments are being driven to diversify into many loosely related activities which most are not all that good at. Universities and Polytechnics are not business enterprises. They do not have the structures, the skills or the cultures to operate as such. And if they succeed in turning themselves into entrepreneurial businesses, they will no longer be educational establishments turning out that well-educated raw material which later experience and focused training will turn into effective managers.

A third concern is the attempts being made in the Polytechnics, and later no doubt to be made in the Universities, to change the terms and conditions of teachers so that they become equivalent to those of office workers. This can only make it even more difficult to attract skilled teachers, those who could command much higher salaries by working in real offices.

So, by taking a number of steps which may facilitate the practical and the relevant in those areas where they are needed, such as post-experience management development, we may well be destroying tried and tested approaches where such practical, immediate relevance is not relevant at all. A more sensible answer would surely be some degree of separation of pre- and post-experience types of education.

Recommendation 5
The need for development programmes for your managers in a setting wider than your own company, or even your own industry, is vital to your competitive advantage in the 1990s. You need to become more involved in how Business Schools are run and what they teach, when it comes to post-experience training, if this need is to be met. You need to see Business Schools as an important part of your management development programmes. You need to become an active stakeholder, perhaps a shareholder, in your local Business School. You need to press actively for Business Schools which have some measure of independence from the academic institution of which they are a part, rather than a shotgun approach which hits everything in sight and could seriously damage the early fundamental education of future managers.

More open-ended change requires a larger quantity of management

No matter how good the quality of the managers in a company, control will still be defective if there are not enough of them. This is so obvious that it should hardly be worth saying. But the trends of the 1980s towards lean management structures and small staff support have now been carried so far, in so many companies, that they suffer in an extremely detrimental way from shortage of this essential instrument of control.

Management today is typically put under much greater pressure than it was in

the 1970s or before. It is now far more common to find managers who arrive for work before eight in the morning and do not leave until after eight at night. And they appear at the office during the weekends too. In fact working these unrealistic hours has, in many places, already become embedded in the 'macho culture'. You will hear approving stories over business dinners about how late this manager has stayed and little digs and jokes at the expense of that manager who went home early.

To run so tight a management resource that this kind of behaviour becomes common, and widely approved of, is to pay a serious and hidden price. Most human beings do not think as clearly, they are not as imaginative or as perceptive when they are tired and burned out, as they do when they experience the relaxation which comes from pursuing other interests as well. On top of that there will not be much time for perception and imagination in such tightly run situations.

If there is no management slack there will be no one competent to develop an innovative opportunity. Every new opportunity or acquisition will distract someone from what he was doing before and the existing business will suffer. Management and staff morale will suffer.

The purposeful use of political processes to handle open-ended change takes up management time. Training and development of management takes up time. Effective communication and mutual exploration of opportunities, problems and perceptions all take up time. You cannot handle the disturbance arising in open-ended change on a shoe string. It requires investment. Investment in management; investment which you may well now be seeing as expensive slack. This investment in extra management resource, in some management slack, is absolutely vital to the effective handling of open-ended change.

Recommendation 6

Review the quantity of your management resource. If managers are working all hours, if you never start meetings on time, if you keep postponing them because some other urgent matter has come up, if you cannot hold control review meetings because you are all too busy, then something is seriously wrong. You will be holding costs down admirably and boosting profit. But it is short-term profit. In the long term you will not be able to handle open-ended change effectively. You must invest in what looks like some management slack. You must create enough time so that your managers can participate effectively in the group processes which are vital to effective innovative experimentation.

Separating the existing business from the cutting edge of innovation

Specialization by hierarchical level

The tension created by the conflicting demands which control places on structures,

culture and management are so severe that there is a strong motivation to separate the existing business, with its day-to-day control needs, from the cutting edge of innovation. This is the oldest approach to resolving control tension. Separation is traditionally achieved by hierarchical specialization, with the top levels of management dealing with innovative experimentation in open-ended change situations, and layers of middle and supervisory management confined to the day-to-day.

Such rigid separation does not work today and will not work in the 1990s. First the volume of disturbance arising in open-ended change situations is now too great and its impact on the organization too widespread. Second, pressures to install more and more effective short-interval control in decentralized units means that more and more layers of management are now exposed to open-ended change. Third, the education and expectations of managers today are such that they seek involvement and participation; they have become vital to motivation and commitment. An approach which tries to deal with control tension by hierarchical specialization is therefore becoming increasingly unsatisfactory. There will always be a change in the balance of concern away from the day-to-day towards the open-ended as one moves up the hierarchy, but there need not, and in the 1990s there should not, be a rigid separation.

Specialization by type of activity

Since the old recipe of rigid hierarchical specialization is no longer a very appropriate means of resolving control tension, it is now recommended by many[3] that a form of specialization by activity should be adopted. This means that the existing business is kept separate from innovative activity. It is advocated that special committees to vet new ideas should be set up outside the normal top management meetings, with some independent members from outside the organization. It is suggested that special funds be established to finance such ideas. It is recommended that task forces should consist of members taken away from existing business. Specialization in innovative experimentation should be created.

This form of specialization to deal with different change situations also has considerable drawbacks. Strategy is built by backing successful experiments at the boundaries of the existing business; it is coherent, clear, continuing direction from the existing business. Much of strategy develops from the carrying out of the existing business in many small new ways: improvements in control systems; changes in operational techniques; repackaging and re-presentation of existing products. Innovation rarely relates to the completely new.

This makes it impractical always to define management roles in terms of either the new or the existing, somehow separating innovation into a functional specialism for a few bright people no longer in touch with the existing business.

Major experiments will require full-time task forces, but they should be temporarily withdrawn from the existing business. The day-to-day and the open-ended are so intertwined that separate committees looking at new ideas may miss important interconnections.

In the end there is no simple way of resolving fundamental control tension. It is a continuous, almost ad hoc, process in which tensions are continually resolved in a manner which is reasonably satisfactory at a particular point in time, in the particular circumstances of that time. The greatest value which management adds to the business organization arises from dealing with interconnected open-ended change and control tension in a continuing and innovative way.

Notes

[1] See the Litton Industries and Texas Instruments case in J Quin, H Mintzberg and R James, *The Strategy Process*, Prentice-Hall (1988).

[2] C Bartlett, *MNCs: Get off the Reorganisation Merri-Go-Round* in R Buzzel and J Quelch, *Multi-National Marketing*, Addison-Wesley (1988).

[3] P Drucker, *Entrepreneurship and Innovation*, Heinemann (1985).

10
Review: Balancing Opportunism and Planning

This book has sought to explore what I perceive as the great divide in approaches to the strategic management of a business enterprise — the opportunistic and the rational planning approaches. It has also considered the sharp distinction which is usually made between strategic and operational, or day-to-day management.

Business planning

Those adopting the conventional approach to strategic management are in essence claiming that noticeable benefits are yielded by a prominent degree of formality and a significant element of regularity in the preparation of long-term plans. Such plans set clear objectives to be achieved a number of years hence and map out comprehensive routes to achieve those objectives. Fundamentally, this approach is based on the belief that control can be exerted, that change occurring now and having long-term consequences can be managed, using a 'grand design' for the future.

Increasingly, those advocating this approach are adopting a healthy cynicism towards it. Most would now proclaim a weaker version — the regular preparation of formal plans focuses attention and effort on a coherent, analytically based search for new opportunities and new competitive edges. In other words, formal long-term planning harnesses enterprise in a rational, systematic manner; it provides occasions for systematically collecting and examining data; it provides occasions for and facilitates communication, particularly between business unit and corporate levels; it provides exercises in developing the strategic skills of the management team.

Practical limitations are recognized and to overcome them what is prescribed is flexibility in the whole process, a willingness to change objectives and routes to them as circumstances require. But the basic approach, the formality and regularity, the heavy emphasis on rational, analytical processes, remains the philosophical cornerstone of the conventional approach. In the end some form of rational, long-term planning, inevitably based on some form of forecasting, is retained by those who advocate this approach.

Opportunism

Others, however, adopt a diametrically different approach, one which is philosophically inconsistent with conventional, rational, strategic management. This entrepreneurial approach is based on the view that control can only be exerted, that changes occurring now with longer-term, uncertain consequences, can only be managed using intuitive processes and experimental action — in short, opportunism. Rational analytical processes may assist in posing questions and exploring some of the potential consequences of experimental actions, but the essence here is an intuitive, experience-based feel for markets and the business, in which formality and regularity play little part. Indeed, regularity and formality are the enemies of intuitive, fast-acting responses, which cannot be based on forecasts because of the high level of uncertainty.

The two approaches are poles apart and philosophically at odds with each other. The use of the word entrepreneurial in conventional strategic management means something completely different from what it means in the opportunistic approach — in the former it is an explicitly rational activity and in the latter it most emphatically is not. In this sense Planning and Entrepreneurial strategic management are not simply different modes, they are diametrically opposed philosophies. And such different philosophies lead to completely different types of organization, different ways of thinking, different management styles, different ways of responding to strategic challenges.

The conflict in context

To put the conflict into context, this book started from basic principles and asked what kinds of change situation have to be managed by a business. The answer is a spectrum of change situations ranging from the closed at one extreme, where what is causing the change and how it is causing it are both clear cut, to open-ended change at the other extreme, where the what and the how are both far from clear. And all businesses have to manage change now which covers the full range of that spectrum.

The central problem which this need simultaneously to manage different kinds of change creates, is that the meaning of control changes as one moves across the change spectrum. In fact control at one end of the spectrum has a meaning which is diametrically opposed to what it means at the other end. No evidence is required for this statement — it is a simple logical proposition. Control, if it is to satisfy its full definition as systematic behaviour which is not haphazard, has to include three elements — planning, monitoring in its sense of detecting change and checking progress, and action. Drop one element and it is no longer control in the fullest sense.

In closed change situations control has a precise definition — it means setting objectives, specifying and forecasting routes to them, monitoring outcomes against forecast and taking corrective action. The appropriate form of control is control by variance, or short-interval control. And that set of processes which we call Management Information and Control Systems is the appropriate instrument.

In open-ended situations, forecasting is by definition impossible. The only ways the human race has so far discovered for dealing with such situations, true uncertainty, are that of exploration, experiment, trial and error. But such behaviour is still controlled — planning means choosing and designing sensible experiments; monitoring means detecting the changes which prompt the experiment in the first place and then checking the conduct of the experiment; action means abandoning the experiment, continuing with it or backing successful experiments with resources and energy. This is control by trial and error, and the instrument which allows and encourages it to take place at all, which supports and finally backs successful experiment, is the political system of the business. It is the political system which provides the framework for the activities of champions who identify and push strategic issues, for the formation and operation of special interest groups who support the inclusion of issues on the strategic agenda, the functioning of the task forces which progress responses to the issues, the management teams which back successful responses with resources.

Between the extremes of closed and open-ended change there is that probabilistic change where some degree of forecasting is possible and statements can be made about what is more or less likely to happen. These statements can be made because such events have occurred before, they are to some extent repetitive, past experience is a reasonably reliable guide. Here, a watered-down version of short-interval control, control by grand design, is the appropriate form of control.

Resolving the conflict

Which of these forms of control is appropriate for the 1990s? Well, that depends on the change situations which will characterize the 1990s. Chapter 2 argued that change is polarizing and will continue to polarize at the closed and open-ended extremes. Consequently, success in the 1990s will demand the simultaneous application of short-interval control with its requirement for precise comprehensive business planning, and control by trial and error with its politically driven opportunism.

Applying diametrically different forms of control at the same time creates enormous control tensions. These different forms of control impose diametrically opposed demands on organization and behaviour — they require different objectives time-frames and constraints, different processes of control, different role

definitions and perceptions, different interpersonal relationships, structures and cultures. Continually resolving these control tensions lies at the heart of strategic management.

And strategic management comes to mean simultaneous control in closed and open-ended situations, simultaneously employing the short-term business planning of control by variance and the opportunism of control by trial and error. Strategies become the outcomes of successful experiments which are backed by the organization, not the starting point for everything else.

In all this there is little place for the core prescriptions of conventional strategic management, with its fundamental emphasis on explicit rationality and its doomed attempts to set and monitor long-term objectives and preordained strategies in highly uncertain environments. Furthermore successful companies with long-range planning systems recognize this implicitly because they do not use their long-term plans as a form of control in uncertain situations. They behave as opportunistically as any other successful company when it actually comes to the unknowable.

My evidence for this contention is first my own personal experience — I have yet to find a company actually using its long-term plans. Such plans are usually found in a filing cabinet, while management identifies and progresses the real strategic issues through political means. The studies which Peters and Waterman[1] made of a number of organizations came to a similar conclusion. And a careful reading of the Goold and Campbell study suggests this conclusion too.[2] But there is a purely logical reason for the statement as well. Successful companies have by definition been dealing adequately with open-ended change — they have survived. It is only possible to deal with such change in a trial and error way. Successful companies must, therefore, have employed trial and error control approaches.

Instead of installing and using long-range planning systems which are on balance harmful, the need is to focus on improving both short-interval control and control by trial and error. The focus should be on developing a control style which balances short-term business planning and intuitive opportunism. This means installing and using effective Management Information and Control Systems, which is relatively easy. And it means examining and improving those political processes which either block or foster the kind of intuitive team responses required by open-ended change and the continual resolution of control tension. It means improving the total control system of the business to enable it to respond to a spectrum of change situations.

Summary of recommendations

The following is a brief summary of the 18 recommendations made in this book. They can be found in more detail, together with the reasoning which leads up to

them, in Chapters 8 (for the first 12 recommendations) and 9 (for the following 6).

1 Abandon any intention to install formal long-term planning systems and procedures. Scrap them if you already possess them. What you need to do instead is improve your company's ability to innovate, experiment, be opportunistic, play dynamic business games. The instrument for doing this is the political system of your business, the framework which fosters or impedes the activities of champions who identify strategic issues, special interest groups which get issues on to the strategic agenda of the organization, task forces which progress responses to the issues and management teams which back success with resources to build strategies.

2 Do not be persuaded that a turbulent and rapidly changing environment makes the application of tight, short-interval control to the day-to-day less relevant. It is even more vital. But this kind of environment will require frequent changes to Management Information and Control Systems. It will also require more and more managers in the business to develop the ability to judge when to apply tight, short-interval control and when it is more appropriate to utilize flexible, innovative responses.

3 If you recognize your organizational control style as that of the Informal Monitor, Firefighter or Bureaucrat, then without delay, you must install modern Management Information and Control Systems. You must do this to secure the benefits of consistent quality, reliability, flexibility, high service levels and tight cost control. A more detailed, hard to copy Management Information and Control System than your rivals' is a major source of competitive advantage.

4 Clarify the purpose of your budget and make sure that all who are using it as a control instrument are involved in its preparation and have a common understanding of its purpose. Its preparation must not be dictated by laborious reporting requirements of top management. Especially do not get it all tied up with the preparation of long-term plans. Scrap that intensive annual budget ritual and move to much tighter short-interval control with five-quarterly, rolling budgets. When reviewing budgets, focus on the issues which variances are identifying, not on lengthy discussions of and excuses for, past performance.

5 Tie staff and management performance appraisal firmly to a rolling five-quarterly budget. But performance in the long term is just as important. You have to make judgements about the weight to be attached to these different types of performance. There are no mechanistic systems to do this.

6 Focus your monitoring processes on variables which measure what is really

important to your business, variables which also direct your attention to the future rather than to the past. Concentrate on a few of the most vital indicators — order books, order flows, quickly obtainable volume measures of activity, indicators on quality, responsiveness, adaptability and so on. You must be able to answer the question — Where are you making money and where are you losing it?

7 Strategy is about innovation. If innovation is conspicuously infrequent in your organization consider where the few innovative ideas come from. Do they always come from a small number of people at the top? If they do then find out why. What is blocking the emergence of a wider range of champions? Explicitly examine the manner in which political power in your business is concentrated or dispersed. And seriously ask whether too much power is concentrated in the hands of a few at the top. Explicitly examine the personality balance of the top management team. Consider how the most senior managers stay in touch with the market place and the shop floor — scrap the ceremonial visit and make real contact. Instead of continually shelving potentially important strategic items because you have insufficient time, set up middle management groups to develop them and to suggest items which they think should be commanding attention. Review the support you give to champions. Appoint one of the organization's most senior managers to a position where the main duties relate to the promotion of new ideas, a business development director who trawls the organization for suggestions on how to do things more effectively.

8 Use task forces to progress the key issues facing your business. Do not leave major reorganizations, product developments, technology changes or even small new ideas to the uncontrolled cooperation of those most affected by the change. The way to control trial and error is through multi-discipline task forces across functions and business units. Having set up the task force, take a strong and continuing interest in it. Set milestones and keep reviewing them.

9 Appoint one person to listen to what goes on at your senior management meetings, to measure the time spent on different items and track what happens to issues raised. Hold special meetings to hammer out the purpose of the meetings. Get team members to write out their views of the informal rules which govern their behaviour at the meetings. Get them to discuss whether these are helpful or not. Get team members to consider their personality differences explicitly and what distinctive contributions such differences make. Use the above programme of meeting analysis to change the format and composition of the meetings so that they become relevant to building the necessary strategic agendas.

10 Make your strategic agenda explicit, check its relevance and comprehensiveness in a manner which recognizes the inherent difficulties of handling open-ended change — ill-structured problems and opportunities which are difficult to identify; which by their very nature cannot be foreseen; which call for up-to-date information locked in managers' heads. Do this by setting up a series of workshops when events come together to make it necessary. Avoid regular, formal and eventually boring planning conferences. Workshops surface and develop issues when there is a real need — they do not prepare plans.

11. Explicitly examine the key features of the top leadership of your business: style of interpersonal relationships; personal work style. Review your understanding of the role of the chief executive and the chairman or woman. Leaders, be aware of your personality and the impact it is having. The rapidly changing competitive environment of the 1990s and the inherent difficulty of handling strategic issues point strongly to strategic facilitation as the appropriate role for the top levels of management in the processes of strategic control.

12 Ensure that you do have a resource to gather sensible and practical information and to provide analytical support for effective strategic management. See this support not as some form of staff usurpation of management roles, but as a support and a serious contributor to the political process.

13 Ensure that your formal organizational structure is as simple as possible. Push decentralization to profit centres, related to market segments, as far as is consistent with delivering competitive advantage to those segments. Keep your organization structure as flat as possible, but not so flat that you remove the management resource you will require for the political processes demanded by effective handling of open-ended change.

14 Develop attitudes and behavioural rules, that is, an organizational culture, which supports decentralized structures operating in the interests of the whole corporation. Do this by more widespread use of task forces and workshops which range across business units and functions and cover a number of rungs in the management hierarchy, involving more people in an orderly way in the 'big issues'.

15 Review your management selection procedures. Recognize that for the 1990s you need more managers with competences in wider ranging thinking, balanced judgement and flexibility. Recognize that you are looking for people who will fit the role, fit in with the team and provide the necessary balance of personalities within it.

16 Review your management development policies. Give one of the politically

most powerful figures in your organization specific responsibility for management development. Accord it high organizational attention — it is a vital link in your total control of the business. Put it on the agenda of your regular meetings. Monitor what is being done. Make sure you have the expertise to do it. Above all specifically tie your management development programmes to the attributes which your control system requires of management roles.

17 The need for development programmes for your managers in a setting wider than your own company, or even your own industry, is vital to your competitive advantage in the 1990s. You need to become more involved in how Business Schools are run and what they teach if this need is to be met. But what may be appropriate for post-experience management may be disastrous for fundamental undergraduate education upon which business depends for future managers. Push for focused rather than shotgun approaches to educational changes.

18 Review the quantity of your management resource. If managers are working all hours, if you never start meetings on time, if you keep postponing them because some other urgent matter has come up, if you cannot hold control review meetings because you are all too busy, then something is seriously wrong. You will be holding costs down admirably and boosting profit in the short term. But in the long term you will not be able to handle open-ended change effectively.

Notes
[1] T Peters and R Waterman, *In Search of Excellence*, Harper and Rowe (1982).
[2] M Goold and A Campbell, *Strategies and Styles*, Blackwell (1988).

Index